The Faith of the Faithless

The Faith of the Faithless

Experiments in Political Theology

———————◆———————

SIMON CRITCHLEY

VERSO
London • New York

First published by Verso 2012
© Simon Critchley

1 3 5 7 9 10 8 6 4 2

Verso
UK: 6 Meard Street, London W1F 0EG
US: 20 Jay Street, Suite 1010, Brooklyn, NY 11201
www.versobooks.com

Verso is the imprint of New Left Books

ISBN-13: 978-1-84467-737-5

British Library Cataloguing in Publication Data
A catalogue record for this book is available from the British Library

Library of Congress Cataloging-in-Publication Data
A catalog record for this book is available from the Library of Congress

Typeset in Bembo by MJ Gavan, Cornwall
Printed in the US by Maple Vail

For Jamieson Webster, with love

Contents

1

Introduction

I'd like to begin with a story, a parable of sorts. On May 19, 1897, Oscar Wilde was released from Reading Gaol after two years' detention for acts of gross indecency. He left England for the last time on the same day and traveled to Dieppe. On his arrival in France, Wilde was met by Robert Ross, his loyal friend and sometime lover. Ross was handed a manuscript of some 50,000 words on eighty close-written pages. Wilde had apparently written it during the last months of his imprisonment: his gaolers allowed him one sheet of paper at a time and, after it was filled, took the completed sheet and handed him a new one. It was Wilde's last prose work before his death in shambolic circumstances in Paris three years later, and the only piece that he wrote in prison.

An expurgated version of Wilde's text, a long and at times bitter epistle to his inconstant lover Lord Alfred Douglas, was published in 1905 with the title *De Profundis*, which is the *incipit* of Psalm 130 in Latin, "From the depths I cry to thee, O Lord." It is the religious dimension of this letter that interests me, and in particular Wilde's interpretation of the figure of Christ. I think that this text by Wilde illuminates extremely well the shape of the dilemma of politics and belief that will guide the various experiments in this book.

De Profundis is the testimony of someone who knows that he has ruined himself and has squandered the most extraordinary artistic gifts. Yet the text is also marked by a quiet but steely audacity. Having lost everything (his children, his reputation, his money, his freedom), Wilde does not bow down before the external command of some transcendent deity. On the contrary, he sees his sufferings as the occasion for a "fresh mode of self-realization." He adds, "That is all I am concerned with."[1] That is, Wilde's self-ruination does not lead him to look outside the self for salvation, but more deeply within himself to find some new means of self-formation, of self-artistry. As he endures incarceration, Wilde seems to be more of an individualist than ever. As we will see, matters become more complicated still.

For such an act of self-realization, Wilde insists, neither religion nor morality nor reason can help. This is because each of these faculties requires the invocation of some sort of external agency. *Morality*, for Wilde—the antinomian par excellence—is about the sanction of externally imposed law and must therefore be rejected. *Reason* enables Wilde to see that the laws under which he was convicted and the system that imposed them are wrong and unjust. But, in order to grasp the nature of what has befallen him and to transcend it, Wilde cannot view his misfortunes rationally as the external imposition of an injustice. On the contrary, he must internalize the wrong—but this requires an artistic, not a rational, process. For Wilde, this means that every aspect of his life in prison—the plank bed, the loathsome food, the dreadful attire, the silence, the solitude and the shame—must be artistically transformed into what Wilde calls "a spiritual experience."[2] The various degradations of Wilde's body must become "a spiritualizing of the soul," the transfiguration of suffering into beauty, or what psychoanalysts call "sublimation": passion transformed.

But it is Wilde's views on religion that are so interesting in connection to the themes of politics and belief. Where others might have faith in the unseen and intangible, the great unknown or whatever, Wilde confesses a more aesthetic fidelity to "What one can touch and look at."[3] His, then, is a sensuous religion. He goes on to make an extraordinary pronouncement that describes the dilemma I would like to confront in this book:

> When I think of religion at all, I feel as if I would like to found an order for those who *cannot* believe: the Confraternity of the Faithless, one might call it, where on an altar, on which no taper burned, a priest, in whose heart peace had no dwelling, might celebrate with unblessed bread and a chalice empty of wine. Everything to be true must become a religion. And agnosticism should have its ritual no less than faith.[4]

It is the phrase, "Everything to be true must become a religion" that is most striking. What might "true" mean? Wilde is clearly not alluding to the logical truth of propositions or the empirical truths of natural science. I think that he is using "true" in a manner close to its root meaning of "being true to," an act of fidelity that is kept alive in the German word *treu*: loyal or faithful. This is perhaps its meaning in Jesus's phrase when he said, "I am the way, the truth and the life" (John 14:6). Religious truth is like *troth*, the experience of fidelity where one is affianced and then betrothed. What is true, then, is an experience of faith, and this is as true for agnostics and atheists as it is for theists. Those who cannot believe still require religious truth and a framework of ritual in which they can believe. At the core of Wilde's remark is the seemingly contradictory idea of the *faith of the faithless* and the *belief of unbelievers*, a faith which does not give up on the idea of truth, but transfigures its meaning.

I think this idea of a faith of the faithless is helpful in addressing the dilemma of politics and belief. On the one hand, unbelievers still seem to require an experience of belief; on the other hand, this cannot—for reasons I will explore below—be the idea that belief has to be underpinned by a traditional conception of religion defined by an experience or maybe just a postulate of transcendent fullness, namely the God of metaphysics or what Heidegger calls "onto-theo-logy."[5] The *political* question—which will be my constant concern in the experiments that follow—is how such a faith of the faithless might be able to bind together a confraternity, a consorority or, to use Rousseau's key term, an *association*. If political life is to arrest a slide into demotivated cynicism, then it would seem to require a motivating and authorizing faith which, while not reducible to a specific context, might be capable of forming solidarity in a locality, a site, a region—in Wilde's case a prison cell.

This faith of the faithless cannot have for its object anything external to the self or subject, any external, divine command, any transcendent reality. As Wilde says: "But whether it be faith or agnosticism, it must be nothing external to me. Its symbols must be of my own creating."[6]

We appear to be facing a paradox. On the one hand, to be true everything must become a religion, otherwise belief lacks (literally) credibility or authority. Yet, on the other hand, we are and have to be the authors of that authority. The faith of the faithless must be a work of collective self-creation where I am the smithy of my own soul and where we must all become soul-smiths, as it were.

The apparent paradox is resolved through Wilde's interpretation of the figure of Christ. In his 1891 essay "The Soul of Man under Socialism," Wilde describes Christ as a "beggar who has a marvelous soul," a "leper whose soul is divine." Christ is a "God realizing his perfection through pain."[7] Wilde's captivity might, then, best be understood as an extended *imitatio* of Christ, where he becomes who he is through the experience of suffering. It is through suffering and suffering alone that one becomes the smithy of one's soul. Wilde's suffering in Reading Gaol is thus the condition for his self-realization as an artist. At the core of Wilde's understanding of Christ is an almost Schopenhauerian metaphysics of suffering: "For the secret of life is suffering. It is what is hidden behind everything."[8] The truth of art, according to Wilde's expressivist romantic aesthetics, is the incarnation of the inwardness of suffering in outward form, the expression of deep internality in externality. It is here that Wilde finds an intimate connection between the life of the artist and the life of Christ.

For Wilde, Christ is the supreme romantic artist, a poet who makes the inward outward through the power of the imagination. Wilde goes even further, saying that Christ makes himself into a work of art through the transfiguration of his suffering in his life and passion. Christ creates himself as a sublime work of art by rendering articulate a voiceless world of pain:

> To the artist, expression is the only mode under which he can conceive life at all. To him what is dumb is dead. But to Christ it was not so. With a width and wonder of imagination that fills one almost with awe, he took the entire world of the inarticulate, the voiceless world of pain, as his kingdom, and made of himself its external mouthpiece.[9]

In his compassion for the downtrodden and the poor, but equally in his pity for the hard, empty hedonism of the rich, Christ is the incarnation of love as an act of imagination, not reason, the imaginative projection of compassion onto all creatures. What Christ teaches is love, and, Wilde writes, "When you really want love you will find it waiting for you."[10] The decision to open oneself to love enables a possible receipt of grace over which one has no power and which one cannot decide.

Wilde's extraordinary panegyric to Christ culminates in what he calls Christ's "dangerous idea."[11] This turns upon the treatment of a sinner like Wilde himself. Christ does not condemn the sinner—"Let him of you who has never sinned be the first to throw the stone"—but rather sees sin and suffering as "being in themselves beautiful holy things and modes of perfection."[12] By this, Wilde does not mean that the act of sin itself is holy, but that the transfiguration of this act follows from the experience of long repentance and suffering. To this extent—and Wilde finds this a deeply un-Hellenic thought—one can transform one's past through a process of aesthetic transfiguration or sublimation. As he concludes: "It is difficult for most people to grasp the idea. I dare say one has to go to prison to understand it. If so, it may be worth while going to prison."[13]

It is only in and through the experience of imprisonment that Wilde is able to become himself, to deepen what he relentlessly calls his individualism into a subjectivity defined by the transfiguration of suffering, the transformation of passion. In this, Wilde's artistic exemplar is Christ: "He is just like a work of art. He does not really teach one anything, but by being brought into his presence one becomes something."[14]

This Wilde Christianity finds its political expression in *socialism*. Wilde's argument for socialism prior to his imprisonment is singular, to say the least. For him, the chief advantage of socialism is that it would relieve us of that "sordid necessity of living for others."[15] That is, socialism would relieve us of the constant presence and pressure of the poor: the bourgeois burdens of charity and the so-called altruistic virtues. In eliminating poverty at the level of the political organization of society, socialism "will lead to individualism."[16] That is, it will allow individuals to flourish in a society that will permit and positively encourage self-artistry and self-formation.

But is such socialism possible without the experience of pain, suffering, and imprisonment, that is, without the whole *imitatio* of Christ that we have followed in *De Profundis?* In "The Soul of Man under Socialism," Wilde imagines an Arnoldian Hellenism in which the sheer joy of life would replace painful lamentation for the suffering God. In 1897, after the experience of imprisonment and degradation, Wilde is not so sure. And this is what gives the lie to his aesthetic individualism. In my view, what is being articulated in *De Profundis* is not individualism at all but what, in my parlance, I call "dividualism."[17] The self shapes itself in relation to the experience of an overwhelming, infinite demand that divides it from itself—the sort of demand that Christ made in the Sermon on the Mount when he said: "Love your enemies, bless them that curse you, do good to them that hate you, and pray for them which despitefully use you, and persecute you" (Matt. 5:44).

When Christ says this, when he makes this infinite ethical demand, he is not stating something that might be simply fulfilled or carried out. Whether he was the incarnation of God or just some troublesome rabbi in occupied Palestine, Christ was presumably not simply stupid and expressed this infinite demand for a purpose. When, in the same sermon, he says, "Be ye therefore perfect, even as your Father which is in heaven is perfect" (Matt. 5:48), he does not imagine for a moment that such perfection is attainable—at least not in this life. Such perfection would require the equality of the human and the divine, a kind of mystical glorification. What such a demand does is to expose our imperfection and failure: we wrestle in solitude with the fact of the infinite demand and the constraints of the finite situation in which we find ourselves. Otherwise said, ethics is all about the experience of failure—but in failing something is learned, something is experienced from the depths, *de profundis*. What is exposed here—an idea I will return to throughout this book—is the nature of *conscience*, or what I will call that powerless power of being human.

The infinite ethical demand allows us to become the subjects of which we are capable by dividing us from ourselves, by forcing us to live in accordance with an asymmetrical and unfulfillable demand—say the demand to be Christlike—while knowing that we are all too human. Although we can be free of the limiting externalism of conventional morality, established law, and the metaphysics of traditional religion, it seems that we will never be free of that "sordid necessity of living for others." The latter requires an experience of faith, a faith of the faithless that is an openness to love, love as giving what one does not have and receiving that over which one has no power. It is the possible meaning of such faith that constitutes the horizon for this book.

A SIMPLE ENOUGH SUMMARY OF THE ARGUMENT

The return to religion has become perhaps the dominant cliché of contemporary theory. Of course, theory often offers nothing more than an exaggerated echo of what is happening in reality, a political reality dominated by the fact of religious war. Somehow we seem to have passed from a secular age, which we were ceaselessly told was post-metaphysical, to a new situation in which political action seems to flow directly from metaphysical conflict. This situation can be triangulated around the often-fatal entanglement of politics and religion, where the third vertex of the triangle is violence. Politics, religion, and violence appear to define the present through which we are all too precipitously moving, in which religiously justified violence is the means to a political end. How to respond to such a situation? Must one either defend a version of secularism or quietly accept the slide into some form of theism? This book refuses such an either/or option. *The Faith of the Faithless* consists of four historical and philosophical investigations into the dangerous interdependence of politics and religion, and is framed by two brief parables.

I begin with a discussion of Rousseau, whose work provides an exemplary index for thinking through the relation between politics and religion in the modern era. The turn to Rousseau is motivated both by the inherent fascination of his work—which has long been a personal obsession of mine—and its prescience with regard to the triangulation mentioned above. I identify a paradox of sovereignty in Rousseau. *The Social Contract* of 1762 arguably provides the definitive expression of the modern conception of politics, an egalitarian conception of association rooted in popular sovereignty: the only sovereign in a legitimate polity is the people itself. In other words, Rousseau provides an entirely *immanent* conception of political legitimacy. This finds its clearest expression in his conception of law: the only law that can be followed in a legitimate polity is the law that it gives itself through acts of the general will. In other words, law must be self-authorizing and correspond to autonomy. Yet, what authority can a law have if it is self-authorizing? This question leads Rousseau to the famous problem of the legislator: in order for law to have authority over a community it becomes necessary to posit the existence of a legislator who stands outside that community: a foreigner, a stranger who initiates the constitutional arrangements of a polity. The autonomy of law needs a heteronomous source in order to guarantee what some see as law's empire.

The dependence of an immanent conception of legitimacy on some transcendent instance becomes even more acute in Rousseau's treatment of the relation between politics and religion. On the one hand, as we will see in detail below, in an early draft of *The Social Contract* Rousseau insists that the question of legitimate political institutions is a philosophical issue that must not be resolved theologically. Yet, on the other hand, the published version of *The Social Contract* concludes with an infamous discussion of civil religion, those political articles of faith—which include a belief in a beneficent deity and an afterlife—that Rousseau believes are necessary in order to provide the motivational set of moral intuitions that will affectively bind together a polity and ensure that its citizens will take an active interest in the process of collective legislation that constitutes a self-determining political life. Such is the source of Rousseau's appeal to Voltaire that there should be a catechism of the citizen, analogous to the articles of Christian faith, which would underpin the functioning of any legitimate polity.

Following Althusser, I see Rousseau's extraordinarily inventive thinking as marked by a series of *décalages*—displacements, moments of tension, ambiguity or seeming contradiction—which find a focus on three key concepts: politics, law, and religion. An avowedly immanent conception of political autonomy requires an appeal to transcendence and heteronomy that appears to undermine it. My hunch is that these *décalages* do not simply define the intricacies of Rousseau's texts, but can be used to cast light on the intrication of politics and religion in the contemporary world. Politics is indeed conceivable without religion: the question is whether it is practicable without some sort of religious dimension. This will be explained in greater historical detail below, combined with examples from Madison's arguments for federalism, the constitution of the European Union, and the role of religion in Barack Obama's political liberalism. But, to be clear, I do not see the relation between religion and politics in terms of some purported passage or even progress from the pre-modern to the modern, where religion would be that unwelcome pre-modern residue in modern political life. Rather than seeing modernity in terms of a process of secularization, I will claim that the history of political forms can best be viewed as a series of *metamorphoses of sacralization*.

In whatever genre he worked within, or indeed invented, Rousseau's exemplarity consists in his acknowledgement of the constitutive function of fiction. Chapter 2 culminates in a discussion of fictions of political belief, or fictions of the sacred, which is at once diagnostic and normative. Diagnostically, I seek to show how the history of political forms—notably the passage from monarchical to popular sovereignty—can be approached through the category of fiction: the reason why, in the overwhelming majority of cases, the many submit to the governance of the few can be traced to what Hume saw as the power of opinion, or what I will call "fictional force." I then turn to the speculative hypothesis, borrowed from Wallace Stevens, of a supreme fiction in politics—namely, a fiction that we know to be a fiction, yet one in which we still believe—and approach the problem of political legitimacy through poetic categories. The chapter concludes with a discussion of Alain Badiou's understanding of politics, which, I argue, is best approached in Rousseauian terms.

Continuing on from the discussion of civil religion, "mystical anarchism" begins with a discussion of Carl Schmitt, perhaps the major source of the contemporary renewal of interest in political theology. Schmitt's predilection for Catholic counter-revolutionaries like Joseph de Maistre and Juan Donoso Cortés allows the central question of Chapter 3 to be raised: what is the relation between politics and original sin? The latter is the theological name for an essential defectiveness in human nature which cannot be put right by any act of the will, and which explains the human propensity to wickedness, violence, and cruelty. If human beings are defined by original sin, then politics becomes the means of protecting human beings from themselves, something that justifies the forms of dictatorship and state authoritarianism defended by Schmitt. I argue that updated versions of the concept of original sin are still very much with us, and seek to explore this thought through an engagement with the work of John Gray. I contend that Gray provides a powerful naturalization of original sin as part of his compelling critique of liberal humanism. The political analogue to this critique is what Gray calls "political realism," which is more benign—indeed Burkean—than Schmitt's authoritarianism, but which maintains the latter's deep pessimism about the human condition. After mounting a critique of what I see as Gray's passive nihilism, I begin an investigation into the target of Schmitt's and Gray's political polemic: namely, forms of utopian politics based on an essential optimism about human nature that have been historically connected with forms of millenarianism.

The question posed at the center of Chapter 3 is the following: how might the thinking of politics and community change if it is believed that the fact of original sin can be overcome? This leads to a discussion of the political form that such a sinless union with others might take, what Norman Cohn calls "mystical anarchism." The latter is the occasion for an experimental investigation into the revolutionary eschatology at the basis of millenarian belief: the conviction that these are the end times, in which a conflict between the forces of good and evil, in the person of the Anti-Christ, will culminate in the triumph of good and the establishment of God's kingdom on earth. Although I am highly skeptical of such eschatological belief, I try to show how what animates it is a form of faith-based communism that draws its strength from the poor, the marginal, and the dispossessed. I examine the most radical version of such communism, the so-called heresy of the free spirit that gained great popularity in the thirteenth and fourteenth centuries, and which was violently suppressed by the Catholic Church. To my mind, the most compelling version of this "heresy" is the French mystic Marguerite Porete's *The Mirror of Simple and Annihilated Souls*, which has interesting connections with Meister Eckhart's mystical theology. Porete was burned at the stake in Paris in 1310 for heresy. The core of her book is an account of the seven stages by which the soul can overcome the limitations of the human condition defined by original sin and achieve a union with the divine: once annihilated through a daring and dramatic process of love, the soul becomes God, a version of faith that I also seek to track in relation to other female mystics. The political form of this overcoming of sin is a communism that seeks to annul the institution of private property, which is viewed as the basis for social inequality. In place of Cohn's questionable polemic against the morally licentious and politically pernicious character of mystical anarchism, I try to identify a lineage of radical political thinking that can be found in the anarchism of Gustav Landauer, the communal experiments of Georges Bataille, and the Situationism of Raoul Vaneigem. In conclusion, I turn towards contemporary manifestations of experimental communism in two fields: in the collaborative, collective practices of contemporary art and in the insurrectionism of anonymous groups like The Invisible Committee. Although I am critical of both tendencies, I try to track what has shifted in the aesthetic and political practices of resistance and how the latter has begun to mobilize around concepts of invisibility, opacity, anonymity, and resonance. I conclude by bringing out what I see as most valuable in mystical anarchism, namely its politics of love, in which love is understood as that act of absolute spiritual daring that attempts to eviscerate existing conceptions of identity in order that a new form of subjectivity can come into being.

It is this conception of love and its connection with faith that provides the link to Chapter 4. The focus here is the recent resurgence of interest in Saint Paul shown in the work of thinkers like Jacob Taubes, Giorgio Agamben, and Badiou. Paul's political theology has been employed negatively as a critique of empire, and positively as a means of finding new figures of activism and militancy based around a universalistic claim to equality. I begin by arguing that the return to Paul is nothing new and that the history of Christianity, from Marcion to Luther to Kierkegaard, can be understood as a gesture of reformation whereby the essentially secular order of the existing or established church is undermined in order to approach the religious core of faith. Paul has, I argue, always been the figure for a reformation motivated by intense political disappointment. The double nature of the address in Paul is fascinating: both in his address by the call that transformed him from a persecutor of Jewish Christians into a preacher of Christ's gospel; and in the addressee of Paul's call, namely the various churches or communities that he established and which are identified as the refuse of the world, the scum of the earth. But the central concern of this chapter is the idea of faith understood not as the abstraction of a metaphysical belief in God, but rather as the lived subjective commitment to an infinite demand. Faith is understood here as a declarative act, as an enactment of the self, as a performative that proclaims itself into existence in a situation of crisis where what is called for is a decisive political intervention. I examine how this conception of faith as proclamation is outlined in Agamben's reading of Paul before turning to Heidegger, the central focus of the chapter.

Through a close reading of Heidegger's 1920–21 lectures on Paul, I try to show how the decisive insights of the project that would come to be called, in the following years, "fundamental ontology" were powerfully shaped by his engagement with Paul's Epistles. Heidegger's central question is: how is Christian life enacted? His answer is that it is enacted in a proclamation or a gospel that arises in a situation of crisis and which is marked by a mood of anguish. With this idea of anguish as the proof of the calling, I consider Paul's subtle relation to mysticism before turning to Heidegger's discussions of the figures of *parousia*, or second coming, and the Anti-Christ, which are the source of his later insight into the theme of falling. It is in the intricacy of Heidegger's reading of texts like Second Thessalonians that his thinking of temporality takes shape. Against Agamben's critique of Heidegger, I show how Heidegger's reading of Paul has a plausibly Messianic dimension. The latter turns on the double imperative of what will be called *meontology*: seeing what is as if it were not, and seeing what is not in what is. What emerges—surprisingly—from Heidegger's lectures on Paul is not a reading defined by the figure of autarchy and resoluteness understood as potentiality, but a conception of the human being defined by an experience of enactment that exceeds the limits of potency and strength, and in which authenticity is rooted in an affirmation of weakness and impotence.

On this basis—and this is the theoretical core of the second half of *The Faith of the Faithless*—a reinterpretation of Heidegger's *Being and Time* becomes possible. I give a close reading of Heidegger's discussion of the call of conscience. The call has a double function in Heidegger that is strongly analogous to Paul: it both calls me away from entanglement in fallen everydayness and towards the uncanniness or strangeness that, for Heidegger, defines the human condition. I am called away from what Heidegger calls "the nothing of the world" towards the nullity of the call. I show how Heidegger's *Dasein*, his term of art for the human being, is an entity that is stretched between two nullities and how this constitutes the experience of guilt. The latter is not to be understood as moral culpability, which appears later in *Being and Time* as "wanting-to-have-a-conscience," but as the essential onto-logical structure of indebtedness. If Dasein always has its being to be, as Heidegger repeats, then its being is constituted by debt. The strangeness of what it means to be human, in Heidegger's view, consists in the affirmation of a double nullity: the nullity of thrownness and the nullity of projection. This double nullity is nothing less than the experience of freedom, a freedom that does not evade responsibility but which constitutes it.

In the penultimate section of the chapter, I turn back to the question of faith more closely and consider a further heresy, namely that of Marcion in the second century. The radicality of Marcion's position lies in his hyper-Paulinian affirmation of faith, one which comes at the price of a disavowal of the experience of law, in particular as it is expressed in the Hebrew Bible. This leads Marcion to cut the cord that connects "Old" and "New" Testaments—the orders of creation and redemption—and replace the affirmation of one god with two. Monotheism becomes dualism: the god of creation is not the same being as the god of redemption proclaimed by Paul. Following closely Harnack's reading of Marcion, I show how the seductive power of this heresy becomes clear: what is announced in Paul's Epistles is something absolutely new, for which the only proof is the proclamation of faith. This brings us back to the contemporary return to Paul and the disavowal of the figure of law that is at its core. I argue that the Paulinism of Agamben and Badiou is actually a crypto-Marcionism that risks a radical antinomianism in its attempt to break the connection between law and faith. Against this tendency, I give a reading of Romans 7 and 8 that tries to provide a different and, I hope, more plausible understanding of the relation between faith and law: if law and sin were not within me, then faith would mean nothing. Our wretchedness is our greatness.

Returning to the triangulation outlined above, while the interdependence between politics and religion dominates the three preceding chapters, the focus shifts in Chapter 5 to the question of violence and its relation to the ethics and politics of nonviolence. This chapter uses my polemical debate with Žižek as its guiding thread and argumentative foil. I begin by giving a reading of Žižek's views on violence, and in particular his understanding of Walter Benjamin's conception of divine violence. After identifying a series of deadlocks—at once philosophical and political—in Žižek's thinking, I turn to Benjamin's famous 1921 essay "Critique of Violence," and the series of distinctions at its heart: between law-making and law-preserving violence, the political strike and the general strike, and mythic and divine violence. What Žižek misses in his interpretation of "Critique of Violence" is the dimension of nonviolence and Benjamin's question as to whether and to what extent a nonviolent resolution of conflict is possible.

Of particular interest in Benjamin is the question of the relation between divine violence, on the one hand, and the biblical commandment "Thou shalt not kill"—the injunction to nonviolence—on the other. Does the prohibition of murder preclude acts of violence? As we will see, matters are more complex than they might first appear and much more nuanced than Žižek allows. The biblical commandment is not an impersonal, coercive law addressed in the third person—for example, "Murder is the unlawful killing of a human being with malice aforethought" (US Code, Title 18). The commandment is a more fragile, but insistent, guideline or plumb-line for action, addressed in the second person, "Thou shalt not kill." Also, crucially, the force of the commandment is non-coercive and requires our assent. In my jargon, it is an ethical demand that requires approval. By virtue of its noncoercive force, the commandment of nonviolence is a guideline for action with which we are obliged to wrestle in solitude and, in certain exceptional cases, to take responsibility for ignoring. The commandment that prohibits murder does not, then, exclude the possibility of murder, but neither does it condone such killing.

My interpretation of the commandment in Benjamin occasions a sideways move into a series of reflections on the question of violence in relation to Levinas. It will allow us to interpret the otherwise inexplicable fact that the first ethical injunction—for Levinas, "you shall not commit murder" (*tu ne tueras point*)— necessarily arises in a situation of war and violence, and is indeed an act of violence itself. The face of the other is both the temptation to kill and the call to peace. Levinas, like Benjamin, must acknowledge violence in his attempts to give expression to the nonviolent relation to the other. This leads to a very different picture of Levinasian ethics than we are accustomed to, where the face of the other is both the temptation to kill and the call to peace. Levinas gives us a fragile ethics with dirty hands, a difficult pacifism.

The political implications of what is called, following Judith Butler, "nonviolent violence," are laid out in terms of a historically embedded conflict between authoritarianism and anarchism, which recalls the analyses of Chapter 3. Here, I turn to the specifics of my political disagreement with Žižek. This is not a question of the narcissism of petty personal differences, but of a clear political cleavage that recalls Bakunin's critique of Marx and the anarchist critique of Leninism. I argue that the only choice in politics is not, as it is for Lenin and Žižek, between state power or no power. Rather, politics consists in the creation of interstitial distance within the state and the cultivation of forms of cooperation and mutuality most powerfully expressed in the anarchist vision of federalism. The central question at stake here is our widely differing evaluations of political resistance and its relation to the state. Against Žižek's claim that resistance is surrender, I will argue for the efficacy of infinite ethical demands for a politics of resistance. Although I am strongly critical of what I see as the mannerist nostalgia for revolutionary violence in thinkers like Žižek, I conclude with a critique of abstract and ahistorical conceptions of nonviolence. Violence is of course a phenomenon with a history, broadly the history of exploitation and expropriation. History, indeed, is a seemingly unending cycle of violence and counter-violence, and to refuse its overwhelming evidence in the name of some *a priori* conception of nonviolence is to disavow history, risking ideological abstraction and dogmatism. On this account, politics is action guided by an ever-compromised infinite ethical demand that arises in the conflict between a commitment to nonviolence and the historical reality of the violence into which one is inserted. Political action is caught in a strictly context-dependent double bind that negotiates between the responsibility for the commandment of nonviolence and the responsibility of being drawn into a situation in which that commandment might have to be violated. In a world such as ours, simple-minded, blanket denunciations of violence not only risk missing the point, they defuse the very possibility of resistance and transformation in the concrete struggles in which we are engaged. I conclude with some remarks on the relation between finite and infinite demands in politics.

The book ends with a second parable on the question of faith in Kierkegaard's *Works of Love*. Kierkegaard places great emphasis on the *rigor* of faith that seeks to persist with the commandment to love, "you shall love your neighbor." As I show in my discussion of Paul and Heidegger, faith is a proclamation that enacts life. Such a proclamation is as true for the non-Christian as for the Christian—indeed, it is arguably *truer* for non-Christians, because their faith is not supported by any creedal dogma, the institution of the church, or metaphysical beliefs in matters like the immortality of the soul and the afterlife. Paradoxically (and here I return to Oscar Wilde's question with which I began), the faith of the faithless reveals the true nature of faith: the rigorous activity of the subject that proclaims itself into being at each instant without guarantees or security, and which seeks to abide with the infinite demand of love. Faith is the enactment of the self in relation to an infinite demand that both exceeds my power and yet requires all my power.[18]

For those readers with some acquaintance with my work, the foregoing might begin to explain the seemingly odd fact that I have written a book that deals with questions of religion and faith. Elsewhere, of course, I assert that philosophy begins in disappointment, notably religious disappointment—that is to say, crudely stated, the death of God. Nothing in this book contradicts this claim. When I talk about faith, it is not at all a matter of belief in the existence of some metaphysical reality like God. My conception of faith—as fidelity to the infinite demand—is not just shared by the denominationally faithless or unbelievers, but can be experienced by them in an exemplary way. Faith is not, then, necessarily theistic. However, and this has also been a constant concern of my work, an atheistic conception of faith should not be triumphalist. I have little sympathy for the evangelical atheism of Richard Dawkins or Christopher Hitchens that sees God and religion as some sort of historical error that has happily been corrected and refuted by scientific progress. On the contrary, the religious tradition with which I am most familiar—broadly Judeo-Christian—offers a powerful way of articulating questions of the ultimate meaning and value of human life in ways irreducible to naturalism. Thinkers whose company I have long valued, like Augustine and Pascal, raise exactly the right questions, even if I cannot accept their answers. Furthermore—and this is something that Rousseau understood better than anyone—when it comes to the political question of what might motivate a subject to act in concert with others, rationality alone is insufficient. In order that a legitimate political association might become possible—that is, in order that citizens might pledge themselves to the good—reason has to be allied to questions of faith and belief that are able to touch the deep existential matrix of human subjectivity, what William Connolly calls its "visceral register."[19]

In short, neither traditional theism nor evangelical atheism will suffice. What is needed, as James Wood rightly puts it, is a "theologically engaged atheism that resembles disappointed belief. Such atheism, only a semitone from faith, would be like musical dissonance, the more acute for its proximity."[20] For me, if philosophy is inconceivable without religion, then it is equally inconceivable with religion. The idea of the faith of the faithless seems close to Dietrich Bonhoeffer's famous idea of a "religionless Christianity." In a letter to Eberhard Bethge from April 1944, Bonhoeffer writes, "We are moving toward a completely religionless time," where even those who honestly describe themselves as religious "do not in the least act up to it."[21] True enough, one might say, and perhaps even truer now than in 1944. Bonhoeffer's question is "How do we speak of God—without religion, i.e. without the temporally conditioned presuppositions of metaphysics, inwardness and so on?" My question, however, is the opposite: it is not a matter of how we speak of God without religion, but rather how we speak of religion—as that force which can bind human beings together in association—without God.

Although the four main chapters of this book constitute a developing and interrelated set of concerns that seek to respond to the above-mentioned triangulation of politics, religion, and violence, each of them is relatively self-contained. I see the chapters as a series of essays in the sense of an "assay" or experiment. Indeed, if the form of this book resembles anything I've written before, then it is probably closest to *Very Little ... Almost Nothing*, which also had an experimental structure and adumbrated the themes of mortality and literature from a number of different perspectives rather than providing the kind of single, overarching argument that can be found in a book like *Infinitely Demanding*. However, although it is my hope that this book is not in complete contradiction with my earlier work, I do not want to give the impression that nothing has changed. The reader will find that my views on violence and nonviolence have shifted significantly, as has the centrality of philosophers like Rousseau and Heidegger to the development of the set of theoretical concerns outlined below. But what is perhaps most novel here is the emphasis on the idea of love, in particular the idea of mystical love, which is understood as that act of spiritual daring that attempts to eviscerate the old self in order that something new might come into being. The concept of love, explored in Chapter 3, is developed in relation to the experience of faith in Chapter 4 and underpins Chapter 5 and the opening and closing parables. The question motivating much of my previous work can be simply stated: how to live? The response to this question obviously turns on the relation to mortality: to philosophize is to learn how to die. For reasons that are still slightly obscure to me, but which this book begins to clarify, the question "how to live?" has become the question "how to love?" Love is not just as strong as death—it is stronger.

2

The Catechism of the Citizen

I would wish, then, that in every State there were a moral code, or a kind of civil profession of faith, containing, positively, the social maxims everyone would be bound to acknowledge, and negatively, the fanatical maxims one would be bound to reject, not as impious, but as seditious.[1]

Jean-Jacques Rousseau,
The Discourses and Other Early Political Writings

Rousseau's observation, in a letter to Voltaire of August 18, 1756, is, of course, the germ of the argument for civil religion that he would go on to elaborate six years later in *The Social Contract*. The context of Rousseau's letter—and one knows that whatever fellow feeling might have existed between the two men was rapidly turning to enmity during these years—is Voltaire's response to the Lisbon earthquake of 1755 (the super-tsunami of its day) about which he had published a poem in March the following year. "In your *Poem on Natural Religion*," Rousseau wrote, "you gave us the Catechism of man: give us now, in the one I am suggesting to you, the *Catechism of the Citizen*."[2]

Voltaire, of course, did no such thing and went on to write his *Candide* in 1759, which Rousseau in his paranoid megalomania saw as the true response to his 1756 letter, which had received only a brief, albeit conciliatory reply. However, in this chapter I want to explore the idea of a *catechism of the citizen* or a civil profession of faith as a way of thinking about the relation between three interconnected terms: politics, law, and religion. Obviously, the theological concept of catechism—from *catechesis* or instruction specifically in the elements of Christian faith—is being deliberately politicized by Rousseau in a way that unwittingly anticipates later tracts, such as Bakunin's "Revolutionary Catechism" of 1866 and, four years later, Nechayev's splendidly nihilistic "Catechism of a Revolutionary."[3]

My argument will continually cut in two directions at once:

1. On the one hand, I want to follow closely at the textual and conceptual level Rousseau's claim that what is required to solve the problem of politics and law is a civil profession of faith, a civil catechism. I want to show how the problem of politics in Rousseau—the very *being* of the political, understood as the act by which a people becomes a people—is articulated around what we might call a paradox of sovereignty that draws it ineluctably towards a religious solution.

To borrow Louis Althusser's word, the functioning of Rousseau's thought is only possible because of the play of a series of *décalages*, displacements or dislocations. Althusser claims that it is the play of these *décalages* that both makes possible and at the same time impossible what Rousseau calls his "sad and great system."[4] The conditions of possibility for Rousseau's system are at once its condition of impossibility, which of course is a definition of the quasi-transcendental in Derrida's sense.

That is, Rousseau's solution to the problem of politics, which goes by the name or, more accurately, as we will see, the *misnomer* of the social contract, attempts to cover over a series of *décalages* that make the articulation of that problem possible. Rousseau's thought

—and, for me, this is an important methodological caveat—is a self-conscious play of dislocations and displacements, a reflexive series of contradictions that make both the articulation and disarticulation of that thought possible. Rousseau's text is thus a sort of *machine à décalage* of which he was utterly self-conscious and which makes him in my view, along with Nietzsche, the supremely *fictive* philosopher. I use the adjective "supreme" to modify the noun "fiction" advisedly and will return to this point presently.

This play of *décalages* is one explanation of the multiplicity of possible, plausible, and deeply contradictory interpretations of Rousseau, whether Kantian or Hegelian, liberal or communitarian, not to mention totalitarian.[5] Incidentally, I think all classical philosophical texts from Plato onwards are *décalage* machines, which is why they are able to sustain a number of plausible yet contradictory interpretations. Perhaps this is one of the reasons why we define such texts as canonical.

If the problem that Rousseau is trying to solve in *The Social Contract* is the problem of politics, then the solution to that problem requires religion. This means, of course, that we have to read *The Social Contract* and arguably Rousseau's entire sad system back to front.[6] That is, the political argument of *The Social Contract* requires the account of civil religion, which otherwise looks like an addendum to the book. Which is to say that Rousseau's purportedly purely internal or *immanentist* conception of the being of politics requires a dimension of externality or *transcendence* in order to become effective. Or again, a conception of the political based on the absolute primacy of autonomy seems to call for a moment of heteronomy for its articulation and authorization.

2. However, I also want to use Rousseau's thought in order to show how his conception of the political can throw some light on the present situation, that is, on the darkness of our times. What I mean is that if Rousseau's sad system is a *décalage* machine, then I wonder whether something analogous might be said of our world, defined as it is by a series of nightmarish intrications of politics

and religion: politics of religion and religions of politics, where we have entered nothing less than an epoch of new religious war. Thus, my hope is that following Rousseau's thinking on politics and religion will somehow allow us to think through and think against our present.

This leads me to the following series of general—maybe too general—questions: Is politics conceivable without religion? The answer is obviously affirmative as the evidence of various secular political theories testifies. But is politics *practicable* without religion? That is the question. And it is the question that Rousseau's thinking of politics faces. Can politics become effective as a way of shaping, motivating, and mobilizing a people or peoples without some sort of dimension—if not foundation—that is religious, without some sort of appeal to transcendence, to externality, to what we called above, with Charles Taylor, "fullness," however substantive or otherwise that appeal might be? I do not think so.

The exemplarity of Rousseau, to my mind, consists in the fact that he gives us the definitive expression of the modern conception of politics: that is, politics is the break with any conception of nature and natural law and has to be based in the concepts of popular sovereignty, free association, rigorous equality, and collective autonomy understood as the self-determination of a people. And yet in order for this modern conception of politics to become effective it has to have a religious dimension, a moment of what the Romans used to call *theologia civilis*, civil theology. The *secularization* that seems to define modern politics has to acknowledge a moment of what Emilio Gentile calls *sacralization*, the transformation of a political entity like a state, nation, class, or party into a sacred entity, which means that it becomes transcendent, unchallengeable, and intangible.[7]

So, can a political collectivity maintain itself in existence, that is, maintain its unity and identity, without a moment of the sacred, without religion, rituals, and something that we can only call *belief*? Once again, I do not think so. The presidential campaign of Barack Obama in 2008—sometimes reduced to one word: "BELIEVE"—comes to mind here. I have turned a critical eye towards Obama elsewhere, but it is worth noting that his political genius—the word is not too strong—lies in his combination of the rhetorical force of religion, in particular the eloquence of historically black Christianity, with a defense of classical constitutional American liberalism.[8]

Might we not conceive of the possibility of redefining the secularization that is believed to be definitive of modernity with the idea of modern politics as a metamorphosis of sacralization, where modern forms of politics—whether liberal democracy, fascism, soviet communism, national socialism and the rest—have to be grasped as new articulations and mutations of the sacred, as *metamorphoses of sacralization?*

Before continuing, it should be noted that I have come to this conclusion with no particular joy. We are living through a chronic re-theologization of politics, which makes this time certainly the darkest period in my lifetime, and arguably for much longer. At the heart of the horror of the present is the intrication of politics and religion, an intrication defined by violence, and this is what I would like to begin to think through in this book. I want to do this not in order to break the connection between politics and religion, but to acknowledge the limitations of any completely secularist politics, particularly on the left.

It seems to me that the left has all too easily ceded the religious ground to the right and it is this ground that needs to be regained in a coherent, long-term, and tenacious political war of position, as Gramsci would say; indeed, he famously wrote that "socialism is the *religion* that is needed to kill off Christianity."[9] The relation of politics to religion raises the question of the necessity of *fiction* in the political realm, of the need for a new version of Bentham's "theory of fictions," both the seeming necessity for a divine fiction at the basis of politics and the possibility of what Wallace Stevens, after Santayana, would call a *supreme* fiction in politics. But I am getting ahead of myself.

ALTHUSSER AND BADIOU ON ROUSSEAU

Permit me a word on methodology. Louis Althusser's extraordinarily intelligent reading of *The Social Contract* will be constantly on my mind as I write, as will that of Alain Badiou in *Being and Event*. Along with Jacques Lacan, Althusser was the other of Badiou's two masters as a young philosopher. A claim to be developed below is that part of the difficulty in understanding Badiou's political thought stems from too great an emphasis being placed on his relation to Marx and the misunderstood and maligned phenomenon of French Maoism and too little on his debt to Rousseau. In my view, matters become much clearer if Badiou is approached as a Rousseauist rather than a Marxist.

There is a strong formal similarity between Althusser's and Badiou's interpretations of Rousseau, although it conceals significant differences between the two interpretations at the ontological level. Both Badiou and Althusser display a similar formalism in picking out the contradictions or *décalages* that both define and divide Rousseau's text, but they take this in very different directions.

For Badiou, the originality of Rousseau consists in thinking the being of politics in terms of the category of the *event*, understood as a subjective (but not individual—becoming a subject for Badiou can be described as a trans-individual act) moment of creation whose radicality consists in the fact that it does not originate in any structure supported within being or the situation, such as the realm of the socio-economic. In Badiou's jargon, the social pact of association is the supernumerary or ultra-one of the event that is in excess of the pure multiplicity of being.

For Althusser, by contrast, Rousseau's project is defined by a failure to understand the socio-economic constitution of the political. Rousseau is unable to think what Althusser calls the *real*, understood as the objective dialectic of forces and relations of production. Linked to this is Rousseau's failure to acknowledge the specificity of factional or class interests as politically emancipatory, i.e., the revolutionary potential of the proletariat. In Althusser's view, these failures lead Rousseau towards an entirely ideological politics which is ineluctably drawn back towards an artisanal socio-economic primitivism and has no way of facing up to the savage potentiality of capitalist relations of production.

Obviously, the key figure behind both of these interpretations is Marx. Althusser's critique of Rousseau is that of an orthodox base-superstructure Marxist. Badiou's "Marxism" is political or evental and can find no support from the situation, i.e., it cannot simply be deduced from socio-economic causes; such is Badiou's break with orthodox Second International versions of Marxism. It also has to be articulated at a distance from the state, which is the reason for his break with Lenin and all forms of Leninism.

With this in mind, it is also worth mentioning that Althusser's views on Marx—and indeed Rousseau—undergo a significant recalibration in his late work on "The Underground Current of the Materialism of the Encounter," written in the early 1980s, when he was mostly in psychiatric care after having murdered his wife.[10] This text, at times strangely painful to read, develops a philosophy of transcendental contingency which combines an Epicurean materialism of atoms and the void with a Heideggerian account of the formation of worlds out of this void, or what Althusser calls the "aleatory encounter," understood as the moment of unification. The text presents a philosophical history of the encounter from Machiavelli, Spinoza, Hobbes, Rousseau, Marx, Heidegger, and indeed Althusser's student Derrida. In this late text, a very different picture of Marx emerges to that found in Althusser's earlier work—what we might call an evental Marx, a Marx dedicated to the surprise of the event, a much more Machiavellian Marx. For the later Althusser, there appear to be two philosophical categories: the void, which is the name of being; and the encounter, which is concerned with the constitution of a world. The process Althusser describes, adducing his historical examples, is the way in which a world is constituted out of the transcendental contingency of the void. This is how he reads Rousseau, in terms of the passage from the void of the state of nature full of disparate individuals in the *Discourse on Inequality*, to the formation of a world in a moment of legitimate unification in *The Social Contract*. In other words, late Althusser advances an ontological dualism in Rousseau that begins to resemble Badiou or perhaps, more properly, vice versa.

WHY ARE POLITICAL INSTITUTIONS NECESSARY? THE "VIOLENT REASONER" AND THE PROBLEM OF MOTIVATION IN POLITICS

There are two versions of the book that has come to be known as *The Social Contract*, although, as already mentioned, this title is a misnomer. For the book's publication in 1762, Rousseau finished a clean handwritten draft, to be sent to the printer. It has come to be known as the *Geneva Manuscript*. Precise dating of this text is difficult, although it might well date from 1755, and thus follows hard on the heels of the *Discourse on Inequality* and the *Discourse on Political Economy* that were both published in that year—though the writing of the Second Discourse was completed in 1754. What is fascinating about this first version of *The Social Contract* is the *décalage* that opens up around the question of politics and religion.

Let us consider two philological puzzles. First, Rousseau writes a compelling opening chapter to the *Geneva Manuscript* on the necessity for political institutions, which is simply suppressed in the published version. Second, although the text of the *Geneva Manuscript* is written in Rousseau's best hand, a chapter called "On Civil Religion" is scribbled in an almost indecipherable hand on the text's verso. It is probable that this text was written in 1761 as Rousseau was drafting the final version of *The Social Contract*. So, Rousseau's doubts and uncertainties about whether the subject of politics can be raised without reference to religion frame the entire agonized writing and conceptual organization of *The Social Contract*.

In addition, Rousseau's doubts extend to the very title of his book on politics. He initially thought of it as a work on the need for and nature of political institutions. Rousseau begins the *Geneva Manuscript* with the words, "Let us begin by inquiring why the necessity for political institutions arises."[11] The fair version of the *Geneva Manuscript* has the Platonic subtitle "Essay about the Form of the Republic," where "form" would seem to recall the concept of *eidos*. Although Rousseau changes the published subtitle of *The Social Contract* to "Principles of Political Right," he retains the allusion to Plato. The new subtitle is a variation on the *Republic*'s subtitle, *peri dikaion politikos*: concerning the right or just ordering of human affairs in the state or republic. But the full extent of Rousseau's wavering about the title of his book on politics is brought out by Gourevitch, who writes that the manuscript title page of the *Geneva Manuscript*

> shows "Of the Social Contract" crossed out and replaced by "Of Civil Society," which is again crossed out and replaced by the original "Of the Social Contract"; the second line reads "or"; and the third line gives as subtitle "Essay on the Constitution of the State"; "Constitution of the State" is then crossed out and replaced by "The State," which is then also crossed out, to leave the subtitle to read "Essay on the Form of the Republic." In the definitive version, the subtitle became "Principles of Political Right."[12]

In order to bring out the full extent of Rousseau's uncertainty about the relation between politics and religion, I will lay out the argument of the initial chapter of the *Geneva Manuscript*, "On the General Society of Mankind," in a series of sixteen steps. Rousseau's question is this: Why does the need for political institutions arise?

(i)   The initial answer is that "Nature's gentle voice is no longer an infallible guide for us."[13] That is, human beings have become denatured and alienated. This, of course, is the argument of the *Discourse on Inequality*. Furthermore, life in the innocence of nature would leave human beings without any society as there is no communication. We would live without feeling anything: "we would die without having lived; our entire happiness would consist in not knowing our misery."[14]

(ii)   We have become social and therefore—according to Rousseau's logic in the *Discourse on Inequality*—miserable and wicked. We have entered Hobbes's state of war, which Rousseau equates with the state of nature.

(iii)   Nature cannot be a guide to how society should be run: this is a "true illusion" or "veritable chimera."[15] Rousseau is resolutely against any conception of natural law, as he was in the *Discourse on Inequality*.

(iv)   We therefore find ourselves in a social state of independence or a violent individualism governed by private interest alone. Contra Mandeville in "The Fable of the Bees" or Pope in "An Essay on Man," there is no alliance between private interest and the public good. On the contrary, for Rousseau, private interest and the public good pull in opposite directions.

(v)   So, the question becomes: how do we persuade the personage that Rousseau calls "the independent man"?[16] That is, how might the person of private interest—the Hobbesian rational egoist, the character that Rousseau identifies with Diderot's "violent reasoner"—be persuaded to act out of the common good rather than private interest?[17]

(vi)   One powerful option is divine will. This is rejected, as Rousseau asserts that it will lead to fanaticism. The multitude will never grasp the sublime morals that God imposes upon us, but will create "Gods as senseless as itself."[18]

(vii)   Therefore, Rousseau suggests, "Let us set aside the sacred precepts of the various Religions whose abuse causes as many crimes as their use may prevent."[19] He goes on to argue that we should not appeal to theology in determining the good, but should return to the philosopher what the theologian has imperfectly understood. He continues: "Let us restore to the Philosopher the examination of a question which the Theologian has never dealt with except to the prejudice of humankind."[20]

(viii) Yet the philosopher will send us back to the concept of the human race or humankind (*le genre humain*), which is a concept that rightly invites Rousseau's suspicions. The philosopher will claim that the human being should address himself to the greatest good or—and this is how the central term of Rousseau's political theory is casually dropped into the *Geneva Manuscript* in a seeming allusion to Diderot—the general will.

(ix) How does the "violent reasoner" or "independent man" respond to the philosopher? He will assert that it is not a question of teaching him what justice is, "But of showing me what *interest* I have in being just."[21] What is the connection between justice and the interest in justice? *Cui bono?* as Hobbes writes, recalling Cicero.[22] In other words, what is at stake is not a question of the philosophical justification of the good, but rather the subjective motivation to act on the good. Recall that Hobbes's answer to this question in *Leviathan* is that my interest in justice is in order to leave behind "that miserable condition of Warre."[23]

(x) There are other obvious problems with an overly philosophical approach to politics. The general will is "a pure act of understanding" that requires that each citizen become a philosopher of sorts. For egalitarian reasons, Rousseau wants to avoid Plato's elegant solution to this problem with the idea of the "philosopher king." He asks, "Will the average man be capable of deriving his rules of conduct from this manner of reasoning?" Also, might we not mistake our inclinations for the general will? "Will he listen to the inner voice?"[24] But if such an "inner voice" or conscience is only formed through the habit of judgment in relation to the laws that govern a given society, then such a conscience cannot serve to establish such laws. How, therefore, do we avoid error in moral reasoning?

(xii)   There is no obvious way of avoiding error. There is no Socratic *daimon* or Augustinian divine voice to which we can appeal, as conscience is only formed when human beings become sociable—that is, when they have already become narcissistic and miserable. We cannot, for the same reason, appeal to the principles of right that may govern the society we live in, for we might well be the dupes of that society, as we do not know anything else. Mushrooms grown in the dark cannot be trusted to judge the quality of sunlight.

(xii)   What to do, then? Rousseau writes, in an extraordinarily eloquent passage that concludes the chapter, and I quote at length:

> But although there is no natural and general society among men, although men become unhappy and wicked in becoming sociable, although the laws of justice and equality mean nothing to those who live both in the freedom of the state of nature and subject to the needs of the social state; far from thinking that there is neither virtue nor happiness for us and that heaven has abandoned us without resources to the corruption of the species, let us endeavor to draw from the ill itself the remedy that should cure it. By means of *new associations* let us correct, if possible, the lack of a general association. Let our violent interlocutor himself be the judge of our success. Let us show him in *perfected art* the redress of the evils which beginning art caused to nature: let us show him all the misery of the state which he believed happy, all that is false in the reasoning which he believed solid. Let him behold in a better constitution of things the worth of good deeds, the punishment of bad ones, the endearing harmony of justice and happiness. Let us enlighten his reason with new knowledge, fire his heart with new sentiments, and let him learn to

increase his being and his felicity by sharing them with his fellows. If my zeal does not blind me to the enterprise, let us not doubt that if he has the fortitude of soul and upright sense, this enemy of humankind will in the end abjure his hatred along with his errors, that the reason which led him astray will bring him back to humanity, that he will learn to prefer to his apparent interest his interest rightly understood; that he will become good, virtuous, sensitive, and in sum, finally, instead of the ferocious brigand he wanted to be, the most solid bulwark of a well-ordered society.[25]

What is being imagined here is an art of politics. Such an art attempts to show "in perfected art" the reparation of the ills that "beginning art caused to nature." The logic of Rousseau's argument recalls Derrida's analysis of the *pharmakon*, which means both poison and cure. Rousseau insists that we must endeavor to "derive from the evil the remedy which will cure it." The art of politics is not *creatio ex nihilo*, or a work of genius, but the imagining of what Rousseau calls "new associations" that will remedy the lack of a general association. That is, given that we live in the aftermath of the catastrophe that "beginning art caused to nature"—namely the development of society away from a state of nature towards a state of war and violent inequality—the cure is not a return to nature, but a turn to art: an art of politics that is capable of shaping new associations. Art against art, then. Of course, this is nothing new. In the Introduction to *Leviathan*, Hobbes compares the commonwealth to "an Artificiall man."[26] If God said during creation, "Let us make man," then the art of politics is the fiction of an artificial man complete with an "Artificiall soul" that will animate the "Body Politique."[27]

(xiii) What is fascinating about the opening chapter to the *Geneva Manuscript* is that we can see how the argument of *The Social Contract* was initially intended to persuade the skeptic, the violent reasoner, the social narcissus living in state of war described at the end of the *Discourse on Inequality*. It is a question of providing something that will motivate the violent reasoner to act in the light of the general will and that will "bring him back to humanity,"[28] in relation to public rather than merely private interest.

(xiv) The argument about religion comes full circle here. In order to force the violent reasoner to act on the general will we cannot rely on religion, on the coercive power of will of God, as this would lead to fanaticism. What seems to be required is a philosophical answer to a practical dilemma. Yet, at the end of *The Social Contract*, in the chapter on civil religion scribbled on the verso of the *Geneva Manuscript*, Rousseau acknowledges the motivational inadequacy of a purely philosophical account of politics and offers the picture of a political religion. In so doing, Rousseau implicitly accepts the limits of any Platonism in politics and comes much closer to Hobbes than is usually thought.

(xv) Perhaps this is why Rousseau eliminated the original introduction to his book on politics and the chapter on religion was added to *The Social Contract*. Is the necessity for religion the Platonist's cry of despair? Is that faint noise we hear at night from the downstairs apartment the sound of Socrates's sobbing? Or is it rather the quiet ironic Straussian chuckling at the very idea that philosophers might be kings? It is difficult to discern through the floorboards of the millennia of interpretation and misunderstanding.

(xvi) These are unanswerable, indeed paralyzing, questions. This much is clear, though: there is a need for fictions other than philosophical in order to unite the general will with the interest to act on that will, and to bring the "enemy of mankind ... back to humanity." The "perfected art" of politics that will permit the formation of "new associations" requires new forms of what I will call *fictional force* that might address the problem of motivation in politics. As we will see presently, these fictional forms are described with disarming honesty in the *Discourse on Political Economy*. For those tempted to see Rousseau as what Gourevitch nicely calls "a lisping Kant,"[29] it should be noted that this is the problem Kant never solves in his ethics: namely, how to combine the legitimacy of practical reason—the universality of the moral law—with the motivation to act on that law. Insofar as Kant's critical system is written under the sign of the primacy of practical reason, the problem of motivational force is arguably what undoes that system, the rationalism of Kant's ethics, and any Neo-Kantian moral rationalism such as Habermas's discourse ethics. As Rousseau writes in a political fragment reminiscent of Hume: "The mistake of most moralists has always been to consider man as an essentially reasonable being. Man is a sensitive being, who consults solely his passions in order to act, and for whom reason serves only to palliate the follies his passions lead him to commit."[30]

THE BEING OF POLITICS, OR THE MISNOMER OF THE SOCIAL CONTRACT

Man is born free, and he is everywhere in chains. One believes himself the others' master, and yet is more a slave then they. How did this change come about? I do not know. What can make it legitimate? I believe I can solve this question.[31]

Jean-Jacques Rousseau, *The Social Contract*

Perhaps the most obvious way of reading Rousseau's opening words to *The Social Contract* is to imagine that he is recommending that we throw off our chains and return to a state of original freedom, or what he elsewhere calls natural freedom. This is the romantic or indeed classical anarchist Bakuninesque reading of Rousseau, where revolutionary political activity is justified insofar as it returns us to the allegedly free and original condition of humanity without the shackles of law and government.

However, to read Rousseau in this manner is to misread him. Let's look at those words more closely: man is everywhere in chains, that is, everyone everywhere is in chains, not just the oppressed, the exploited, and the poor. Rousseau is clear: "One believes himself the others' master, and yet is more a slave than they." Thus—and this is the dialectical logic that Hegel will develop to full effect in the *Phenomenology of Spirit*—the master who believes himself free because of his ability to oppress the poor and disadvantaged and bend them to his will is mistaken in his belief. On the contrary, his very being as master is utterly dependent upon its recognition by the slave from whom he believes himself independent and superior. The master is paradoxically less free than the slave because the former's entire being is constituted through his purported superiority to the latter. Rousseau's point is that everyone is a slave—especially the master who believes that he is free.

Rousseau goes on, "How did this change come about?" That is, how is it that human beings all ended up wearing chains? How did we lose our natural freedom, our natural equality? In other words, to coin a phrase, what is the origin and foundation of inequality amongst human beings? "*Je l'ignore,*" Rousseau curtly responds, "I do not know," or, "I am ignorant or unaware of the reason for this transformation." Rousseau uses a more impersonal version of this sentence in the *Geneva Manuscript*, where he writes "*On n'en sait rien*" (No one knows).[32] Now, this is a peculiar thing for Rousseau to say given that, a few years earlier, he had provided a quite breathtakingly original answer to this question in the 1755 *Discourse on Inequality*. Either Rousseau is being inconsistent—and as readers of the *Confessions* are aware, consistency was never a virtue he claimed to possess—or what is going on in *The Social Contract* is not of the order of knowledge or epistemic certainty, but something else.

Returning to the opening quotation from *The Social Contract*, we can note an intriguing and important separation of the realm of knowledge from the realm of legitimacy. The political question of the transformation from freedom to bondage is not an epistemic or empirical question that can be resolved with reference to the state of nature or natural law. It is rather a question of the *legitimacy* of this transformation that presupposes a break between the orders of nature and politics. This means that the order of politics begins, to paraphrase Rousseau, by "setting aside all the facts,"[33] by disregarding the realm of being, of that which is, and establishing a domain where a new political subject comes into existence: a domain of art or fiction in the strong sense, the realm of what Badiou calls the *event*. Badiou criticizes Rousseau's recourse to the language of legitimacy and replaces it with talk of truth—by which he means not empirical or propositional truth, but the order of the new, of creation.[34] The distinction between truth and knowledge is, of course, inherited from Lacan, where truth is what bores a hole in knowledge.

With the question of legitimacy, understood as the emergence into existence of an evental political subject that breaks with the realm of facts and knowledge, we arrive at the problem of politics as conceived by Rousseau. In many ways, it feels more like a riddle than a problem, a riddle that is subject to a series of *décalages* that I will attempt to track. Slightly later in *The Social Contract*, in words set apart in the text with quotation marks, he states the problem in the following terms: "To find a form of association that will defend and protect the person and goods of each associate with the full common force, and by means of which each, uniting with all, nevertheless obey only himself and remain as free as before."[35]

How can human beings live according to a law that they recognize as equally binding on all citizens, as legitimate for the collective as a whole, and yet at the same time a law to which they freely submit because they see it as the expression of their own freedom? If there is no question of a return to nature, to an original freedom where we are finally free of our chains—the anarchist dream of society without the state—then the problem of politics is: how can those chains be made legitimate? Or, better, how can citizens wear legitimate chains? To put it crudely, the problem of politics is the relation between non-consensual and consensual forms of bondage, and the transition from the one to the other. How can we organize society so that freedom and equality might exist in some sort of equilibrium? "This," writes Rousseau, "is the fundamental problem to which the social contract provides the solution."[36]

But what do the words "social contract" mean for Rousseau? Is it, as I have already suggested, a misnomer for what he imagines as the being of politics? Firstly, the matter of politics is about the establishment of a form of association and the "new associations" that we noted above. This requires a convention or covenant, Rousseau thinks, but one that is not based on the family or any form of patriarchy *à la* Filmer, or the right of the strongest where the conqueror simply enslaves the conquered *à la* William the Conqueror—options that he discusses and dismisses in Book 1, Chapters 3 and 4. Importantly, it also excludes the possibility of a primary covenant between a people and a king of the kind imagined by Grotius or, in a more subtle way, by Hobbes. For Rousseau, crucially, "Before examining the act by which a people elects a king, it would be well to examine the act by which a people is a people. For that act, being necessarily prior to the other, is the true foundation of society."[37] Thus, the essence of politics or the being of the political consists in an act whereby a people becomes a people, an original covenant that presupposes that there has been at one time unanimity.

Althusser usefully illuminates this issue with an opposition between obstacles and forces: the obstacles that stand in the way of such a form of association and the forces that might enable it—a distinction that obviously echoes Marx's distinction between relations and forces of production. This is also where we are obliged to consider the relation between *The Social Contract* and the *Discourse on Inequality*. Part Two of the Second Discourse gives an extraordinarily powerful account of the obstacles that stand in the way of a legitimate politics, namely the vicious state of war described in its final pages, which it is tempting to translate as the present state of the world, or what Agamben in characteristically understated manner describes as "global civil war."[38] In this state of war, human beings exist in a state of total alienation and the previous history of humanity, for Rousseau as for Marx, is the history of the growth of that alienation. The force that can face and possibly overcome these obstacles is the combined bodily power of alienated individuals, not working for particular interests but for the common interest. This is the force that is described in *The Social Contract*, a force that can only take effect as a transformation of human beings' manner of existence, what Rousseau refers to on many occasions as a "change of nature."[39]

This entails that the relation between the Second Discourse and *The Social Contract* is complimentary but disjunctive: the radically unequal state of the world in the former, the possibility of a legitimate politics in the latter; being—or the state of the situation—in the former, the theory of the event in the latter. Politics, then, is about the creation of a force that can overcome obstacles, which requires an act of aggregation or what Denis Guénoun calls "pure assembly," where a people unites and decides to act.[40] Let me leave to one side the vast question as to where this force might come from. (Where does it come from? Does it come? Always?) We can say for sure that it is not given in the situation, but in excess of the situation as a vital but fleeting supplement, a fictional force, an artful force. Yet Rousseau is crystal clear, and such is his pessimism—a tone that one finds echoed in Sartre, Badiou, Rancière, and others—this force is rare and can only exist in very few places: Geneva for a while, Corsica for a while, Poland as a theoretical possibility, and so on. I feel certain that he would not find it in the contemporary regimes that go by the misnomer of democracy. True politics is rare, the obstacles are vast and the force required to bring it about is exceptional.

Now, is this act of association a contract? If it is, then it is a very strange contract. Usually, a contract is understood as a relation entered into by two pre-existing parties, like a marriage. But this does not begin to describe Rousseau's "social contract." There is no pre-existing second party. Indeed, there is not even a first party. Let me try to be clear here as the logic of this "contract" is difficult to grasp. To begin with, there is the first party of the contract, which exists in the state of total alienation described in the Second Discourse, which is to say that it is not free at all but totally enmeshed in systems of social inequality. Yet this radically unfree, alienated individual still possesses the force—that peculiar, rare but ever-potential force I mentioned just now—to give itself in an act of association with others, that is, with others who also exist in a radically alienated state. Yet, in giving itself to others the subject contracts with no one except the generality, the imagined association, which is the expected outcome of such self-giving. Rousseau is crystal clear on this point: "each, by giving himself to all, gives himself to no one."[41] Thus, there is no contract, I give myself to no one. Indeed, there is no self to give, as it exists in a state of total alienation and only becomes a subject through an act of force where it associates with others. The subject of politics is the consequence of the act of association. This is what I would like to call *the fiction of an alienation from alienation*. In other words, the essence of politics is a fiction, an act of creation that brings a subject into existence. Once again, Rousseau is clear: "These clauses [i.e., of the social contract], rightly understood, all come down to just one, namely the total alienation of each associate with all of his rights to the whole community."[42]

The so-called social contract begins with the *fact* of total alienation, which is overcome by an *act* of total alienation whereby I give myself to the community, to an imagined generality, to a people which does not in fact exist. That is, I totally alienate myself in the name of a fiction of association that would allow me to overcome the total alienation of social inequality. As Althusser rightly underlines, total alienation is the solution to the state of total alienation.[43] Thus—and here is a first *décalage*—Rousseau's "social contract" does not correspond to its concept: it is not a contract based on an exchange between parties, but an act of constitution, of fictive constitution, where a people wills itself into existence. That such a people exists, that it might exist, that the fictional act might become fact, is what Althusser calls Rousseau's "dream."[44] One of the important goals towards which this inquiry is trying to grope its way is that of establishing the necessity of such dreams, such supreme fictions, in the political realm and providing a key to their interpretation. Let me now turn to law.

THE GENERAL WILL, LAW, AND THE NECESSITY FOR PATRIOTISM

Let us ask, very generally: what is the problem to which law is the solution? As we have seen, the problem that Rousseau is trying to solve in *The Social Contract* is the problem of legitimacy. How can we imagine a form of association or "new associations" that would balance the claims of freedom and equality, of individual freedom on the one hand and the interests of the collective on the other? Such is, I have claimed, the problem of politics for Rousseau and for us.

How can my freedom be just one amongst many freedoms? If I am free, then any law to which I submit must be my law; it must be a law that I give myself. It must be consistent with my autonomy, that is, it is a question of a law to which I freely bind myself. So, how is my autonomy compatible with equality, with the demand that the laws that I freely choose should be binding on myself and other free agents? Rousseau elegantly solves the problem by simply denying that there is an opposition between freedom and equality and making a distinction between the general will and the will of all.

The will of all is the sum of private interests, of particular freedoms, the interests that can be aggregated together—for example, in the mechanism of the vote in a liberal democracy. The entire problem of liberal democracy from a Rousseauian perspective consists in the fact that one is asked to vote or exercise one's freedom on the basis of one's private interest as an individual rather than the public interest which might well simply conflict with one's private interests, depending upon one's wealth, class, status, property, and so on. This entails that Rousseau has an entirely negative relation to what we might call "actually existing liberal democracy" and that *The Social Contract* should not be read, as is sometimes the case in the English-speaking world, as an apologia for a liberalism which is supposedly based on a social contract. On the contrary, I see *The Social Contract* as a radical critique of liberal individualism, which is what is called in the Second Discourse "*le faux contrat*":[45] the false or fraudulent contract, based on radically unequal private interests and property ownership, and which culminates in a state of war. The will of all in an electoral democracy is simply the aggregation of particularities rather than the construction of association based on generality.

The general will, by contrast, is not private interest but the common interest that tends towards the public good. It is one's will as a citizen. To choose in accordance with the general will is not to choose in relation to my particular, private interest, but in line with what I see as good for the form of political association as a whole. To act in such a way is consistent with what Rousseau calls our civil liberty as distinct from our natural liberty. In passing from the state of nature to society I give up my natural freedom, which has no limitation other than my physical power, and I gain civil liberty. The latter is a notion of moral freedom that is only acquired in society with others and consists in obedience to a law that I give myself, i.e. which is consistent with my autonomy. As Rousseau writes, "the impulsion of mere appetite is slavery, and obedience to a law one has prescribed to oneself is freedom."[46]

The same argument goes for equality, where one gives up the rough natural equality of the state of nature and the vicious social inequality of the state of war for the political equality of all with all. To choose freely is to choose in accordance with the general will which means that one chooses for all. Therefore, there is no conflict between freedom and equality, and the latter is the expression of the former when it is rightly understood. Collective autonomy is the only legitimate political expression of individual autonomy.

To approach matters in this way also solves the problem

of sovereignty because the only being who is sovereign in a legitimate polity is the people itself. The core of *The Social Contract* is a defense of popular sovereignty, and I will come back to this theme in the later parts of this chapter. Popular sovereignty consists in acts of legislation by the general will, where the people determine themselves by themselves and not through the mediation of any monarch, prince, aristocracy, or unrepresentative body. For Machiavelli, the true citizen loves the city more than his own soul. Rousseau's hyper-Machiavellian twist to this wisdom is to add that the city—and this was his hope for Geneva and why he proudly described himself on the title pages of the *Discourse on Inequality* and *The Social Contract* as "Citizen of Geneva"—is nothing else but the expression of one's own soul; it is the civic incarnation of the animate. As in Plato's *Republic*, the order of the city reflects the order of the soul and the transparency of the latter is reflected in the former. One is a political subject only by virtue of the association of which one forms a part. For Rousseau, and this was the core of Jean Starobinski's famous interpretation, in a legitimate polity there exists a sheer transparency between my freedom and those of my fellow citizens.[47] Freedom and equality are two sides of the same coin (although Rousseau detested money, which he always saw as a mere simulacrum and supplement). But the metal that melds the two sides of the coin is a love of one's city, of one's *patrie*, and Rousseau vigorously defends the need for civic patriotism.

On this point—and I think the question of patriotism is an important but troubling issue for many readers—let me make a brief excursus into Rousseau's extraordinary 1755 entry to Diderot and D'Alembert's *Encyclopédie* on "Political Economy" in order to restate the argument about politics and establish the link to law. For Rousseau, political association is conceived as a body politic, and the soul that animates this body is the general will. The most important maxim of legitimate government is following the general will and this means that all private, particular interests have to be excised from the body politic. But how, then, do citizens freely subjugate their freedom to the general will? "How can it be," Rousseau asks, "that they obey and no one commands, that they serve yet have no master; all the freer in fact that in apparent subjection, no one loses any more of his freedom than might harm someone else's?" For him, the answer is clear: "These marvels are the work of law. It is to law alone that men owe justice and freedom."[48]

Rousseau continues to wax lyrical over law, describing it as a "celestial voice." But the question this raises is simple and vast. Indeed, it is the problem of the "vicious reasoner" that we discussed above: how can citizens take an *interest* in the law? For Rousseau, unlike Kant or indeed Habermas, rationality is not a sufficient nor even reliable guide. Citizens have to be formed: "Therefore, form men if you want to command men: if you would have the laws obeyed, see to it that they are loved."[49]

Citizens must be formed, that is, they must be taught to *love* the law, something that requires virtue. By the word "virtue," Rousseau simply means that which enables the particular will to conform with the general will. Virtue is the becoming-general or, with Badiou, the becoming-generic of the particular will. How can this be achieved? The answer is clear: love of the *patrie*, the fatherland, a "gentle and lively sentiment which combines the force of *amour propre* with all the beauty of virtue, endows it with an energy which, without disfiguring, makes it into the most heroic of all the passions."[50]

Therefore, it is patriotism that is the key to making people virtuous, it is love of the fatherland, the love of what Rousseau queerly calls "*la mère patrie*" (the mother fatherland), which is the passion that forms citizens and teaches them to love the law. This is why the issue of public education is of such political importance for Rousseau, for without it there would be no way of constituting and maintaining a legitimate polity.

Can there be a legitimate or a true politics without patriotism? Habermas recognizes the force of this question in speaking of "constitutional patriotism."[51] However, Rousseau's view is that we need a more widespread affective basis to patriotism than the constitution—one grounded, say, in a web of practices, habits, and traditions, what he calls *les moeurs*. Yet, constitutional patriotism is not irrelevant, particularly in the American context. To take two diametrically—indeed comically—opposed examples: as we will see in the next chapter, Obama—who taught constitutional law at the University of Chicago—proposes a providentialist political theology that is based on love of the US Constitution, which receives a compelling analysis in an entire chapter of *The Audacity of Hope*.[52] At the other end of political spectrum, Sarah Palin's brand of "commonsense conservatism" concludes with the following patriotic paean: "Whatever your gender, race, or religion, if you love this country and will defend our Constitution, then you're an American."[53]

The connection between law and civic patriotism becomes even clearer in Rousseau's posthumously published 1770–71 text, "Considerations on the Government of Poland." Any project of constitution-writing must, for Rousseau, be guided by the following question. "No constitution will ever be good and solid unless the law rules the citizens' hearts. So long as the legislative force does not reach that deep, the laws will invariably be evaded. But how can men's hearts be reached?"[54]

The answer appears shocking. The only way of getting citizens to love the law and the *patrie* is: "Dare I say it? With children's games; with institutions which appear trivial in the eyes of superficial men, but which form cherished habits and invincible attachments."[55] These games would be what we might call *ceremonies of nationhood*: spectacles, games, and festivals which are always conducted "in the open,"[56] like the public festivals described in Rousseau's denunciation of theatre in his 1758 *Letter to D'Alembert*, an idea that had a direct influence on Robespierre's *fêtes nationales civiques* in the years after the French Revolution.[57] In such spectacles, as we will see below, nothing would be represented, as in conventional theatre where we watch the sufferings of Oedipus or whatever. Rousseau recommends horsemanship as "an exercise well suited to Poles," which might play a similar role to that of bullfighting in Spain, whose role in maintaining "a certain vigor in the Spanish nation is not negligible."[58] Interestingly, for both Obama and Palin, basketball plays precisely this role in the formation of a virtuous and vigorous American character.

It is not difficult for non-basketball playing, non-bullfighting, post-Kantian, metropolitan, cosmopolitan metrosexuals like ourselves to ridicule such ideas. But the issues that they raise are more serious. If human rationality is fallible, if it cannot be assumed that citizens will always will the good, then what is required is a political account of formative passions that might force citizens to love the law, that is, to overcome the obstacles of alienation and inequality through an act of association. Now, is such a thing practicable without fairly robust notions of civic patriotism and public education? I don't think so. The question is: how? This is where it might be helpful to turn in more detail to Rousseau's critique of theatre.

THEATRE IS NARCISSISM

What is the connection between narcissism and inequality? For Rousseau, the great sea change in the history of inequality is the institution of private property, where someone said "this is mine" and found people simple enough to believe him.[59] Yet, even prior to the establishment of private property, when human beings first gathered together, socialized and looked at one another— Rousseau imagines this taking place around a tree in a purported state of nature—there was engendered a desire for distinction, to be distinct and different from others. It is with this desire for distinction that the healthy *amour de soi* or self-love that defines human beings in a natural state begins to be transformed into a narcissistic *amour propre* or pride. For Rousseau, the origin of narcissism consists in this desire for social distinction, from a sense of one's own importance. Thus, inequality and narcissism derive from the same source.

This is the kernel of the drama that unfolds in Rousseau's play *Narcisse, ou l'amant de lui-même (Narcissus, or the Self-Admirer).*[60] Rousseau wrote seven plays, in various stages of completion or incompletion. *Narcisse* was the only one to be performed publicly —and even then, it received only a single performance, by Les comédiens du Roi, on December 18, 1752. *Narcisse* found its way to the stage because of the considerable success of *Le Devin du village*, Rousseau's one-act pastoral opera, which had been performed before the French king, queen, and court at Fontainebleau the previous October. Louis XV was so impressed that he demanded an audience with Rousseau. Rousseau, however, was so neurotically plagued by a weak bladder that he was terrified he would wet himself during the audience. He therefore declined, complaining of his *"infirmités."*

Narcisse was described by Rousseau's sometime friend Grimm as *"une mauvaise comédie,"* and although one might perhaps expect more loyalty from a friend, he is not incorrect in his judgment. The play is in the style of Marivaux, who read, commented on, and even made some changes to the text. Sadly, *Narcisse* is not up to the quality of Marivaux's plays, which is perhaps explained by the fact that Rousseau claimed in the *Confessions* to have written it when he was just 18 years old. This, though, is certainly not the whole truth: it is clear that Rousseau periodically and significantly redrafted the play between his youth and the time of its only performance, when Rousseau was 40. Indeed, he admits as much in the *Confessions:* "when I stated in the preface to that play that I had written it at eighteen I lied to the extent of some years."[61] Nonetheless, it is probable that *Narcisse* was his first extended piece of literary composition.

The action of *Narcisse* is very simple. It concerns a man, Valère, who falls in love with a painting of himself dressed as a woman. The drama begins with Valère's sister, Lucinda, devising a plan to trick the incurably vain protagonist, who is engaged to be married to Angelica. The trick is to test his love for her—something which backfires horribly as Valère falls completely in love with his own feminized portrait, his objectified self-image. There is much playful, if predictable, dramatic irony, when Valère sends off his man, Frontin, in search all over Paris for his new beloved—who is in fact himself.

> Lucinda: Frontin, where is your master?
> Frontin: Gone in search of himself.
> Lucinda: In search of himself?
> Frontin: Ay, to be married to himself.

Eventually Valère realizes his mistake and the error of his ways, is scolded by his father, and decides to marry Angelica after all. There is also a second love story in *Narcisse*, which is curiously unresolved and unsatisfactorily presented in the play, between Lucinda and Leander, which mirrors the main dramatic relationship.

So, the play is a little lesson in the failings of narcissism that ends with a moral: "when we truly love another, we cease to be fond of ourselves." As such, it is a derivative, slight, and nicely inconsequential piece, just the sort of thing that Rousseau thought might gain him some sort of a literary reputation when he moved to Paris in 1742, in his thirtieth year.

However, matters become more compelling when the play is read alongside the long preface that Rousseau wrote to accompany its publication in 1752. In his *Confessions*, Rousseau declares the preface to be "one of my best pieces of writing."[62] In this way, the play is placed in between the arguments of Rousseau's First and Second Discourses, in 1750 and 1755. In 1749, when Rousseau was 37 years old, he went to see his friend and fellow encyclopedist Denis Diderot, who at that time was imprisoned at Vincennes outside Paris, for expressing opinions contrary to religion and the state. Short of money, Rousseau used to walk the five miles to the prison and to entertain himself on the journey would read a journal or newspaper. On one occasion, reading the literary gazette *Mercure de France*, he came across a subject proposed by the Academy of Dijon for an essay competition: "Has the progress in the arts and sciences done more to corrupt or to purify morals?" In a sudden Pauline flash, Rousseau realized that progress in the arts and sciences had, in fact, corrupted morals. In a letter to Malesherbes from 1762, Rousseau writes of this experience with characteristic emotional overstatement:

> If ever anything resembled a sudden inspiration, it is what that advertisement stimulated in me: all at once I felt my mind dazzled by a thousand lights, a crown of splendid ideas presented themselves to me with such force and in such confusion, that I was thrown into a state of indescribable bewilderment. I felt my head seized by a dizziness that resembled intoxication. A violent palpitation constricted me and made my chest heave. Unable to breathe and walk at the same time, I sank down under one of the trees in the avenue and passed the next half hour in such agitation that when I got up I found that the front of my jacket was wet with tears, although I had no memory of shedding any. Ah, Monsieur, if ever I had been able to write down what I saw and felt as I sat under that tree, with what clarity would I have exposed the contradictions of our social system, with what force would I have demonstrated all the abuses of our institutions, with what simplicity would I have demonstrated that man is naturally good, and has only become bad because of those institutions.[63]

The central belief of what is all too glibly called the Enlightenment, which derives from Bacon and which is absolutely decisive for figures like Voltaire and Diderot, is the belief in progress. That is to say, the development of science, technology, art, and culture has led to the amelioration of humanity—or, in Kant's formulation, Enlightenment is freedom from man's self-incurred tutelage. For Rousseau, on the contrary, rational and scientific progress is moral and political regress. Civilization is decline. The so-called progress in the arts and sciences has made humanity worse: less human, more depraved, selfish, and greedy. What we see in Rousseau is an early version of nineteenth-century theories of history, in particular that of Marx and Engels in *The German Ideology* and the opening pages of *The Communist Manifesto*, where the seeming progress of humanity has led to progressive alienation from our true condition, what the young Marx called "species-being." But we equally see an anticipation of Nietzschean genealogy in Rousseau, where the history of morality is the crushing of the active forces of life-affirmation by the cringing *ressentiment* of Judeo-Christian morality. For Rousseau, human history, society, and so-called civilization have all conspired to the degradation of the human condition.

However, if such is Rousseau's position, then isn't it hypocritical of him to publish and indeed permit the performance of a play like *Narcisse*—not to mention his more or less successful experiments with opera, ballet, music, and poetry? Betraying early signs of the paranoia that would painfully suffocate him in later life, seeing spies at every turn, Rousseau spends much of the Preface responding polemically to this objection. First comes his implausible claim that *Narcisse* is merely a work of his youth and shouldn't be taken seriously. Secondly, and more compellingly, he argues that given that Parisian society is so utterly and irredeemably corrupt with regard to morals (*les moeurs*), it is better to divert them with such trifles as the theatre, as this might prevent them from engaging in more harmful, wicked activities like violence and warfare. "My advice," he continues with caustic irony

> is therefore—and I have said this more than once—to leave alone and even to support the academies, the colleges, the universities, the libraries and the theatres, and all the other amusements which are capable of producing some diversion from the wickedness of men and which might prevent them from filling their idleness with more dangerous things. For in a country where there are no decent men and good morals, then it is better to live with mere rascals than violent ruffians.[64]

From this perspective, the failure of *Narcisse* to extend beyond its opening performance offers Rousseau a perverse vindication of his views: "My play had the fate that it merited and which I foresaw. But because of the tedium that I felt in watching it I left the performance much more content with myself than if it had been a success."[65] Thus, the manifest failure of *Narcisse* is transformed into success and its mediocre tediousness is an inverted triumph for Rousseau's assault on culture.

If we place *Narcisse* in the context of Rousseau's arguments in its preface and the *Discourses*, then the question of narcissism takes on a rather different, deeper aspect. If narcissism is the experiential effect of inequality—or rather its lived affect—then the very idea of theatre is thereby condemned. This becomes clear if *Narcisse* is linked to the *Letter to D'Alembert*, where Rousseau denounces D'Alembert's proposal for a theatre in Geneva.

Rousseau makes two main accusations against theatre. First, he says, theatre is morally and socially dangerous because it reverses the purportedly natural relation between the sexes, permitting women to take power over men through the play of theatrical representation. Theatre—and here Rousseau is thinking of the playful comic ironies of Molière—reverses the hierarchy of the sexes and is essentially effeminizing. Seen in this light, the travesty of *Narcisse*, where the male protagonist falls in love with his own cross-dressed feminized image, enacts the entire sexual threat of theatre.

The second strand of his attack concerns representation. In it, he restates Plato's critique of the tragic poets in the *Republic* where theatre is excluded from the well-ordered *polis* because it is the *mimesis* or imitation of a mere appearance, rather than an attention to the true form of things which should be the proper concern of the philosopher.

This critique of theatre as feminization and representation runs together with Rousseau's proposal to replace theatre with civic spectacle. What is essential to such spectacles is precisely that they are not representations but the presence to itself of the people coming together outdoors in daylight and not dallying in the darkness of the theatre, whose very architecture, says Rousseau, is reminiscent of Plato's cave:

> Plant a stake crowned with flowers in the middle of a square, gather the people together there, and you will have a festival. Do better yet; let the spectators become an entertainment to them-selves; make them actors themselves; do it so that each see and loves himself in the others so that all will be better united.[66]

In the civic spectacle, the people do not passively watch a theat-rical object of representation, but rather become the actors and enactors of their own sovereignty. Rousseau's defense of popular sovereignty in *The Social Contract* is of a piece with his critique of any and all forms of representative government. The only way of attaining political legitimacy is to root sovereignty in the will of the people—not in some external, representative authority. The people should be the actors in the theatre of their state. In this context, festival becomes the lived manifestation of popular sovereignty, the reinforcement of the people's individual and col-lective autonomy that allows for the identification between law and patriotism, where the latter is the glue connecting the people to the former.

The civic festival is the enacting of the general will without the mediation of representation. As such, Rousseau's idea of the civic festival finds a powerful echo in Schiller's conception of the aesthetic revolution that must accompany any political revolution, a vision that finds its most dramatic and aphoristic expression in the sensuous political organicism of his *Oldest System-Programme of German Idealism* and its call for a "new mythology."[67] By contrast, the theatre is a veritable temple to Narcissus, a cavernous hall of mirrors that reflects nothing more than the desire for distinction and the hypocrisy of *amour propre*. The theatre is a place where actors are not subjects, but objectify themselves in their desire to see and be seen. Theatre is the very crucible of narcissism and the temple to inequality. If narcissism, pride, and the desire for distinction were powerful features of life in the eighteenth century, then this is arguably all the more true at the present time, in a world that has become a vast and spectacular surface of simulacra.

All of which means that the status of Rousseau's theatre is peculiar, perhaps without precedent though with many subsequent imitators, right the way down to Brecht and Beckett: it is theatre against theatre; it is theatre against the very idea of theatricality. Matters can be distilled here into three questions and answers:

(i)   What is theatre? It is narcissism.
(ii) What is theatre for? It allows human beings to experience their cave-like captivity in the order of representation and objectification and to become alienated from their true subjectivity, both individual and communal.
(iii) What, then, might be the purpose of Rousseau's theatre? It is nothing less than a means for diagnosing and criticizing the essential narcissism of modernity and subverting its drama of inequality.

Theatre is narcissism. What's more, theatre does not arise *ex nihilo* from some vacuum—society itself is narcissism. But also, insofar as it feeds and feeds upon intellectual *amour propre*, philosophy is narcissism. Rousseau makes the case crystal clear in the 1752 Preface:

The taste for philosophy weakens all the bonds of benevolence and mutual regard that attach men to society. In fact, this is the greatest of the evils that philosophy engenders. The delights of study render any other attachment rather insipid. What's more, by dint of observing and reflecting on humanity, the philosopher learns to appreciate human beings according to their true value; and it is difficult to have affection for something that one despises. Soon, all the interest that so-called virtuous men share with their fellows is reunited in the person of the philosopher:

his contempt for others is transformed into arrogance; his pride increases in direct proportion to his indifference for the rest of the universe. Words like family and country become for him completely meaningless. He is neither a parent, nor a citizen, nor a man, he is a philosopher.[68]

THE AUTHORITY OF THE LAW

Now I will return to the argument about law. If the social contract, understood as the coincidence of freedom and equality in the general will, is what breathes life into a legitimate polity, then it is law that gives that polity the motivation and legs to get up and walk: "By the social pact we have given the body politic existence and life: the task now is to give it motion and will by legislation."[69] Rousseau defines law in the following way:

> But when the whole people enacts statutes (*statue*) for the whole people it considers only itself, and if a relation is then formed, it is between the entire object from one point of view and the entire object from another point of view, with no division of the whole. Then the matter with regard to which the statute is being enacted is general, as is the enacting will. It is this act which I call law.[70]

In French, the verb that is doing the work here is *statuer*, to decree, ordain, rule or enact: to make law. The final sentences are much more precise and interesting in French than in English, where Rousseau writes, "Alors la matière sur laquelle on statue est générale comme la volonté qui statue. C'est cet acte que j'appelle une loi." For Rousseau, laws are acts of the general will. If one accepts Rousseau's analysis then it becomes immediately clear that we can longer ask who makes the laws, because laws are the expression of the general will. Laws are acts by virtue of which a people legislates for itself and where sovereignty is entirely popular.

It is clear that this conception of law stands opposed to Hobbes's conception of the sovereign monarch as he who legislates for a society, but who stands outside the social order in a kind of state of nature. If the total alienation of the state of war requires, for Hobbes, the externality of the monarch, the "mortall god," then Rousseau has a purely internalist conception of law and sovereignty, in which a people contracts with itself in the act of association or assembly. But the obvious difference between Hobbes and Rousseau disguises a deeper similarity in their logic of sovereignty. Althusser is correct when he writes that

> Rousseau's theoretical greatness is to have taken up the most frightening aspects of Hobbes: the state of war as a universal and perpetual state, the rejection of any transcendental solution and the "contract" of total alienation. But Rousseau's defense against Hobbes is to transform total alienation in externality into total alienation in internality.[71]

If Rousseau's logic of sovereignty is entirely immanent, based on an identity between subject and sovereign, then Hobbes's monarch is the factual transcendence of the sovereign, where the sovereign is distinct from the subject over whom he has power.

But the important point here is that the political opposition between monarchical sovereignty and popular sovereignty is a transformation of the modality of the Hobbesian logic: God the monarch becomes God the people. The paradox of sovereignty in Rousseau is that his avowedly immanentist conception of politics is also drawn towards transcendence in two instances: (i) the person of the legislator and (ii) the doctrines of civil religion. This entails that Rousseau is far more Hobbesian than is usually imagined.

For Rousseau, no one in the political realm stands outside of the law, for the law must be willed by everyone within that realm. This line of thinking has the peculiar consequence that subjects of the general will can no longer ask, "Whether the law can be unjust, since no man can be unjust toward himself; nor how one is both free and subject to the laws, since they are merely records of our wills."[72]

In this conception of law, there is a perfect transparency or mirroring of my will in the general will. If, in Hobbes, the authority of monarchical sovereigns lies in their being both inside and outside the society for which they legislate, for Rousseau sovereignty is purely internal and immanent. This is why sovereignty cannot be represented in an external body: a monarch, the state, or even parliament. Sovereignty is the pure presence to itself of the body politic animated by the general will. In Book 3 of *The Social Contract*, in a passage that seems to anticipate Schopenhauer on the will, Rousseau writes: "Sovereignty cannot be represented, for the same reason that it cannot be alienated; it consists essentially in the general will, and the will does not admit of being represented: either it is the same or it is different; there is no middle ground."[73]

As we have just seen in relation to theatre, Rousseau is the source of the modern critique of representation whose *locus classicus* is Plato's critique of *mimesis*, and which extends into thinkers like Heidegger (despite his ridiculous underestimation of Rousseau) and Guy Debord: the true "subject" cannot be the subject of representation and all forms of representation conceive of the subject as subject *to* the spectacle and its theatre of war and inequality.[74] In the civic festivals that Rousseau recommends in the *Letter to D'Alembert*, nothing gets represented and there is no spectacle: "But what then will be the object of these entertainments? What will be shown in them? Nothing, if you please."[75]

As such, politics is not about representation, but is rather, as Badiou writes, the manifestation of "the 'collective being' of citizen militants."[76] If it is asked: how does this being show itself? Then the answer is: as nothing, if you please. What takes place in the festival is just the presence to itself of the people in the process of its enactment.

As Rousseau tirelessly points out in his tirades against

England—and I self-hatingly love him all the more for this reason, "I have never liked England or the English"[77]—this is the error of parliamentarianism:

> The English people thinks it is free; it is greatly mistaken, it is only free during the election of Members of Parliament; as soon as they are elected, it is enslaved, it is nothing. The use it makes of its freedom during the brief moments it has fully warrants its losing it.[78]

As Edmund Morgan points out, the idea of political representation is a magical enigma: in a representative government, so the story goes, the people are not just the governed, they are also the government, which somehow happens through the miracle of representation.[79] But how exactly can a few be said to represent the many? They cannot. The truth of the situation, rather, is that the spurious legitimacy of representative government rests on the simple fiction of the few *believing* that they represent the many and, if the fiction is believed, vice versa.

Sovereignty cannot be represented because it is the people alone who have legislative authority and who make the law: "the instant a People gives itself Representatives," writes Rousseau, "it ceases to be free; it ceases to be."[80] The only representation possible in a legitimate polity is at the level of executive power, namely the magistrates who are elected by the people to carry out its will. But the executive does not make the law, as in representative government; it only carries it out. Yet, this move in Rousseau's argument establishes the distinction between sovereignty and government, which opens a further *décalage*: the distinction between generality and particularity.

How is government instituted? It can only be instituted through an act of the general will which flows from the sovereignty of the people. How does this take place? How does the sovereign, who is by definition general, become government, which is particular—especially when those people chosen to govern also, by necessity, form part of the sovereign people? Rousseau faces the contradiction head-on: "The difficulty is to understand how there can be an act of Government before the Government exists."[81] The answer he provides to this conundrum is astonishing: it is through the sudden conversion of sovereignty into democracy. It should be recalled that Rousseau described democracy in Book 3 of *The Social Contract* as "a Government without a Government" and rejected it as being suited to a nation of gods, but not human beings:

> Here again is revealed one of those astonishing properties of the body politic by which it reconciles apparently contradictory operations. For this reconciliation is accomplished by a sudden conversion of Sovereignty into Democracy; so that without any perceptible change, and simply by a new relation of all to all, the Citizens having become Magistrates pass from general to particular acts, and from the law to its execution.[82]

Thus, without any visible change, the sovereign people transforms itself into a government. That is, each of the individuals that constitute the body of the people becomes a magistrate, if only temporarily. Having refused democracy as being too god-like, Rousseau acknowledges that the establishment of legitimate government necessarily requires a passage *through* democracy, and from there into the elective aristocracy that he recommends as the most felicitous form of government. Thus, the passage from the general to the particular requires a sudden god-like moment of transfiguration.

This opens up a fault-line in Rousseau's argument that runs through the remainder of Book 3 and into Book 4, and that perhaps explains its overlong meander through Roman political history. Which is to say that, having begun *The Social Contract* with a series of arguments that have a precise, almost geometrical formality—even using the language of ratios—it becomes a book that Rousseau doesn't seem to know how to finish. Such doubts are compounded in his final chapter on civil religion and the question of the relation between politics and religion that frames *The Social Contract* and, moreover, the book you are presently reading. Having insistently argued that the only legitimacy possible in a polity is through acts of generality, the passage from sovereignty to government—from the general to the particular—means that we have to speak of a qualified generality, or of a divided and particularized universality. This is nowhere clearer than in the enigma of voting procedures outlined in Book 4 of *The Social Contract*. Rousseau is forced into the contradictory conclusion that the general will has to be manifested in the majority—generality only finds expression in a particularity—which leaves him open to John Stuart Mill's objection that there is no political room for the minorities which also make up the sovereign body of the people. We will come back to this contradiction below in relation to Rousseau's account of dictatorship, which is nothing less than the suspension of the sovereign authority of the people by the very agency that claims to speak in its name.

THE PARADOX OF SOVEREIGNTY

For Rousseau, the problem that law appears to solve is that of the relationship between freedom and equality. If he is right, then he has solved the problem of politics—which is a problem, as he puts it in his "Considerations on the Government of Poland," akin to "squaring the circle in geometry."[83] However, my view is not that Rousseau succeeds in squaring that circle, but rather that his text is articulated around a series of conceptual *décalages* of which we are the inheritors, e.g., the relation between sovereignty and government, internality and externality, generality and particularity. Rousseau's thinking enacts a series of contradictions that any serious conception of the being of politics is obliged to confront. This is nowhere clearer than in the problem of the authority of the law.

The problem might be posed in the following way: if the only law that I can follow is a law that I give myself—a law that is the expression of the general will, a law that is consistent with my autonomy yet binding on all members of the social group—then by virtue of what does this law have authority? The obvious answer is that if law is nothing else but the act of the general will, then authority becomes self-authorship. That is, there can be no higher court of legal authority than autonomy. Yet, if authority becomes self-authorship, then doesn't a legitimate polity end up as a collective narcissus?[84] Despite the immanentist logic of Rousseau's argument, isn't there a need for a moment of transcendent authority in law in order to bind subjects to the law, a moment of radical externality or heteronomy, like the function of the monarch in Hobbes? If that is the case, if Rousseau also seems to need a mortal god to animate his politics, then is such an authority conceivable without religion? I think these problems will take us to the very heart of the paradox of sovereignty that forces Rousseau into his argument for the legislator, and from there into the dependency of politics and law on religion. It is my hope that in this way we might begin to get a little closer to the heart of our current political and legal situation.

Of course Rousseau, being the most supremely fictive and self-conscious of philosophers, recognizes precisely the problem that I have raised. In Book 2 he writes, "The People subject to the laws ought to be their author." Yet he goes on seemingly to contradict himself: "How will a blind multitude, which often does not know what it wills because it rarely knows what is good for it, carry out an undertaking as great, as difficult as a system of legislation?"[85]

That is, how can an uninformed and ignorant multitude will the good? How can they learn to act not simply on the basis of private interest but of common interest, not the will of all but the general will? Rousseau concludes: "By itself the people always wills the good, but by itself it does not always see it."[86] Therefore, he claims, the people need a guide, something or someone that will, in the fatefully misunderstood words of Book 1 of *The Social Contract*, force the people to be free.[87]

This leads Rousseau to the beautiful fiction of what he calls the "legislator" or "lawgiver," an "extraordinary man" or "genius."[88] The legislator is described by Rousseau as the engineer of the state machine. He is the person who legislates for society, but who has to stand apart from society. The legislator belongs neither to the order of nature, as he intervenes in politics by establishing the constitution, nor to the political order, because he is not subject to the laws that he declares. The office of the legislator is strictly paradoxical: "This office which gives the republic its constitution has no place in that constitution."[89] That is, in order for the internalist laws generated by the general will to have authority, they have to be decreed or "statuted" by a quasi-external lawgiver, who belongs neither to the realm of politics nor nature, but who exists in a "no place" (like Augustine's God in Book X of the *Confessions*[90]). It is by occupying this quasi-external, quasi-divine "no place" that the lawgiver gives a fictional majesty to the law. Rousseau writes:

> When Lycurgus gave his fatherland laws, he began by abdicating the Kingship. It was the custom of most Greek cities to entrust the establishment of their laws to foreigners. The modern Republics of Italy often imitated this practice, the Republic of Geneva did so as well and to good effect. Rome in its finest period witnessed the rebirth of all the crimes of Tyranny in its midst, and found itself on the verge of perishing, for having united the legislative authority and the sovereign power in the same hands.[91]

Of course, if we lived in a society of gods and not human beings—a democracy—then this problem would not arise. Although, as we have just seen, there is a miraculous god-like moment in the transition from sovereignty to government, we are not gods—at least not for more than a moment. Therefore, what is required is a separation of sovereign power, which resides in the people, from legislative authority, which belongs to the lawgiver.

Here we approach the paradox of sovereignty: it is only through the strangeness of the foreigner that the laws are seen to have authority and to be binding on an autochthonous people. On the one hand, the law is and has to be the free expression of the general will, the perfect interiority of a people to itself, but on the other hand, there has to be a lawgiver, someone who stands outside society and by virtue of which the law has authority beyond the self-authorizing acts of the general will. The only legitimate law is one that we give ourselves, yet the law has to be given to us. As we know, Rousseau—the troubled Genevan, the internal exile and the foreigner in France—wrote revealing projects for the constitutions of Poland and Corsica (all of which—appropriately given Rousseau's paranoia—failed). One has to invent the fiction of a legislator from outside in order to lend authority to the law, even if that law is only legitimate if it is a law that society gives to itself. Such is the paradox of sovereignty at the heart of political legitimacy. Rousseau confesses the point, and here one feels the ground begin to slip away under his feet: "So that one finds at one and the same time two apparently incompatible things in the work of legislation: an undertaking beyond human force, and to execute it an authority that is nil."[92]

As Groucho Marx might have said, don't let appearances deceive you: these "two things" do not just look contradictory, they *are* contradictory. Such is the *décalage* machine of Rousseau's text. The authority of the law whose essence is the general will requires the fiction of a lawgiver who overrides the will of the people. The people cannot give the law to itself without the fiction of the law being given to them by an outside agency. Political self-authorship has to be underwritten by a ghost author, a quasi-divine legislator.

The vast question that this raises is the relation of politics, law, and legal authority to religion and religious authority. This is the problem that Rousseau tackles in the final pages of *The*

Social Contract, which deal with civil religion. To say that this is a contemporary political problem is to risk considerable understatement. If it is the fiction of the legislator that provides the necessary authority for a people to self-authorize itself through the general will, then can we have such authority without religion? That is, can we have law without religion, without some moment of sacralization? Rousseau puts the problem much more sharply: in order to establish a legitimate political order, there would need to exist a "superior intelligence who saw all of man's passions and experienced none of them, who had no relation to our nature yet knew it thoroughly." In short, "It would require gods to give men laws."[93]

In an intriguing footnote, Rousseau turns to Machiavelli (not the evil "Machiavel" of Shakespeare, but "an honest man and a good citizen"[94]) when he writes: "The truth is that there has never been in any country a lawgiver who has not invoked the deity; for otherwise his laws would not have been accepted. A wise man knows many useful truths which cannot be demonstrated in a way that will convince other people."[95] Every legislator has to authorize the law with reference to the beautiful fiction of a divinity.

Rousseau's reasoning at this point is subtle and revealing, involving a further *décalage*, this time an inversion of the order of cause and effect: "Each individual, appreciating no other scheme of government than that which bears directly on his particular interest, has difficulty perceiving the advantages he is supposed to derive from the constant privations required by good laws."[96]

In order for the individual to understand the beneficial effects of submitting to the general will, he or she would already have to live in the legitimate polity that those effects bring about: "The effect would have to become the cause ... men would have to be prior to laws what they ought to become by means of them."[97]

It is only the effect of the law that might bring the privately interested individual to will the cause, to will generally. In order for this conundrum to be solved, the lawgiver must appeal to "an authority of a different order, one which might be able to compel without violence and to persuade without convincing." "This," Rousseau continues, "is what has at all times forced the fathers of nations to resort to the intervention of heaven and to attribute their own wisdom to the Gods."[98]

If the privately interested citizen can be compelled to believe that the laws which govern political life have the same divine source as those which govern the universe—for example, in the fiction of natural law—then he or she might be persuaded to assume the yoke of the general will without being in a position to be rationally convinced by it, for this rationality will only follow from entering a legitimate political association. The beneficial effects of a subject submitting to the law can only lead that subject to will the cause when appeal is made to a divine cause.

Of course, reasoning in this way also contains the seeds of what Rousseau sees as the Caligula solution to political authority, that one declares oneself a god at the same time as declaring that the people are animals. The exquisite historical irony of *The Social Contract* comes with Rousseau's question as to "which people, then, is fit for legislation?" He assembles a characteristically Rousseauesque list of criteria. It would be a people "Whose every member can be known to all ... one that can do without all other peoples and without which every other people can do."[99]

A people fit to receive laws should live on the edges of history and not at its center, possessing customs that are solid but also malleable. This sounds very nice, but where might one find such a place? Rousseau casts around and declares that Corsica is the one country in Europe fit to receive laws. He goes on, "I rather suspect that this small island will one day astound Europe."[100] Of course, not too many years later something came out of Corsica that did astonish Europe: Napoleon, who dramatically limited the legislative power of the French Republic in order to allow for a massive expansion of imperial, executive power which culminated in his breathtakingly narcissistic self-coronation as emperor in 1804. It would seem that there is little to prevent the legislator from becoming a tyrant, from believing that he is a mortal god who incarnates the general will. Such is the risk that is always run when politics is organized around any economy of the sacred, where the deeper and more searching question is whether politics is practicable without a moment of sacralization.

In this regard, Rousseau's argument for dictatorship in Book 4 is extremely revealing. He asserts that the legislator should not frame the constitution and establish political institutions too rigidly, "to the point of depriving oneself of the power to suspend their effect."[101] That is, the laws which issue from the sovereign authority of the people must be able to be suspended: what Roman jurists called *iustitium*, and which Agamben has interestingly analyzed.[102] Rousseau writes that such *iustitium*—a suspension or literally a standstill—is only permitted in the case of an emergency, *un danger*, which arises when the safety of the *patrie* is at stake. When national security is threatened by external attack or—although Rousseau doesn't mention it explicitly—internal dissent, then the sovereign authority of the general will can be suspended: "If however the peril is such that the laws as an instrumentality are an obstacle to guarding against it, then a supreme chief (*chef*) is named who silences all the laws and provisionally suspends the Sovereign authority."[103]

This supreme chief is the dictator who does not have the power to make laws, but can suspend their operation. What Rousseau is envisaging here is the state of exception, in which *iustitium* is required in order to preserve the security of the political order of the *patrie*. The obvious questions this raises are as follows: who decides on the state of exception, for how long, and what is permitted—or, more accurately, forbidden—in such a state? Rousseau turns once again to Roman history for guidance, noting that the senate both decided upon the choice of the dictator and stipulated that the period of dictatorship should not exceed six months, otherwise it would become tyrannical. The corollary of this position, particularly for contemporary devotees of so-called civic republicanism, is the necessary co-implication of republicanism

and dictatorship. For Rousseau—and this is the classical view—
one cannot have one without the other. The sovereign authority
of law cannot exclude the possibility of its suspension: no justice
without *iustitium*.

Of course, the contemporary dilemma concerns whether—as
Agamben thinks, following Benjamin—in modern bio-politics
"the state of exception … has become the rule."[104] If this is the
case—and Agamben provides compelling, if partial, legal evidence
to justify his claim—then dictatorship is the generalized form
of contemporary government. This entails that in a situation of
declared danger or peril to the "homeland"—after a "terrorist"
attack, say—the executive power of a president can override the
legislative authority of the other organs of government, not to
mention international legal institutions like the UN and nice-
ties like the Geneva Conventions. In a time of war, particularly
something as vague and indefinite as a "war on terror," justice
becomes *iustitium* and the republic slides into dictatorship. It is
difficult to think of a more plausible interpretation of the novel
category of "unlawful combatant" than in the case of the detainees
in Guantanamo Bay, where the legal framework of the Geneva
Conventions that protect the rights of prisoners of war was suspended by the invention of a new legal category that permitted
the extension of executive power during the period of the Bush
administration.

Agamben's description of the contemporary geo-political situation as a "global civil war" can, I think, be heard as an echo of
Rousseau's analysis in the Second Discourse of inequality that culminates in a state of war. It is hard to disagree with such a diagnosis
at the present time. For Rousseau, the necessity for the passage
from popular to dictatorial sovereignty arises when there is a purported threat to national security. At such moments, the dictator
can declare *iustitium* and legitimately banish or put to death those
who threaten the nation: the internal or external enemy. It is at
this point that the entire sacred underpinning of sovereign power
turns on the determination of the figure of *homo sacer*, as he who

can be legitimately killed without being sacrificed. It is curious to note that, as part of a critique of theocracy in the final pages of *The Social Contract*, Rousseau observes that "to die for one's country is to become a martyr, to break the laws is to be impious, and to subject the guilty man to public execration is to deliver him to the wrath of the Gods: *sacer estod*, be accursed."[105]

We will return persistently to the question of dictatorship in the course of this book. For Schmitt, the concept of sovereignty finds its definition with the notion of *iustitium* or state of exception (*Ausnahmezustand*), where the sovereign is that subject who is capable of a decision on the state of exception. This entails that dictatorship reveals the essence of the political insofar as the latter is identified with the power of decision. I will try to assess the implications of this conception of the political in debates with Badiou at the end of this chapter and with Žižek in Chapter 5 where I will examine the possible meaning of Benjamin's idea of "divine violence." These questions will reverberate in our discussions of mystical anarchism and the Pauline *ecclesia* where what is at stake is the possibility of the passage from the *Discourse on Inequality* to *The Social Contract*, from dictatorial sovereignty and a state of war to popular sovereignty and the possibility of "new associations."

THE PROBLEM OF CIVIL RELIGION

The conclusion to Rousseau's argument for the legislator is clear: there can be no legal authority, and hence effective political legitimacy, without an appeal to religious authority. There can be no legitimate polity—and legitimacy implies immanence and an internalist conception of sovereignty—without an appeal to transcendence, ultimately transcendence in the form of the sacred. It is this problem that leads Rousseau towards the issue of civil religion with which *The Social Contract* concludes.

Although, as discussed, the extraordinary pages on civil religion were in all likelihood added to the *Geneva Manuscript* as Rousseau was redrafting the text for publication in 1761, they are by no means an addendum to the main argument about politics. On the contrary, they are its transcendental condition of possibility. This is the reason why *The Social Contract* has to be read back to front. However, it is my contention that Rousseau's argument about civil religion is also the condition of *impossibility* for his conception of politics. His text wavers between the *décalages* of politics, law, and religion that make its very articulation possible.

Once again, I am not suggesting that Rousseau was unaware of these *décalages*. On the contrary—supremely self-conscious fictor that he was—he was acutely aware of what he was doing. A system of thought, even and especially Rousseau's "great and sad system," is a consequence of the articulation and disarticulation of a series of *décalages*. This is true of any and every system of thought worthy of the name. Such is my *a priori* hermeneutic claim.

As there is often much misunderstanding of the concept, let's begin by asking: what is civil religion? The latter can be thought of as a profession of faith that is paradoxically both transcendent and subordinate to the immanentism of popular sovereignty. In Robert Bellah's classic formulation in *The Broken Covenant* from 1975, a civil religion is that religious dimension that is arguably found in the life of every people, through which that people interprets its internal, historical, and social experience in the light of some transcendent reality, usually God.[106] Bellah's book makes two powerful claims, historico-conceptual and polemical, as follows.

From the historico-conceptual point of view, Bellah proposes, the United States is the first country to be based on a creed or covenant. American civil religion is a fusion of two traditions. First is the biblical, puritanical tradition of Winthrop's "shining citty [*sic*] on the hill" (which Sarah Palin fallaciously but revealingly ascribed to Ronald Reagan during the 2008 presidential campaign), the upbuilding of the "New England." This is what we might call the Massachusetts myth of origin. The second is the republican model of virtue whose model is Roman. We might think of this as the Virginian, Jeffersonian myth of origin. American civil religion, then, is a combination of the biblical and the republican, the Christian and the pagan. It is an amalgam of the prophetic and providential idea of America as the chosen land for a chosen people, and a classical idea of civic virtue. However improbable this combination—expressed architecturally in the governmental buildings of Washington DC—might be, there is no denying its success in the constitution of American identity.

It should not be overlooked that Bellah's book was written during the years of America's fatal involvement in Vietnam, a period Bellah saw as "a time of trial" as serious as the Revolution in the eighteenth century and the Civil War in the nineteenth. If the US was based on the covenant described above, then, says Bellah, that covenant has been broken and needs to be renewed. It is interesting to note the recurrent connection between a state of war and the attempted renewal of civil religion, a situation that found a powerful parallel in Barack Obama's presidential campaign in 2008, in which the context of the so-called war on terror provoked the claim that the covenant between government and the people had been broken by the Bush administration and gave rise to an overwhelming need for belief at the political level, a need that was powerfully channeled through Obama's quasi-religious rhetoric of hope, change, and the reconciliation of a "house divided." Of course, what is taking place here is a clear reenactment of the basic hope of arguably the greatest American civil theologian, Abraham Lincoln. As Lincoln said during the speech in which he accepted the nomination to stand as candidate for the US Senate in June 1858, against the backdrop of virulent disputes about slavery that culminated in the American Civil War, "A house divided cannot stand." In his Second Inaugural Address as president of the United States, delivered in March 1865—the month before the end of the American Civil War and his assassination—Lincoln seeks to justify the Emancipation Proclamation of 1863 and the ending of the Civil War in terms of the theology of divine Providence. He poses the following rhetorical question:

> If we shall suppose that American slavery is one of those offenses which, in the providence of God, must needs come, but which, having continued through His appointed time, He now wills to remove, and that He gives to both North and South this terrible war as the woe due to those by whom the offense came, shall we discern therein any departure from those divine attributes which the believers in a living God always ascribe to him? Fondly do we hope, fervently do we pray, that this mighty scourge of war may speedily pass away.[107]

As we will see in the next chapter, Obama's entire push for the presidency was a *mimesis* of Lincoln's providential political theology, right down to the location where his candidacy was announced in February 2007: outside the State Capitol in Springfield, Illinois, Lincoln's last resting place.

What Rousseau tackles with courageous directness in his chapter on civil religion—much more radically than in his other writings on religion, and more than a century before Nietzsche—is the problem of Christianity and politics, namely the Christian separation of theological and political authority. His reward was the public burning of his books in Geneva, and attempted imprisonment in France. In the religions of antiquity there was an identity of theological and political authority. One need only read the *Oresteia* or the tragedies of Sophocles to realize that the gods of the Athenians were gods of the city, civic gods without universal jurisdiction. Although cities and peoples were fiercely proud of their local gods, this pride seems to have gone hand in hand with the recognition of the relativity of religious belief; namely, that the gods of Sparta were not the gods of Athens, Corinth, or Thebes, and furthermore that the adoption of another city's gods would not be good for the Athenians, the Corinthians, the Thebans, or anyone else. Oddly, this relativity of belief never seems to have led to religious war.

By contrast Christianity, which requires universality of belief, has led to little else but religious war for much of the last millennium. Christianity divides political and theological authority, declaring that the kingdom of God is not of this world, but of the next. It is, for Rousseau, an essentially anti-political religion: "far from attaching the Citizens' hearts to the State, it detaches them from it as from all earthly things. I know of nothing more contrary to the social spirit." He goes on: "after all what does it matter in this vale of tears whether one is free or a serf?"[108] In an eerie anticipation of Nietzsche's argument in *On the Genealogy of Morals*, Rousseau writes that Christianity is slave morality: "True Christians are made to be slaves; they know it and are hardly moved by it; this brief life has too little value in their eyes."[109] The task of a civil religion is that of "reuniting the two heads of the eagle,"[110] that is, bringing together political and theological authority.

Let's examine Rousseau's argument more closely. The 35 paragraphs of the chapter on civil religion fall into three distinct parts. In the first part, which was added by Rousseau when he was redrafting the text for inclusion in *The Social Contract*, he gives a thumbnail sketch of the history of the relation between politics and religion.[111] In the second, he identifies three forms of religion and pursues the above critique of Christianity.[112] In the third— with a rather abrupt transition—he tries to lay out the principles of a civil religion.[113]

The earliest societies were theocratic and the gods were national deities, Rousseau insists. Although this begins to change with Judaism, it is radicalized in Christianity: "Jesus came to establish a Spiritual Kingdom on earth; which, by separating the theological from the political, led to the State's ceasing to be one (*fit que l'État cessa d'être un*), and caused the intestine divisions which have never ceased to convulse Christian peoples.[114]

In dividing the state from itself, the Christian henceforth serves two masters: the rulers of the city of man and of the city of God. Despite the best efforts of the kings and queens of England, who, like the tsars of Russia, are the head of both state and church, the Christian political subject still serves two powers. This is the problem that, as Rousseau notes, Hobbes recognizes: "Of all

Christian Authors the philosopher Hobbes is the only one who clearly saw the evil and the remedy."[115] Hobbes's solution, worked out with probity in Book 3 of *Leviathan*, is that Christian ecclesiastical power is essentially subordinated to the power of the sovereign, and "the Supreme Pastor" in any commonwealth is "the Civill Soveraigne."[116] Of course, using the epithet "Christian" with respect to Hobbes is risky, and Rousseau claims that Hobbes "must have seen that the domineering spirit of Christianity was inconsistent with his system." In the same way as Machiavelli is judged to be "a good man and an honest citizen," so too, "It is not so much what is horrible and false as what is just and true in [Hobbes's] politics that has made it odious."[117] One might speculate whether Rousseau's relation to Christianity invites a similar conclusion.

Rousseau opposes the contrary opinions of Pierre Bayle, who sought to separate religion and politics in a way that foreshadows liberal conceptions of tolerance, and William Warburton, who sought to argue that Christianity is the strongest support of the body politic: "that the Christian, of all religious societies, is best fitted to assist the civil magistrate."[118] The development of Rousseau's own position, and the kernel of the chapter on civil religion, is based on the distinction between two forms of religion: the religion of man and of the citizen. The religion of man, "without Temples, without altars, without rites," is limited to what Rousseau calls "the purely *internal cult* of the Supreme God." This internal cult is identified with "the pure and simple Religion of the Gospel," or "true Theism." By contrast, the religion of the citizen is national, "inscribed in a single country." It possesses dogmas, rites and an "external cult prescribed by laws." Everything that lies outside the city, nation, or republic is regarded as "infidel, alien, barbarous."[119] Such, Rousseau contends, were the religions of the first peoples.

This classical distinction between internal and external cults (*cultus interior, cultus exterior*) recalls Numa Pompilius, the Sabine sage who, according to tradition, succeeded Romulus as king of Rome. As Rousseau writes in his posthumously published "Considerations on the Government of Poland":

Numa was the true founder of Rome. If all Romulus had done was to assemble some brigands whom a reversal could scatter, his imperfect work could not have withstood the test of time. It was Numa who made it solid and lasting by uniting these brigands into an indissoluble unity.[120]

Furthermore, Numa produced the unity of Rome not through the declaration of laws, but through "apparently frivolous and superstitious rites." This armature of an external cult "sanctified" Rome, and it is such sanctification through rites that Rousseau sought to elaborate in the case of Poland in the constitution of a national identity rooted in a legitimate system of government.

From Augustine's furious polemic against Roman *theologia civilis* in the *City of God* in the early fifth century to John of Salisbury's *Policraticus* (1159) onwards, it is precisely this conception of a religion of the external cult that is attacked by Christian theologians and contrasted with the internal cult of the direct love of God revealed through Christ.[121] Rousseau's question in the chapter on civil religion is whether these two forms of religion can be combined. Each has its virtues and vices. The external cult of the religion of the citizen is good insofar as it combines divine worship with love of the laws. To break the laws, therefore, is to be impious and subjected to the wrath of the gods: *sacer estod*. The religion of the citizen affords Rousseau a robust civic patriotism on the model of Numa.[122]

But the external cult is bad because it is "founded on error" and "drowns the true cult of the divinity in vain ceremonial."[123] The religion of the citizen is also pernicious because of its exclusivism. It makes a people bloodthirsty and intolerant by believing that one executes a holy deed in killing whomsoever does not accept the national gods. As such, it produces "a natural state of war." This is crucial, as it might be seen as Rousseau's response *avant la lettre* to a certain *doxa*—call it Arendtian—that dismisses Rousseau's theory of politics by claiming that it was somehow refuted in practice because it inspired Robespierre's neo-pagan cult of republican virtue that is adjudged consistent with the Terror.

Which leaves us with the religion of man or the political problem of Christianity. To begin with, Rousseau makes crystal clear that Christianity is true or veritable religion:

> There remains, then, the Religion of man of Christianity, not that of today, but that of the Gospels, which is altogether differ-ent. Through this saintly, sublime, genuine (*véritable*) Religion, men, as children of the same God, all recognize one another as brothers, and the society that unites them does not dissolve even at death.[124]

We should note the barely concealed polemic against Catholicism in this passage, which only becomes more explicit as the chapter on civil religion continues, particularly in the original *Geneva Manuscript* version. Rousseau is defending evangelical Protestant Christianity—a religion truer to early Christianity than the deca-dent Catholicism visible in France and elsewhere. Although such a true Christianity allows universal fraternity, where "all recognize one another as brothers," the defect of the religion of man is that it has no particular relation to the body politic. A Christian repub-lic is a contradiction in terms, Rousseau insists. Christian soldiers would be crushed in battle by Roman or Spartan adversaries. As we saw above, Christianity is a slave morality that is entirely contrary to social spirit.

So, the overwhelming question hanging over the chapter on civil religion and indeed the entirety of *The Social Contract* is the following: how to combine the virtues of the internal and exter-nal cults, while avoiding their vices. That is, how can love of the supreme, true, and universal God of Christianity be compatible with the love of the laws and the external rites necessary to draw citizens towards that love? What must be avoided is the anti-political nature of Christianity, on the one hand, and the political exclusivism and chauvinism of paganism, on the other. The issue, more generally, is how to combine the virtues of a robust and motivating particularism—a civic patriotism—with the generality of an appeal to equality.

The closest Rousseau gets to a solution to this question is a passage from the penultimate paragraph of the discussion of civil religion in the *Geneva Manuscript* that Rousseau curiously deleted from *The Social Contract*. If Rousseau's political dream is association without representation, in an act where a people becomes a people on the basis of a general axiom of equality, then his theologico-political dream is the following:

> Thus the advantages of the religion of man and the religion of the citizen will be combined. The state will have its cult and will not be the enemy of anyone else's. With divine and human laws always united on the same object, the most pious theists will also be the most zealous citizens, and the defense of the holy laws will be the glory of the God of men.[125]

This is arguably a noble dream; at the very least, it's an open question as to why Rousseau felt he had subsequently to delete this passage.

However, in the third part of the chapter on civil religion, when Rousseau tries to "fix the principles" of his civil religion,[126] the results are at best syncretic, at worst cynical, and arguably a lot less convincing than Hobbes's political theology in *Leviathan*, where Christian ecclesiastical power is essentially subordinated to the power of the sovereign.

It is as if Rousseau doesn't quite know what to do or how to finish the argument of the chapter. He claims that subjects only owe an account of their opinions to the extent that these opinions matter to the community. One's private opinions are one's own business and the sovereign does not have the power to limit them. That is to say, one can believe what one likes as long as it does not interfere with the smooth running of the public realm. This is like the old joke that in America you can believe anything you like, you can be a Muslim, a Buddhist, or a Scientologist just so long as you're a Protestant Muslim, a Protestant Buddhist, or a Protestant Scientologist. At one moment, Rousseau seems to revert to the classical liberal position that one has the right to religious freedom as long as one accepts that this is a private right and one's belief should play no public role. Rousseau argues that "There is therefore a purely civil profession of faith" which it is up to the sovereign, i.e., the people, to fix. The articles of such a catechism are not, Rousseau insists, "dogmas of religion," but "sentiments of sociability" without which it is impossible to be a good citizen or a loyal subject.

However, any apparent liberalism is dispelled when Rousseau comes to stating the dogmas of civil religion, which, he declares, "ought to be simple, few in number, stated with precision, without explanations or commentary."[127]

No explanations or commentary! The articles of the citizen's catechism simply have to be accepted as *catechesis* without argument or interpretation. The positive dogmas include belief in an omnipotent and provident deity, the happiness of the just and the punishment of the wicked, the sanctity of the social contract and the laws, without forgetting the necessity of a belief in the afterlife. It would not, I believe, be an exaggeration to describe this miscellany of dogmas as somewhat opportunistic. (Why, for example, do the sentiments of sociability require a belief in the afterlife, let alone in a prescient and providential divinity?) In addition, anyone who acts against the laws can be banished, "Not as impious but as unsociable, as incapable of sincerely loving the laws, justice, and, if need be of sacrificing his life to his duty."[128] What's more, if someone is found to be a social hypocrite by publicly acknowledging the authority of the laws but behaving as if he did not believe them, then "Let him be punished with death; he has committed the greatest of crimes, he has lied before the laws."[129]

Sacer estod—the sacredness of civil religion requires the execution of the *homo sacer*. If the purpose of civil religion is to provide a transcendent, sacred underpinning to the immanence of the general will, then it does not require much imagination to see how such sacredness might be violently employed to legitimate the most ugly forms of state repression and state terror, particularly when we link them together with Rousseau's argument for dictatorship.

The negative dogmas of civil religion are reduced to just one: intolerance. Again, it is extremely useful to compare the two versions of the chapter on civil religion. In the *Geneva Manuscript*, the discussion of civil religion is followed by a brief section headed "The Marriage of Protestants," which is reduced and significantly rewritten as the final footnote to *The Social Contract*.[130] Rousseau was rightly outraged at a French edict, dating from 1724, which forbade Protestants from having their marriages blessed and their children baptized by Catholic priests, and which also prohibited them from leaving the country to get married or from sending their children abroad. Rousseau describes Protestantism as being "of all the Christian sects ... the wisest and gentlest ... the most peaceful and social."[131] If the prohibition of intolerance is the sole negative dogma of civil religion, then the object of Rousseau's attack, throughout *The Social Contract*, is Catholicism, a doctrine "so manifestly bad that it is a waste of time to amuse oneself demonstrating that it is."[132] Given that it is no longer possible to have a purely national or city-state religion on the model of pagan antiquity, one must tolerate all those who tolerate others insofar as their dogmas are not contrary to the duties of citizenship.

It is in this deeply unsatisfactory way, with Rousseau polemically tilting at the windmills of French Catholic intolerance, that *The Social Contract* ends—with a whimper, not a bang. It simply peters out. Rousseau doesn't seem to have a clue how to finish the book.

Where does this leave us? I have tried to show the "actuality" of Rousseau by tracing the intrication of three concepts in his work: politics, law, and religion. We have followed a series of conceptual *décalages* around which Rousseau's system is staged, where the condition of possibility for any legitimate form of political association requires the externality of the legislator for its authorization and the transcendence of civil religion for its sacralization. Sadly, this condition of possibility is also the system's condition of impossibility, and Rousseau's political argument unravels in a rather improbable conception of civil religion. But it might lead elsewhere.

DOLLAR BILLS, FLAGS, AND COSMIC WAR

It is my belief that there is no way of understanding contemporary political reality without a clear understanding of the nature, history, and force of civil religion, by which I mean the sacralization of politics in its diverse and contradictory forms, which arises when a political unit transforms itself into a sacred entity as a way of buttressing its claim to legitimacy.

This is most obviously the case in American civil religion, which finds banal but compelling empirical confirmation in the weird symbolism of the one dollar bill, complete with the words "In God We Trust"—a phrase added by Eisenhower in 1956.[133] In addition to the Roman eagle of the Great Seal of the United States, we find two allusions to Virgil: the inscription "*Novus ordo seclorum*," "a new order of ages," and "*Annuit coeptis*," "he has approved our undertaking." These allusions bring together the divine source for the polity with a Roman prefiguration of the providential idea of Manifest Destiny. It is the divine source whose radiant sun-like eye stares out at us at the top of the incomplete Masonic pyramid, with its thirteen steps symbolizing the number of the original colonies and the Roman numerals MDCCLXXVI. It is the God of American civil political religion who underwrites the act of republican association, the unification of a disparate plurality, "*E pluribus unum*." Beyond the materiality of the greenback, the articles of American civil religion find expression in the pledge of allegiance, the worship of the flag, and the cult of the war dead—indeed, the entire culture of war.

To move peremptorily, the presence of civil religion can obviously be seen in sundry European nationalisms, but is perhaps most strikingly apparent in the extraordinary symbolism of the European flag, with its crown of 12 yellow stars on a blue background. The flag, based on a design by Arsène Heitz, was adopted by the Council of Europe on December 8, 1955. It seems innocent enough with the stars representing the diverse European peoples (at least, "the Europe of the 12," which existed from 1986–95) on a background of the blue Western sky—apparently a straightforward symbol for European integration.

Heitz was a pious and devoted Catholic and his design was directly inspired by the history of the apparitions of the Blessed Virgin in the Rue du Bac in Paris. In the summer of 1830, the Virgin Mary appeared to Catherine Labouré, a novice in the Sisters of Charity in the Rue du Bac. According to Labouré, the Virgin said, "The times are very evil. Sorrows will befall France; the throne will be overturned. The whole world will be plunged into every kind of misery."[134] Despite the apocalyptic tone, it is truly impressive that the Virgin Mary should have taken such an interest in the internal affairs of nineteenth-century France. The Virgin went on to demand that Catherine have a medal struck, the "Miraculous Medal" that by the time of Catherine's death in 1876 was worn by millions of Catholics. On this medal, the Virgin is depicted with a halo of twelve gold stars around her head in an allusion to the Revelation of St. John, "And a great sign was seen in heaven; a woman arrayed with the sun, and the moon under feet, and upon her head a crown of twelve stars" (Rev. 12:1). Now, if all this seems too much of a coincidence, one might simply note that the day the European flag was adopted by the Council of Europe, December 8, is also the Feast of the Immaculate Conception, adopted by Pius IX on December 8, 1854, exactly 101 years earlier. I am not suggesting—like a paranoid Rousseau—that the European Union is a covert Catholic conspiracy, but there is at the very least a story to tell and a history that requires uncovering.

Without an understanding of the intrication of politics and religion, we have little hope of comprehending the present through which we are all-too-precipitously passing. Ours is a time of new religious war, of what an unpublished report by the Rand Corporation calls a time of "cosmic war," where political actors are religious believers or "cosmic warriors" with a Manichean opposition between Good and Evil. It seems to me that any attempt to understand politics at the present time has to begin from the datum of *sacred violence*, of political violence carried out in the name of the divine.[135] As the authors of the Rand report write: "Religious contestation in Europe before the age of nationalism and Marxism is a better guide to the future than the secular conflict of the Cold War."[136]

In whichever terms we approach the vexed question of the relation of politics to religion, a grim series of parallels is revealed:

(i)   *Zionism*, in which the State of Israel is based on an identity of politics and religion and where any critique of the political regime can therefore be condemned as an anti-Semitic religious slur.

(ii)   *Islamism or Jihadism* in its diverse forms where political action is entirely legitimated in religious terms, where Osama bin Laden justified al Qaeda in terms of an opposition to the "Zionist-Crusaders" and vindicated his own position in terms of a logic of martyrdom.

(iii) *Military neo-liberalism*, where the theology of the free market is combined with a providential understanding of freedom, democracy, and human rights and employs excessive, asymmetrical military power to prosecute a war on terror that is justified in terms of a clash of civilizations.

(iv)   *Social democratic conservatism*, where countries like the Netherlands, Denmark, France, and Switzerland—and throughout western Europe—purportedly defend their traditions of tolerance, integration, and the benefits of the welfare state in a thinly disguised racism against alleged immigrants (though they are often second- and third-generation nationals), who are coded as Islamic and accused of not being willing to integrate into mainstream society.

This list might be continued.

FICTIONAL FORCE: HOW THE MANY ARE GOVERNED BY THE FEW

Rousseau establishes the modern conception of politics: popular sovereignty, or free association rooted in equality. Furthermore, by following the *décalage* machine of Rousseau's text, I think we are afforded a decisive recognition of the fictional force that is essential to politics. In Hobbes's words, what gives life and motion to the body politic is an "Artificiall *Soul.*" Politics is, in the literal sense, a poetic task concerned with the construction of fictions. The question with which I'd like to end is whether we might speak of the possibility of a supreme fiction in politics.

There is a double miracle at work in politics. On the one hand, politics requires a willing suspension of disbelief. It requires that the many believe in the fictions told to them by the few who govern them. That is, government requires make-believe, whether the belief is in the divine right of kings or the quasi-divinity of the people that is somehow meant to find expression through the magic of representative government, the organ of the party, the radiant sun-like will of the glorious leader, or whatever. Government rests on fictions.

But, on the other hand, the extraordinary thing about politics is that it not only requires a willing suspension of disbelief; it also receives it. The force in any polity always lies with the many, with the multitude, yet somehow for most of history—with certain rare and usually brief, glittering, but fleeting exceptions—the many

submit to the will of the few who claim not only to be working
in their interest, but to embody their collective will. Of course, it
might be pointed out that political power is always possessed by
the people with the "guns and sticks," usually the police and the
military, and if the many don't possess them, then they are powerless. That is, of course, incontrovertible: the state is a gendarme and
resistance to it usually requires force of arms. But this doesn't begin
to explain the fictional force whereby the many submits to the
few without the constant threat of physical violence. Considered
closely but disinterestedly, politics is a very curious matter. In
order to understand its operation, all we possess is history—which
is what makes the work of historians of politics so essential.

With that in mind, I'd like to turn to Edmund Morgan's
*Inventing the People: The Rise of Popular Sovereignty in England and
America*. The central theoretical category in this rich historical
account of the transition from monarchical to popular sovereignty
in England and America during seventeenth and eighteenth centuries is fiction. The main concern of Morgan's book is to explain
how it is that the fiction of the divine right of kings gave way
to that of the sovereignty of the people. The interesting thing
about this conjunction of fictions is that whereas it is difficult
from this end of history to see the idea of the divine right of
kings as anything more than an absurdity based on the idea of the
king as the visible god, the overwhelming majority of politicians is
attached to—or at least ventriloquizes—some version of the idea
of popular sovereignty: that all human beings are equal or indeed
created equal, that government should be by the people and for
the people, that government embodies and enacts the will of the
people, and so on.

Morgan's point is that historically one fiction succeeds another
in the extraordinary years of the 1630s and '40s in England, and
in a different but strongly related way in the American colonies
in the 1760s and '70s. What unites both historical moments is the
influence of the radical ideas of the Levellers' "Agreeement of the
People" of 1647 and James Harrington's 1656 *The Commonwealth*

of Oceana. But more importantly, perhaps, conceptually one fiction resembles the other much more closely than we might like to imagine: God the king becomes God the people. As Rousseau writes in his discourse on "Political Economy," "the voice of the people is indeed the voice of God."[137] *Vox populi, vox dei.* Morgan notes how

> The sovereignty of the people was not a repudiation of the sovereignty of God. God remained the ultimate source of all governmental authority, but attention now centred on the immediate source, the people. Though God authorized government, He did it through the people, and in doing so He set them above their governors.[138]

In this connection, the origins of Rousseau's concept of the general will are fascinating. As Patrick Riley shows in great textual and historical detail, the general will was well established in the seventeenth century, not as a political idea, but as a theological idea.[139] Specifically, the concept of the general will referred to the activity of divine will in deciding who would be granted grace sufficient for salvation and who would be sent to hell. The issue was the following: if God wills that all men be saved, then does he have a general will whose consequence is universal salvation? And if not, then does God will particularly that some people not be saved? In 1706, Leibniz writes: "The God of the Christians wills that all men be saved; he has the power necessary to save them all; he lacks neither power nor good will, and nonetheless almost all men are damned."[140]

Rousseau politicizes the theological concept of the general will: the divine is translated into the civic. The general will is transformed from God's supposed will to save all men into the human will insofar as one wills as a citizen and which can provide the key to political legitimacy. What occasioned this translation of the divine into the civic, this transformation of the theological into the political, between the seventeenth and eighteenth centuries?

Riley contends that ideas that were once ascribed to God are turned into human moral ideals made more attractive by "being translated to heaven."[141]

The implications of Rousseau's transformation of divine transcendence into civic immanence can be seen most clearly in the closing pages of Kant's *Critique of Pure Reason*. In the "The Transcendental Doctrine of Method," Kant writes that we will be "acting in conformity with the divine will in so far only as we hold *sacred* the moral law."[142] This, of course, is the problem of moral theology in Kant. "So far, then," he writes, "as practical reason has the right to serve as our guide, we shall not look upon actions as obligatory because they are the commands of God, but shall regard them as divine commands because we have an inward obligation to them."[143]

That is, in order to serve the end of reason in morality and to resist the temptation of what Kant calls "fanaticism" and "impiety," any transcendent employment of moral theology must be avoided. Kant concludes, "Moral theology is thus of immanent use only." In this way, what occurs in Rousseau and Kant is not some assertion of the secular. It is rather a metamorphosis of the meaning of the sacred, which attempts to retain the theological moment by immanentizing the transcendent within moral theology or the general will. The history of modern political forms is not centered on the transition from the religious to the secular—a transition that would allegedly parallel that from the pre-modern to the modern, where the "post-modern" would be the purportedly "post-secular." Rather, the history of modern political forms— republicanism, liberal democracy, fascism, and the rest—is best understood as a series of metamorphoses of sacralization. Modern politics takes place within an economy of the sacral, in particular the passage or ambivalence of the passage between the transcendent and the immanent. As we have seen above in detail in relation to Rousseau, such an immanentizing of the transcendent is fraught with paradox, and modern politics as an economy of the sacral is articulated around diverse stagings of the paradox of sovereignty:

in Hobbes, in Rousseau, in Marx, in Lenin, in Carl Schmitt, even in Barack Obama.

Let's return to the parallel thread of Morgan's narrative about the shift from the fiction of divine right to that of popular sovereignty. Indeed, it might be said that the fiction of popular sovereignty is a more fictional fiction than divine right.[144] A king or a queen is a visible presence with a crown and scepter, and usually a large family with expensive tastes—but where might one see the people? One can see people, but where exactly is *the* people to be found? The fact that some of us might happen to believe in the fiction of popular sovereignty, and the idea or ideal that legitimate government is the expression of the will of the people, in no way diminishes its fictional status.

A moment's thought reveals that popular sovereignty is based on a series of logical *décalages*: namely, that the people are the governed, but also the government, and that this identity of government and the governed somehow happens through the miracle of representation, which is truly the central shibboleth of liberal democracy. But how exactly can a few be said to represent the many? How can a particularity speak for a generality when the latter is not actually present? Of course, it cannot. What is the case, however, is that the legitimacy of the few rests on the fiction of believing that they represent the many. At which point, a dilemma arises: either politics and politicians are entirely cynical—and I am not ruling that out at all; it is the most comforting hypothesis—or they actually believe that they incarnate the will of their voters and the people as a whole through the magic of representation. Similarly, either the electorate believe that their politicians are a group of self-interested, money-grabbing crooks, or they actually believe that their will is miraculously represented through the mechanism of the vote. It would appear that popular sovereignty is a fiction that cannot bear too close an examination or too literal an application. It is a fiction that is extremely useful in giving a patina of legitimacy to representative government where what is essentially at stake is popular consent to a governing aristocracy, oligarchy, political class, or, in the case of the United States, a plutocracy. Popular sovereignty is a lie. Some would argue that, given the wickedness of human nature, it is a noble lie. But I have always been skeptical about the necessity for noble lies.

One tempting option at this point is to return to Rousseau's critique of representation and to ask about the question of size. As we have already seen, in order to minimize the magic of representation, the sovereign authority of the people can only be exercised in a polity that is very small. As Rousseau nicely points out at the end of his critique of political representation: "All things considered, I do not see that among us the Sovereign can henceforth preserve the exercise of its rights unless the City is very small."[145]

For Rousseau, like Montesquieu and Voltaire, small is beautiful in the political realm, as it minimizes the gap between the sovereign legislative authority of the people and the executive power of government. As Voltaire succinctly puts it: "The bigger the fatherland the less we love it, because divided love is weaker."[146] On the basis of this claim, the three classical forms of government can be organized according to the respective scale of the polity: democracy = small; aristocracy = medium; monarchy = large.

In this regard, it is worth considering Madison's reversal of this argument from size in the debates around federalism that found their expression in the great Constitutional Convention of 1787 and in the US Constitution. The problem that Madison grappled with, in the years following independence from Great Britain, was how to bring about a national government that might override the interests of the various states, like Virginia or Rhode Island. Madison's view was that the vigorous and long-established attachment of citizens to their particular states (as a Virginian, a Rhode Islander, or whatever) worked against the forging of a new national identity, what Morgan calls "the invention of an American people." Madison's innovative solution, based explicitly on Hume's ideas on government expressed in "Idea of a Perfect Commonwealth," was to propose extremely large constituencies with relatively few representatives.[147] The assumption was that large constituencies would ensure the election of the right kind of people, namely the "natural aristocracy" of landowning gentlemen—indeed, people rather like Madison and his friends.

For Hume, democracies are prone to factionalism and "the force of popular tides and currents."[148] Democracy is best suited to the turbulence of life in cities and small republics, whereas aristocracy is better "adapted for peace and order," although it often becomes "jealous and oppressive." The most perfect solution, for Hume, is some combination of both and this was the one chosen by Madison for the United States. Hume calls this form of government "refined" democracy, which is a little like refined sugar: whitened and with all the unwanted rough ingredients removed. Hume writes:

> In a large government, which is modeled with masterly skill, there is compass and room enough to *refine* the democracy, from the lower people, who may be admitted into the first elections or first concoction of the commonwealth, to the higher magistrates, who direct all the movements.[149]

Although Madison's "natural aristocracy" eventually gave way to the capitalist plutocracy that still happily governs the United States, it is worth recalling that this system of government is, in Madison's revealingly candid words, "the only defense against the inconveniences of democracy consistent with the democratic form of Government."[150] Representative government prevents the inconveniencies of democracy, namely the genuine sovereign authority of a people, whilst maintaining the appearance of popular sovereignty. Refined democracy presents a patina of popular power from below while genuine legislative and executive power is exerted from above. To borrow a repeated refrain of Rousseau, "This invention is a masterpiece of politics."[151]

There is no doubting what Hume calls the "masterly skill" of the Federalists' arguments. By prefacing the Constitution of the

United States with the words "We the People" rather than "We the States," Federalists like Madison ensured that the fiction of "the People" projected an aura of majesty that allowed it to override the interests of the various states and the vigorous opposition of the anti-Federalists. With a single stroke of the pen, the Constitution circumvented the strong local identification of citizens with their particular states, and what Madison saw as the risk of factionalism and forms of local populism, Hume's "popular tides and currents." Henceforth, identification with a state over the people—which of course was one of the causes of the American Civil War—could be declared to be anti-patriotic. In the same gesture, by making the size of the constituencies in the United States much larger than on any previous model, the Federalists managed to "refine" democracy and avoid its "inconveniences" whilst maintaining its chimera, all the while ensuring that government would be administered by the "higher magistrates," whether patrician Virginian gentlemen like Madison, or the nascent money-making New Yorkers like Alexander Hamilton.

So there is, and always has been, something peculiarly unrepresentative about American representative democracy. At present, for a population of 307 million, there are 100 Senators and 435 members of the House of Representatives. This compares with the current situation in the United Kingdom with 646 members of the House of Commons, plus 617 in the House of Lords in a population of roughly 61.5 million (and, as we have seen, according to Rousseau's criteria the United Kingdom is hardly a model of legitimate government). In the UK, there is one representative for every 100,000 citizens. In the United States, it is one representative for every 700,000. Miraculous indeed! How can so much popular will be squeezed into so few bodies?

Politics, then, is a kind of magic show, where we know that the rabbit has not miraculously appeared in the empty hat and the magician's charming assistant has not been sawn in half, but where we are willing to suspend disbelief and go along with the illusion—believe! This is where Rousseau is so instructive, as he is the most fictively self-conscious of philosophers, whichever genre he works in: the theatrical comedy of manners (*Narcisse*), the sentiment-soaked epistolary novel (*La nouvelle Héloïse*), the didactic treatise in moral education (*Emile*), the quasi-scientific hypothetical history of humanity (*Discourse on Inequality*), the creation of a sexualized subjectivity defined and divided by intimacy (*The Confessions*), or meditative *askesis* (*Reveries*).

The concise, near-geometrical abstraction of *The Social Contract* is a political fiction. It is the formal articulation of the fiction of popular sovereignty understood as association without representation, which is, for Rousseau—and I think he is right—the only form of legitimate politics that can face and face down the fact of gross inequality and the state of war. The being of politics is the act of association without representation. This fiction requires, in turn, other fictions: those of law and religion, which we have traced in this chapter. The fiction of politics has to be underpinned by the authority of a quasi-divine legislator and the dogmas of civil religion. For Rousseau, the binding of a political collectivity has to be the self-binding of the general will and this requires the ligature of *religio*. Such a religion has to be inculcated through mores, shared beliefs, civic values, and what can only be described as political rituals: pledges of allegiance, national anthems, honoring the war dead, the sacredness of the flag, or whatever. Such is the necessary armature of any *theologia civilis* of the kind examined above. For Rousseau, the fiction of politics cannot be sustained without the fiction of civil theology.

So, is my conclusion simply that we cannot and should not enter into discussions of politics without acknowledging the dimension of fiction, particularly legal and religious fictions, in constituting and legitimating political life? That would seem to be what lies behind the skeptical—indeed Humean—historical approach adopted by Morgan. The latter's entire approach is drawn from the opening words of Hume's "Of the First Principles of Government," where he writes: "Nothing appears more surprizing [*sic*] to those, who consider human affairs with a philosophical eye, than to see the easiness with which the many are governed by the few."[152]

Given that "FORCE" (Hume capitalizes the word) is always on the side of the governed, one might ask "by what means this wonder is effected." How, indeed, is the "wonder" of government brought about? Hume is clear: "It is therefore, on *opinion* only that government is founded; and this maxim extends to the most despotic and most military governments, as well as to the most free and most popular."

The many submit to the few that govern through opinions that are very often at odds with fact, myths of origin, providential narratives of progress, historical narratives of victory or defeat or whatever. That is to say, the entire operation of government is dependent upon fiction.

This Humean approach has much to recommend it, particularly at the level of description, diagnosis, and critique of the kind that we find, for example, in Emilio Gentile's work on the religions of politics, especially fascism.[153] Politics requires fictions of the sacred and rituals of sacralization for its legitimation, and these fictions need to be exposed for what they are. Any empire's new clothes need to be stripped away in order to see the old, rotting flesh of the state in the full light of day. At this level, the student of politics is involved in the exposure of the fictions that sustain government and the philosophical analysis of politics is a historical and analytical labor of demythologization.

THE POLITICS OF THE SUPREME FICTION

One could stop here and perhaps it would be prudent to do so. Yet, perhaps simply in the interest of digging my own grave, I would like to push the argument a little further and speculate. It should not be thought that I am opposing fiction to fact here, where the former is adjudged false in the face of the latter's veracity. I do not think that a general critique of political fictions is a mere sacrifice on the altar of empiricism to the god of political realism. In my view, in the realms of politics, law, and religion there are *only* fictions. Yet I do not see this as a sign of weakness, but as a signal of *possible* strength.

The distinction that I would like to advance in closing is not between fiction and fact, but between fiction and *supreme fiction*. In saying this, I allude to Wallace Stevens, and the dim possibility of a fructuous collision between poetry and politics.[154] For Stevens, poetry permits us to see fiction as fiction, that is, to see the fictiveness or contingency of the world. It reveals, in his terms, "the idea of order" which we imaginatively impose on reality. Such is what we might think of as the critical task of poetry, where I understand critique in the Kantian sense, as demystifying any empiricist myth of the given and showing the radical dependency of that which is upon the creative, ultimately imaginative, activity of the subject. More plainly stated, the critical task of poetry is to show that the world is what you make of it. But that does not exhaust the category of fiction.

Paradoxically, a supreme fiction is a fiction that we know to be a fiction—there being nothing else—but in which we nevertheless believe. A supreme fiction is one self-conscious of its radical contingency. For Stevens, it is a question here of final belief. "The final belief," he asserts, "is to believe in a fiction, which you know to be a fiction, there being nothing else. The exquisite truth is to know that it is a fiction and that you believe it willingly."[155]

As he writes elsewhere, "final belief / Must be in a fiction" and the hope of a supreme fiction is to furnish such final belief.[156] In his most important and difficult poem, "Notes toward a Supreme Fiction," Stevens attempts to articulate the conditions for a such a fiction, but only offers notes towards it, something indeed like musical notes. He writes of the supreme fiction that it is not given to us whole and ready-made, but that "It is possible, possible, possible. It must / Be possible."[157]

My hope here is that we might begin to transpose this possibility from the poetical to the political realm, or indeed to show that both poetry and politics are realms of fiction, and that what we can begin to envision in their collision is the possibility of a supreme fiction. This requires that we begin to start thinking about politics as radical creation, as the possibility of what Rousseau called "perfected art," which might repair "the ills that the beginnings of art caused to nature." The cure for inequality is not a return to nature, which is a common misreading of Rousseau, but a turn to art: an art of politics that is capable of conceiving and shaping "new associations."

To choose a nicely tendentious example, this is what Marx attempted in his 1843 "Introduction" to the *Critique of Hegel's Philosophy of Right* where, it seems to me, he gets close to the idea of a supreme fiction. For Marx, the logic of the political subject is expressed in the words "I am nothing and I should be everything" (*Ich bin nichts, und ich müßte alles sein*).[158]

Beginning from a position of nothingness, or what we called above with Althusser "total alienation," a particular group is posited as a generality, which requires "the total alienation of this total alienation" in the act of political association. Marx's name for the supreme fiction is "the proletariat," which he qualifies as communist, that is, as rigorously egalitarian. If politics is the moment of association without representation, then it requires the alienation from alienation, or the shift from the structural inequality under conditions of capitalism to what Marx calls in Volume 1 of *Capital* "an association of free human beings"; what Malatesta calls "free organization."[159] This is the supreme fiction.

To borrow a line of thought from Badiou, what is lacking at the present time is the possibility of such a name, a supreme fiction of final belief around which a politics might organize itself.[160] What is lacking is a theory and practice of the general will understood as the supreme fiction of final belief that would take place in the act by which a people becomes a people or by which a free association is formed. What is lacking is an understanding of how the fiction of political association requires the fictions of law and religion for its authorization and sacralization.

In the absence of a new political name, the political task is the poetic construction of a supreme fiction, what Stevens calls "the fiction of an absolute." Such a fiction would be a fiction that we *know* to be a fiction and yet in which we believe nonetheless. All we have at the present time are some Stevensian notes towards this fiction and the open question with which we began—the question that Rousseau asked Voltaire exactly 250 years ago. A catechism of the citizen would be a supreme fiction, a fiction of final belief. It should be remembered that what Rousseau asks from Voltaire in the 1756 letter is a *poem*: "This work, done with care, would be the most useful book ever composed, it seems to me and perhaps the only one needful to men. Here, Sir, is a subject for you. I passionately wish you might be willing to undertake this work and adorn it with your Poetry."[161] Is the fact that we are still asking for this poem a sign of hope or a symptom of despair? It is possible, possible, possible it is the latter; but it is also possible, possible, possible it is the former.

WHY BADIOU IS A ROUSSEAUIST

In the *Republic*, Socrates wanders out of Athens with Plato's brothers and walks down to the port of Piraeus, leaving the city behind them. After quickly demolishing the prevailing views of justice in Athenian society, Socrates starts dreaming of another city in dialogue, a just city governed by philosophers whose souls would be orientated towards the Good. This is why the standard objection to Plato—that the ideal of the philosophical city is unrealistic, utopian, or impossible to realize—is so fatuous. Of course the philosophers' city is utopian. That's the point. Indeed, one might go further and claim that it is part of the duty of philosophy to construct concepts that allow us to imagine that another city and another world are possible, however difficult that may be to achieve in practice. As Oscar Wilde famously writes in "The Soul of Man under Socialism": "A map of the world that does not include Utopia is not even worth glancing at, for it leaves out the one country at which Humanity is always landing."[162]

In the face of the avowed anti-Platonism of philosophy since the so-called linguistic turn, especially in its Heideggerian version, Alain Badiou proposes a gesture that he calls Platonic, which allows philosophy to return to what he sees as its constitutive triad of concepts in the modern epoch: being, truth, and the subject.[163] It is essential to keep this Platonism in mind when considering Badiou's political thinking.

The source of Badiou's considerable appeal lies in the understanding of philosophy that he defends. He writes that "philosophy is something that helps to change existence."[164] Philosophy, for Badiou, is neither technical and largely irrelevant logic-chopping, nor is it deconstructive, melancholic poeticizing—what Badiou calls "the delights of the margin."[165] On the contrary, philosophy is an affirmative, constructive discipline of thought. As Saint Paul writes in First Corinthians—and we will return to these words closely in Chapter 4—Badiou is concerned with the things that are not, in order "to bring to nothing things that are" (1 Cor. 1:27–8). Philosophy is the construction of the formal possibility of something that would break with the "febrile sterility" of the contemporary world.[166] This is what he calls an *event* and the only question of politics, for Badiou, is whether there is something that might be worthy of the name *event*. If philosophy, with Plato, is understood as a "seizure by thought of what breaks the sleep of thought," then politics is a revolutionary seizure of power which breaks with the dreamless sleep of an unjust and violently unequal world.[167] As such, Badiou is not concerned with the banal reality of existing politics, which he tends to dismiss rather lightly as "the democratic fetish," but with moments of rare and evanescent political invention and creativity. Like Socrates, Badiou dreams of another city in speech and therefore to accuse him of being unrealistic is to refuse to undertake the experiment in thought that his philosophy represents.

Badiou's political writings are marked by a cool rationalism and a biting satire. In addition to withering critiques and witty demolitions of the so-called war on terror, the invasion of Iraq, the bombardment of Serbia, and the pantomime of parliamentary democracy, there is a delightfully Swiftian satire on the Islamic headscarf or *foulard* affair ("Today's republic: down with hats!"[168]) and a savage and poignant denunciation of the racism that led to riots in the Parisian *banlieues* late in 2005 and later in 2007, "We have the riots we deserve."[169] Badiou sees France as a politically "sick" and "disproportionately abject country," whose political reality is not located in the endlessly invoked republican ideal of the revolution, but in the reaction against it.[170] For Badiou, France is the country of Thiers' massacre of the Communards, Petain's collaboration with the Nazis, and de Gaulle's colonial wars. As such, the presidential victory of Nicolas Sarkozy in 2007 is an affirmation of Petainism and Le Penism and a continuation of the long war against the enemy within. Behind what Badiou sees as the transcendental illusion of French politics, its avowed tradition of revolution and republicanism, lies its true reactionary kernel.[171]

As for what Badiou imagines as an alternative to the febrile sterility of the world and its increasingly orgiastic celebrations of social inequality, he describes it as an "Enlightenment, whose elements we are slowly assembling."[172] Such an Enlightenment can neither be understood as what Badiou calls "state democracy," i.e., parliamentarianism, nor "state bureaucracy," the socialist party-state. Political struggle is "A tooth and nail fight to organize a united popular force."[173] This requires "discipline"—an oft repeated word in Badiou's work. It is important to emphasize that this is not party discipline in the old Leninist sense. Rather, what is at issue here is the invention of a politics without a party at a distance from the state, a local politics that is concerned with the construction of a collectivity or group on the basis of an appeal to generality.

But what might this mean? In order to understand Badiou's idea of politics, I think it is necessary to consider his close proximity to Rousseau, another sometime Platonist. In my view, Badiou's understanding of politics is much more Rousseauian than Marxist. Let me list seven reasons in support of this claim.

(i)   *Formalism*—In *The Social Contract*, Rousseau, like Badiou, is trying to establish the *formal* conditions of a legitimate politics. The more Marxist or sociological question of the material conditions for such a politics is continually elided. Although every event requires what Badiou calls "an evental site" (the latter is something that belongs to the situation, but what belongs to it—i.e., the event—does *not* belong to the situation[174]), this is a necessary but by no means sufficient condition for an event.

(ii) *Voluntarism*—In Badiou's view, Rousseau establishes the modern concept of politics which is based in the "act by which a people is a people."[175] For Badiou, the key to Rousseau's idea of popular sovereignty consists in the act of collective and unanimous declaration through which a people wills itself into existence. This act is an event understood as a collective subjective act of creation, whose radicality consists in the fact that it does not originate in any structure supported within "being" or the "situation," such as the socio-economic realm or the dialectic of relations and forces of production in Marx. The event of politics is the making of something out of nothing through the act of the subject. Badiou is a political voluntarist.

(iii) *Equality*—Rousseau is the great thinker of what Badiou calls the "generic," which is a key concept in Badiou's system.[176] The generic is that which is indiscernible in any situation and effects a rupture with the latter. Thought politically, the generic is that collective act or "forcing," as Badiou puts it, whereby a group breaks with the situation by punching a hole in it.[177] Political action is a generic procedure which is conducted with reference not to a relative or particular maxim of action, but to a universal norm: equality. For Badiou, true politics has to be based on the rigorous equality of all persons and be addressed to all. The means for the creation of a generic, egalitarian politics is the general will, conceived as that political subject whose act of unanimity binds a collectivity together. As Badiou writes, politics is "about finding new sites for the general will."[178]

(iv) *Locality*—From this follows a fourth important point of contact with Rousseau. Although Rousseau defends—or more accurately *invents*—a generic politics understood as the act by which a people declares itself a people of equals and addresses itself to all, this can only be realized in a local manner. Badiou insists that true politics has to be intensely local and he is opposed to both delocalized capitalist globalization and its inverse in the so-called anti-globalization movement. But the fact that all politics is local does not mean that it is particular. On the contrary, Badiou, like Rousseau, argues for what we might call a local or situated universalism.

(v) *Rarity*—The issue then becomes one of identifying a locale for politics. As we have seen, Rousseau struggled to find examples of legitimate politics. He pinned his hopes on Geneva, until they started burning his books after the publication of *The Social Contract* in 1762. He held out hopes for Corsica and Poland, both of which ended in failure. If true politics is the act by which a people wills itself into existence as a radical and local break with what existed beforehand, then such a politics is rare. When Badiou responded to an earlier version of this argument, this was his criticism of Rousseau. Namely, that Rousseau's conception of politics is too abstract and lacks an evental site.[179] But the question of abstraction might be returned to Badiou, since the only real example of politics he gives is the Paris Commune, as we will see presently. True politics is always some *mimesis* of the Commune.

(vi) *Representation*—Badiou's reflections on the French elections of 2002 and Sarkozy's victory in 2007 culminate in a rehearsal of Rousseau's arguments against representative, electoral government and majority rule in *The Social Contract*. For Rousseau and Badiou, the general or generic will cannot be represented, certainly not by any form of government. Politics, then, is not about governmental representation through the mechanism of the vote, but about the presentation of a people to itself. Badiou writes, "The essence of politics, according to Rousseau, affirms presentation over and against representation."[180] The general will cannot, of course, be represented. This leads Rousseau to follow Plato in his critique of theatrical representation or *mimesis* and to argue instead for public festivals where the people would be the actors in their own political drama. As we saw above, what takes place in the public festival is the presence to itself of the people in the process of its enactment.

(vii) *Dictatorship*—However, Badiou goes a step further with Rousseau, a step that we saw the latter take above and which Carl Schmitt will take in a more dramatic fashion, as we will see below. It is a step that I refuse to take. Not only does Badiou defend popular sovereignty, which is as controversial as apple pie in the modern era—just so long as no one puts it into practice, that is—he goes on to defend Rousseau's argument for dictatorship. This, we recall, is argued on the basis of Roman history: dictatorship is legitimate when there is a threat to the life of the body politic, and in such moments of crisis the laws which issue from the sovereign authority of the people can be suspended in the act of *iustitium*. Badiou's claim, however, is slightly different. "Dictatorship," he writes, "is the natural form of organization of political will."[181] The form of dictatorship that Badiou has in mind is not tyranny, but what he calls "citizenry discipline."[182] In other words, Badiou is defending what Marx, Lenin, and Mao called "the dictatorship of the proletariat."

The deeply Rousseauian character of Badiou's approach to politics becomes clear in two extended lectures that he gave in 2002–3 on the Paris Commune and the Chinese Cultural Revolution. In order to grasp Badiou's argument, it is essential to understand its precise periodization. What interests Badiou in the Paris Commune is "the exceptional intensity of its sudden appearing."[183] Everything turns here on the moment on March 18, 1871 when a group of Parisian workers who belonged to the National Guard refused to turn over their weapons to the government of Versailles. It is this moment of armed resistance and the subsequent election of the Commune government on March 26 that constitute a political event for Badiou. Politics is the making of something out of nothing through the act of a collective subject, what he calls in many places in his recent work the "existence of an inexistent."[184]

It is this moment that is repeated—and very self-consciously repeated—in the Shanghai Commune of February 1967. This followed upon the intense power struggles within the Chinese Communist Party and Mao's mobilization of the Red Guards against what he saw as the "revisionism" and bureaucratism of the regime. Although Badiou is very well aware that Mao ordered the dissolution of the Shanghai Commune and its replacement with a Revolutionary Committee controlled by the Party, it is this brief moment of the self-authorizing dictatorship of the proletariat that fascinates him.[185]

What takes place in the 1871 Paris Commune is a moment of collective political self-determination. But, crucially, Badiou's understanding of the Commune is freed from Lenin's hugely influential critique in *State and Revolution*, where its alleged failure is used to justify the Bolshevik seizure of state power in 1917.[186] The same political logic is at work in the Shanghai Commune where, after having attempted to mobilize the masses politically, Mao criticizes the Commune for "extreme anarchism" and being "most reactionary."[187] Badiou is acutely aware that the Cultural Revolution led to widespread barbarism, persecution, and disaster.

So, what is politics, then? It is what Badiou calls an "evanescent event," the act by which a people declares itself into existence and seeks to follow through on that declaration.[188] We might say that politics is the commune and *only* the commune. Badiou writes, Platonically, "I believe this other world resides for us in the Commune."[189] It is this sudden *ex nihilo* transformation of the febrile sterility of the world into a fecund something, this moment of radical rupture, that obsesses Badiou, a seizure by thought in the event that is a seizure of power. Furthermore, this event doesn't last. After 72 days, the Paris Commune was crushed by the military forces of the future first president of the Third Republic, Adolphe Thiers. An estimated 20,000 Parisians were slaughtered.

It is this brief moment of politics without party and state that was repeated in a slightly different register in Paris in May 1968.[190] Understood biographically, the category of the event is Badiou's attempt to make sense of the experience of novelty and rupture that accompanied the "events" of '68. The general questions that drive Badiou's project are simple: What is novelty? What is creation? How does newness come into the world? Understood politically, the event is that moment of novel, brief, local, communal rupture that breaks with a general situation of social injustice and inequality through its enactment of equality. Yet, if the event is evanescent, then *fidelity* is the subjective perseverance that persists in looking at the situation from the standpoint of the event, and *truth* is what fidelity constructs in a situation. Badiou's thinking is not at all some blind submission to what is perceived as the event. It is rather the process of subjective fidelity that is only retrospectively named as an event through what Badiou calls an "intervention."[191] Such an intervention brings about something new in the situation in which we find ourselves, and it is this order of generic novelty that Badiou captures with his notion of truth. Truth is not the veridicality of empirical statements or the coherence of logical propositions; it is the order of invention in which something radically new comes to rupture the situation.

Compelling as I find Badiou's understanding of politics, it is his taste for dictatorship that I find distasteful. Despite the protestations of Hannah Arendt in *On Revolution*, I agree that the problem of politics is the formation of the general or generic will, of a popular front or what Sartre called "the fused group."[192] But such a position need not lead to an apology for dictatorship. In *Being and Event*, Badiou powerfully argues that if the error of Marxist politics was the attempt to occupy the terrain of the state, then true politics should operate at a distance from the state.[193] But if that is the case, then why doesn't Badiou at least consider embracing the anarchist politics that he so steadfastly rejects, a politics that is also without party and at a distance from the state? Is there not a willful inconsistency between, on the one hand, Badiou's declaration that "all emancipatory politics must put an end to the model of the party ... in order to affirm a politics 'without party',", and, on the other hand, his assertion that we must not lapse into "the figure of anarchism, which has never been anything else than the vain critique, or the double, or the shadow, of the communist parties."[194] Why is the black flag simply the shadow of the red flag? Might not matters be exactly the opposite? We will come back to these questions below.

For all the apparent optimism and robust affirmativeness of Badiou's conception of philosophy, one might suspect that there is something deeply pessimistic at its heart, which again links Badiou to Rousseau. The formal conditions that define a true politics are so stringent and the examples given are so limited, that it is tempting to conclude that following the Paris and Shanghai Communes and after 1968 any politics of the event has become impossible, or at least extremely unlikely. Politics is like history in Heidegger: it seldom occurs. But such a conclusion forgets where this discussion of Badiou started: with Socrates wandering out of the unjust city to dream of another city in speech. Rousseau concludes his Second Discourse by showing that the development of social inequality culminates in a state of war between persons, tribes, nations, and civilizations. It is difficult to disagree with such a diagnosis at the present time. In the face of such a state of war, the philosopher's dream of another city will always appear unrealistic and hopelessly utopian. To that extent, perhaps the impossibility of Badiou's politics is its greatest strength.

3

Mystical Anarchism

Perhaps no thinker has enjoyed more popularity and has seemed more germane in recent years than Carl Schmitt.[1] In *Political Theology* he famously asserts, "All significant concepts in the modern theory of the state are secularized theological concepts."[2] This is not just true historically, Schmitt insists, but systematically and conceptually. The omnipotent God of medieval Christianity becomes the omnipotent monarch—for example "the Mortall God" of Hobbes's *Leviathan*. As we saw above, until the late seventeenth century, the general will was a theological term of art that referred to the will of God. By 1762, in *The Social Contract*, the general will had been transformed into the will of the people and the question of sovereignty was translated from the divine to the civic. This explains why Rousseau believed that the general will, like the divine will, cannot err. Of course, this entails that the will of the people is always virtuous, and that those who oppose it can be legitimately exterminated as evil. The politicization of theological concepts leads ineluctably to the attempt to purify virtue through violence: the political sequence that begins with French Jacobinism in 1792, through the dreadful

violent excesses of twentieth-century politics that we can sum-
marize with the proper names of Lenin, Stalin, and Hitler, to what
some provocatively call the "Islamo-Jacobinism" of al Qaeda and
related groups.

Yet, such an argument does not exonerate liberal democracy as
a political form free of theology. On the contrary, Schmitt views
the triumph of the liberal-constitutional state as the triumph of
deism, a theological vision that unifies reason and nature by identifying the latter with divinity.[3] As can be seen most obviously
in the deism of the Founding Fathers, at the core of American
democracy—a peculiar confection of Roman republicanism and
puritanical providentialism—is a civil religion which functions as
a powerful sustaining myth and buttresses the idea of Manifest
Destiny. Obama's political masterstroke was to have reconnected
classical liberal constitutionalism with a motivating civil religion focused around the idea of belief and a faith in change and
progress. As he said during his Inaugural Address on January 20,
2009: "These things are old. These things are true. They have been
the quiet force of progress throughout our history."[4]

Schmitt's problem with liberalism is that it is anti-political.
What this means is that for the liberal every political decision
must be rooted in a norm whose ultimate justification flows from
the constitution. Within liberalism, political decisions are derived
from constitutional norms and higher than the state stands the law
and the interpretation of the law. This is why the highest political authority in a liberal state rests with the supreme court or
its equivalent. Political action is subordinated to juridical interpretation. Lawyers and not philosophers are kings in a liberal
democracy.

For Schmitt, a truly political decision is what breaks with
any norm, frees itself from any normative ties and becomes
absolute. This is why the question of the state of exception is
of such importance to Schmitt. The state of exception is that
moment of radical decision where the operation of the law is
suspended. This is what the Romans call *iustitium*, and which I

discussed above in connection with Rousseau. What the decision on the state of exception reveals is the true subject of political sovereignty. Schmitt famously writes: "Sovereign is who decides on the state of exception" (*Soverän ist, wer über den Ausnahmezustand entscheidet*[5]). The sovereign is the person who is exhibited by the decision on the state of exception. The question "who?" is answered by the decision itself. That is, the decision on the state of exception, the moment of the suspension of the operation of law, brings the subject "who?" into being. To put it into a slogan, *the subject is the consequence of a decision*. The subject that is revealed by the decision on the state of exception is the personage of the state, and the core of Schmitt's theory of the political is to show that the true subject of the political is the state, and that the state must always stand higher than the law.

Schmitt observes that the concept of the state of exception is the jurisprudential analogue to the concept of the miracle in theology.[6] The triumph of liberalism as the triumph of deism is the hegemony of a religious view of the world that tries to banish the miracle, as that which would break with the legal-constitutional situation—the order of what Badiou calls the event, and which he sometimes compares with a miracle. Liberal constitutionalists, like Locke, Kant, and Neo-Kantians such as Hans Kelsen and John Rawls, seek to eliminate the state of exception and instead subject everything to the rule of law, which is the rule of the rule itself, namely reason. Schmitt criticizes the rationalism of liberalism in the name of what he calls—and here we find echoes of Wilhelm Dilthey in Schmitt that will resound further in the young Heidegger—a philosophy of concrete life. Such an existential approach embraces the exception, and breaks with the rule and the rule of the rule. Schmitt writes, thinking explicitly of Kierkegaard's *Repetition* from 1843: "In the exception the power of real life breaks through the crust of a mechanism that has become torpid through repetition."[7]

It is not difficult to see why Schmitt's existential politics of passion and concrete life and his critique of liberal democracy should have won him many friends on the left, such as Chantal Mouffe, Ernesto Laclau, and Giorgio Agamben. Sadly perhaps, they are not friends that Schmitt would have chosen. He was much happier in the company of Catholic counter-revolutionaries like Joseph de Maistre and Donoso Cortés, both of whom Schmitt discusses in *Political Theology*.[8] What has to be grasped is that Schmitt's argument for the state of exception as exemplifying the operation of the political is also an argument for dictatorship. If the subject of sovereignty is revealed in the decision on the state of exception, then this decision is the act in which the constitution is suspended and dictatorship is introduced. Dictatorship, then, is justified when there is an actual or imagined danger to the existence of the state. As we saw above in connection with Rousseau, Roman republicanism explicitly allowed for this possibility and led us to ponder above the conceivability of civic republicanism as a political form without the possibility of recourse to dictatorship. In Schmitt's terms, the condition of possibility for legality and legitimacy is the political act that suspends it.

Obama writes in *The Audacity of Hope*: "Democracy is not a house to be built, it is a conversation to be had."[9] At the core of Obama's liberal civil religion is a resolute defense of the primacy of the constitution, an absolute conviction that all political decisions have to be derived from norms, and that the procedure for decision-making is deliberation. It's enough to make Habermas burst into a breakdance. Schmitt, however, would be turning in his grave. For him, the idea of everlasting conversation is a gruesomely comic fantasy. If liberals were presented with the question "Christ or Barabbas?," they would move to adjourn the proceedings and establish a commission of investigation or a special committee of inquiry that would report back sometime the following year. Within liberalism, everything becomes everlasting discussion, the glorious conversation of humankind, the sphere of what Schmitt calls with a sneer, "culture."[10] Such a culture floats like foam over the socio-economic reality of the liberal state which Schmitt, following his teacher Max Weber, compares to a huge industrial plant dominated by capitalism and scientism and incapable of political action. For Catholic counter-revolutionaries, like Donoso Cortés, confronted with the hegemony of a depoliticized liberalism powerless in the face of a capitalist economy, the only solution was dictatorship. Faced with the toothless liberal constitutionalism of Weimar Germany in the 1920s and the reality of economic collapse, it is not difficult to understand the appeal of the argument for dictatorship had for Schmitt with the rise of the National Socialists. The only way to restore the true subject of the political —namely the state—was the suspension of the constitution, and the decision to declare a state of exception.

The political theology of liberalism is the pervasiveness of a weak deistic God. The liberal, like Obama, wants a God, but one who is not active in the world. He wants a God that permits no enthusiasm and who never contradicts or overrides the rule of reason and law. That way, it is assumed, leads to the prophetic radicalism of Obama's former pastor, Jeremiah Wright. In short, liberals want a God that cannot perform miracles, a God who does not intervene in the world. Against this, Schmitt wants to revive the political by imposing the state of exception and restoring the possibility of the miracle. As Schmitt makes crystal clear, this requires a belief in original sin.

For Schmitt, every conception of the political takes a position on human nature.[11] It requires some sort of anthropological commitment: human beings are either naturally good or evil. Schmitt thinks—and I agree—that it is in these terms that one can consider the two most pervasive political alternatives to liberalism: authoritarianism and anarchism. Anarchists believe in the essential goodness of the human being. Their progenitor is Rousseau and his claim that wickedness is the historical outcome of the development of society towards greater levels of inequality. By contrast, on this view, political legitimacy can be achieved by what Rousseau frequently referred to as "a change in nature," from wickedness to goodness, of the kind imagined in *The Social Contract*. Although, as we have seen, this is a caricature of Rousseau—and he could in no way be described as an anarchist—this view is more accurately developed by Bakunin: namely that if human beings are essentially good, then it is the mechanisms of the state, religion, law, and the police that make them bad. Once these mechanisms have been removed and replaced with autonomous self-governing communes in a federative structure, then we will truly have heaven on earth. We will come back to Bakuninesque federalism below, but it is worth noting that arguments for anarchism always turn on the idea that if human beings are allowed to express what comes naturally to them, if the force of life itself is not repressed by the deathly repressive activity of the state that operates through the force of law, then it will be possible to organize society on the basis of mutual aid and cooperation. The latter, of course, was Kropotkin's view.

By contrast, authoritarians believe that human nature is essentially wicked. This is why the concept of original sin is so important politically. For Donoso Cortés and Maistre, human beings were naturally depraved and essentially vile.[12] There is something essentially defective in human nature which requires a corrective at the political and theological level: the authority of the state and of the church. Thus, because the human being is defined by original sin, authoritarianism—in the form of dictatorship, say—becomes necessary as the only means that might save human beings from themselves. Human beings require the hard rule of authority because they are essentially defective. Against this, anarchism is the political expression of freedom from original sin. It is the idea that a sinless union with others in the form of community is the realization of the highest human possibility. It is this idea of a sinless union in freedom that is the core of mystical anarchism.

The idea of original sin is not some outdated relic from the religious past. It is the conceptual expression of a fundamental experience of ontological defectiveness or lack which explains the human propensity towards error, malice, wickedness, violence, and extreme cruelty. Furthermore this defect is not something we can put right—which is why authoritarians think that human beings require the yoke of the state, God, law, and the police. Politics becomes the means for protecting human beings from themselves, that is, from their worst inclinations towards lust, cruelty, and violence. As Hobbes shows, any return to a state of nature is an argument in favor of the war of all against all.

We can find numerous post-Christian attempts to rethink the concept of original sin. For example, Freud advances the Schopenhauerian thesis that there might simply be a disjunction between Eros and civilization, between the aggressive, destructive workings of libidinous desire and the achievements of culture.[13] This disjunction is only held in check through the internalized authority of the super-ego. Heidegger's ideas of thrownness, facticity, and falling were explicitly elaborated in connection with Luther's conception of original sin and the anthropology of the primal Christianity in Paul.[14] It is a phenomenologically refined conception of original sin that allows Heidegger to explain the endless human propensity towards evasion and flight from taking responsibility for oneself. Although such a responsibility can be momentarily achieved in authentic resoluteness, it can never arrest the slide back into inauthenticity. The concept of original sin is still very much with us.

JOHN GRAY: THE NATURALIZATION OF ORIGINAL SIN,
POLITICAL REALISM, AND PASSIVE NIHILISM

The most consequent contemporary defense of the idea of original sin can be found in the work of John Gray. What he gives us is a naturalized, Darwinian redescription of original sin. To put it brutally, human beings are killer apes. We are simply animals— and rather nasty aggressive primates at that, what Gray calls *Homo rapiens*, rapacious hominids. Sadly, we are also killer apes with metaphysical longing, which explains the ceaseless quest to find some meaning to life that might be underwritten by an experience of the

holy or the numinous. Today's dominant metaphysical dogma—
and this is Gray's real and rightful target—is liberal humanism,
with its faith in progress, improvement, and the perfectibility of
humankind: beliefs which are held with the same unquestioning
assurance with which Christianity was held in Europe until the
late eighteenth century. As Gray makes clear, progress in the realm
of science is a fact. Furthermore, it is a good: Thomas De Quincey
famously remarked that a quarter of human misery resulted from
toothache,[15] so the discovery of anesthetic dentistry is an unmixed
good. However, although progress is a fact, faith in progress is a
superstition, and the liberal humanist's assurance in the reality of
human progress is the barely secularized version of the Christian
belief in Providence. Obama is a providential political theologian
for whom, as he said in his Inaugural Address, it is possible to be
"on the wrong side of history."

The most extreme expression of human arrogance, for Gray,
is the idea that human beings can save the planet from environmental destruction. Because they are killer apes, that is, by virtue
of a naturalized version of original sin that tends them towards
wickedness and violence, human beings cannot redeem their
environment. Furthermore, the earth doesn't need saving. This
is where Gray borrows from James Lovelock's Gaia hypothesis.
The earth is suffering from a *disseminated primatemaia*, a plague of
people. *Homo rapiens* is ravaging the planet like a filthy pest that
has infested a dilapidated but once beautiful mansion. In 1600
the human population was about half a billion. In the 1990s it
increased by the same amount. This plague cannot be solved by
the very species who are the efficient cause of the problem, but
only by a large-scale decline in human numbers—say half a billion
or so—back down to manageable levels. This is the exhilaratingly
dystopian vision at the heart of Gray's work: when the earth is
done with humans, it will recover and human civilization will
be forgotten. Life will go on, but without us. Global warming is
simply one of many fevers that the earth has suffered during its
history. It will recover, but we won't because we can't.

Gray writes, with Schmitt explicitly in mind, "Modern politics is a chapter in the history of religion."[16] Politics has become a hideous surrogate for religious salvation. Secularism, which denies the truth of religion, is a religious myth. Specifically, it is a myth of progress based in the idea that history has a providential design that is unfolding. Now, such myths are important. They enable presidents like Barack Obama to get elected. But it doesn't mean that they are true or even salutary. What most disturbs Gray are utopian political projects based on some apocalyptic faith that concerted human action in the world can allow for the realization of seemingly impossible ends and bring about the perfection of humanity. Action cannot change the world because we are the sort of beings that we are: killer apes who will use violence, force, and terror at the service of some longed-for metaphysical project. For Gray, the core belief that drives utopianism, on the right as much as the left, is the false assumption that the world can be transformed by human action and that history itself is progress towards such a transformation. As Gray makes explicit, his critique of utopianism derives in large part from Norman Cohn's hugely influential book, originally published in 1957, *The Pursuit of the Millennium*.

It is Cohn's analysis of millenarianism that is so important for Gray. This is the idea that salvation is not just a possibility, but a certainty which will correspond to five criteria: salvation is collective, terrestrial, imminent, total, and miraculous.[17] In his later work, *Cosmos, Chaos and the World to Come*, Cohn traced the roots of this millenarian faith back to Zoroaster's break with the view that the world was the reflection of a static cosmic order defined by a cycle of conflict. On the Zoroastrian view, sometime between 1500 and 1200 BC, the world was moving, through incessant conflict, towards a conflictless state.[18] A time would come when, during a final bloody battle, God and the forces of good would defeat once and for all the armies of evil. Thus, a marvelous consummation is at hand: the moment when good will triumph over evil and the agents of evil will be annihilated. After that time, Cohn writes,

"The elect will ... live as a collectivity, unanimous and without conflict, on a transformed and purified earth."[19]

This idea finds expression in certain Messianic Jewish sects before finding its most powerful articulation in Christian ideas of the Apocalypse, the Last Days, and the Millennium. On the basis of the authority of the Book of Revelation, it was believed that after Christ's Second Coming he would establish a kingdom of God on earth and reign over it with his elect, the company of saints, for a thousand years until the Last Judgment and the general resurrection of the dead. As we will see in the next chapter, early followers of Christ, like Saint Paul, believed that the Second Coming or *parousia* was imminent, and that they were living in the end times. The search for signs of the Second Coming obviously took on enormous importance. The key clue to the beginning of the end times—and this is crucial—is the appearance of the Anti-Christ: the prodigious, evil, arch-enemy of God.

The Anti-Christ is what Ernesto Laclau would call a "floating signifier" in millenarian political theology.[20] Endlessly substitutable, the Anti-Christ can be personified as the great Satan, the Pope, the Muslims, or the Jews. What is crucial here is the identification of the Anti-Christ as the incarnation of evil that presages the reappearance of Christ or a similarly Messianic figure, and leads to a bloody and violent terrestrial combat to build heaven on earth. This, of course, is the deep logic of the Crusades, which began in 1095 with Pope Urban II's plea to the Church council to go to Jerusalem and, in his words, "liberate the Church of God."[21] This led directly to the "People's Crusade" or "Peasants' Crusade" of 1096–7, and to the formation of a Christian fighting force in Asia Minor that grew to between 50,000 and 70,000 strong. It is a compelling and disturbing historical fact that the recruitment of soldiers for the "People's Crusade" in France, Germany, and the Low Countries established a new and seemingly addictive habit in Western life: pogroms against the Jews. It would appear that the idea of the people requires the external identification of an evil enemy who can be legitimately annihilated in the name of God.

Such, arguably, has always been the justificatory logic of Western military intervention: it is right to exterminate the enemy because it is the incarnation of evil. Such views have always vindicated crusaders from the eleventh century through to their more recent epigones. From the time of Saladin's destruction of the Third Crusade in the last years of the twelfth century, the response has always been the same: *jihad* or war against infidels. It is perhaps not so surprising that Saddam Hussein sought to depict himself in propaganda alongside Saladin. After all, they were both born in Tikrit—despite the awful irony that Saladin was a Kurd.[22]

What is discreetly implied by Cohn and loudly trumpeted by Gray is that Western civilization might be defined in terms of the central role of millenarian thinking. What takes root with early Christian belief and massively accelerates in medieval Europe finds its modern expression in a sequence of bloody utopian political projects, from Jacobinism to Bolshevism, Stalinism, Nazism, and different varieties of Marxist-Leninist, anarchist, or Situationist ideology. Much of John Gray's *Black Mass* attempts to show how the energy of such utopian political projects has drifted from the left to the right. The apocalyptic conflict with the axis of evil by the forces of good was employed by Bush, Blair, et al. as a means to forge the democratic millennium, a new American century of untrammeled personal freedom and free markets. During the first years of the new millennium, a religious fervor energizes the project of what we might call "military neo-liberalism," in which violence is the means for realizing liberal democratic heaven on earth. What is essential to such neo-liberal millenarian thinking is the consolidation of the idea of good through the identification of evil, where the Anti-Christ keeps assuming different masks: Saddam Hussein, Osama bin Laden, Kim Jong-il, Mahmoud Ahmadinejad, and so on.

We saw how Schmitt's critique of liberalism led him towards an argument for dictatorship underpinned by a belief in original sin. Where does Gray's naturalization of the concept of original sin leave us? He powerfully identifies the poison within liberal humanism, and the antidote is what he calls "political realism."[23] We have to accept that the world is in a state of ceaseless conflict. In the face of such conflict, Gray counsels that we have to abandon the belief in utopia and try to cope with reality. This means accepting the tragic contingencies of life and that there are moral and political dilemmas for which there are no solutions. We have to learn to abandon daydreams such as a new cosmopolitan world order governed by universal human rights, or that history has a teleological, providential purpose that underwrites human action. We even have to renounce the Obama-esque delusion that one's life is a narrative that is an episode in some universal story of progress. Against the grotesque distortion of conservatism into the millenarian military neo-liberalism of the neo-conservatives, Gray wants to defend the core belief of traditional Burkean Toryism. The latter begins in a realistic acceptance of human imperfection and frailty, a version of original sin. As such, the best that flawed and potentially wicked human creatures can hope for is a commitment to civilized constraints that will prevent the very worst from happening. Political realism is the politics of the least worst.

The most original feature of Gray's work is the way in which a traditional conservatism underpinned by a deep pessimism about human nature is fused with a certain strand of Taoism. To borrow Rousseau's refrain once again, "This invention is a masterpiece of politics." As Gray points out, "Nothing is more human than the readiness to kill and die in order to secure a meaning for life."[24] Gray believes that the great human delusion is that action—through the means of the will—can achieve a terrestrial salvation. Such political voluntarism has led to nothing but bloodshed, the great slaughter bench of millenarian history. Killer apes like us have to learn to give up the search for meaning and learn to see instead that the purpose of aesthetic or spiritual life is the release from meaning. If seeing one's life as an episode in some universal, emancipatory narrative of meaning is a delusion, then the cure consists in freeing oneself from such narratives. Maybe we just have to accept illusions.

What interests Gray in the subtle paradoxes of the greatest Taoist thinker, Chuang-Tzu, is the acceptance of the fact that life is a dream without the possibility or even the desire to awaken from the dream. If we cannot be free of illusions, if illusions are part and parcel of our natural constitution, then why not simply accept them? In the final pages of *Black Mass* Gray writes: "Taoists taught that freedom lies in freeing oneself from personal narratives by identifying with cosmic processes of death and renewal." Thus, rather than seek the company of utopian thinkers, we should find consolation in the words of "mystics, poets and pleasure-lovers."[25] It is clear that for Gray, like the later Heidegger, the real source of human problems resides in the belief that action can transform the world. As Heidegger writes in a very important collection of post-war notes, published as "Overcoming Metaphysics": "No mere action will change the world"[26]—a statement that finds its rejoinder in the title of Heidegger's posthumously published 1966 interview with *Der Spiegel*, "Only a God can Save Us,"[27] which is to say that we cannot save ourselves. Action simply provides a consolation for the radical insignificance of our lives by momentarily staving off the threat of meaninglessness. At the core of Gray's work is a defense of the ideal of contemplation over action, the *bios theoretikos* of Aristotle or the *ataraxia* of the Epicureans, the state of calm and tranquility of soul where we simply learn to see the mystery as such and do not seek to unveil it in order to find some deeper purpose within.

Schopenhauer, usually read in abridged, aphoristic form, was the most popular philosopher of the nineteenth century. Nothing sells better than epigrammatic pessimism. It gives readers reasons for their misery and words to buttress their sense of hopelessness and impotence. Few things give more refined intellectual pleasure than backing oneself into an impregnably defended conceptual cul-de-sac. Such is what Nietzsche called "European Buddhism."[28] John Gray is the Schopenhauerian European Buddhist of our age. What he offers is a gloriously pessimistic cultural analysis, which rightly reduces to rubble the false idols of the cave of liberal humanism.

Counter to the upbeat progressivist evangelical atheism of Richard Dawkins or Christopher Hitchens—whom Terry Eagleton fused into one composite called "Ditchkins"—Gray provides a powerful argument in favor of human wickedness that is consistent with Darwinian naturalism.[29] It leads to the position that I call "passive nihilism": an extremely tempting worldview, even if I think the temptation must be refused.

The passive nihilist looks at the world with a certain highly cultivated detachment and finds it meaningless. Rather than trying to act in the world, which is pointless, the passive nihilist withdraws to a safe contemplative distance and cultivates his aesthetic sensibility by pursuing the pleasures of lyric poetry, yogic flying, bird-watching, gardening, or, as was the case with the aged Rousseau, botany ("Botany is the ideal study for the idle, unoccupied solitary"[30]). In a world that is rushing to destroy itself through capitalist exploitation or military crusades—which are usually two arms of the same killer ape—the passive nihilist withdraws to an island where the mystery of existence can be seen for what it is without distilling it into a meaning. In the face of the coming decades, which in all likelihood will be defined by the violence of faith and the certainty of environmental devastation, Gray offers a cool but safe temporary refuge. Happily, we will not be alive to witness much of the future that he describes.

I have looked at two interrelated responses to the thought that the modern concepts of politics are secularized theological concepts. Schmitt's critique of constitutional liberalism as anti-political leads him to a concept of the political that finds its expression in state sovereignty, authoritarianism, and dictatorship. Gray's critique of liberal humanism and the ideas of progress and Providence that it embodies leads him to a political realism of a traditional Tory variety. He fuses this critique with a pessimistic anti-humanism spiced with elements of the Gaia hypothesis and Taoism into a compelling position that I have called passive nihilism. Both conceptions of the political are underpinned by ideas of original sin, whether the traditional Catholic teaching or Gray's Darwinian naturalization of the concept. The refutation of any and all forms of utopianism—and here our question begins to take shape—follows from this concept of original sin. It is because we are killer apes that our metaphysical longing for a conflict-free perfection of humanity can only be pursued with the millennial means of violence and terror.

MILLENARIANISM

Is the utopian impulse in political thinking simply the residue of a dangerous political theology that we are much better off without? Are the only live options in political thinking Schmitt's authoritarianism, Gray's political realism, or business-as-usual liberalism; that is, a politics of state sovereignty; an incremental, traditionalist conservatism; or varieties of more or less enthused Obamaism? In order to approach these questions I would like to present the form of politics that Schmitt and Gray explicitly reject: anarchism. I have sought to outline and defend a version of anarchism in some of my work.[31] This is what I call an ethical neo-anarchism, in which anarchist practices of political organization are coupled with an infinitely demanding subjective ethics of responsibility. I will try to extend and clarify this position below, notably in my debate with Žižek in Chapter 5. However, here I want to present a very different version of anarchism, perhaps the most radical that can be conceived: mystical anarchism. The key issue here is what happens to our thinking of politics and community once the fact of original sin has been overcome. To be clear, although I think that mystical anarchism is a compelling political possibility, my approach to it will express significant reservations.

Let's return to Cohn's *The Pursuit of the Millennium*. What Cohn tries to show is the way in which millenarian Christian belief took root amongst significant sectors of the rootless and dislocated poor of Europe between the eleventh and sixteenth centuries. Belief in the Last Days led to a revolutionary eschatology, in which a series of messiah figures, prophets, or indeed "Christs" would spontaneously appear. Cohn gives a catalog of these messiahs, from Tancheln, the Emperor Frederick, the Pseudo-Baldwin, through to John Ball, Hans Böhm, Thomas Müntzer, and the terrifying and bloodthirsty Jan Bockelsen, better known as John of Leyden. What unites these figures is not just their heretical fury and utter self-belief. It is also their capacity to construct what Cohn calls, non-pejoratively but psychoanalytically, a *phantasy* or social myth around which a collective can be formed. The political structure of this phantasy becomes complete with the identification of an enemy. It is always in relation to an enemy that the eschatological phantasy finds its traction. This enemy is always the Anti-Christ, whose identity floats in different historical manifestations of millenarianism. It can be the Muslims or indeed Jews for the Crusaders, but it is more often the forces of the Catholic Church and the state. A holy war is then fought with the Anti-Christ, and violence becomes the purifying or cleansing force through which the evil ones are to be annihilated. Terror is a common feature of life in the New Jerusalem.

Revolutionary millenarianism desires a boundless social transformation that attempts to recover an egalitarian state of nature, a kind of golden age of primitive communism. This requires the abolition of private property and the establishment of a commonality of ownership. As a famous proverb from the time of the English Peasants' Revolt in 1381 puts it, possibly recited by the hedge priest John Ball, "When Adam delved and Eve span, / Who was then the gentleman?[32]

The task of politics was the construction of the New Jerusalem and the model was always paradise, the Garden of Eden before the occurrence of original sin. There was a perfectly obvious reason why such forms of revolutionary millenarian belief should arise amongst the poor: they owned nothing and therefore had nothing to lose. By destroying private property, on the contrary, they had everything to gain. One extant fragment from John Ball, preserved and probably embellished by the French chronicler Jean Froissart, makes the point powerfully:

> Things cannot go well in England, nor ever will, until all goods are held in common, and until there will be neither serfs nor gentlemen, and we shall be equal. For what reason have they, whom we call lords, got the best of us? How did they deserve it? Why do they keep us in bondage? If we all descended from one father and one mother, Adam and Eve, how can they assert or prove that they are more masters than ourselves? Except perhaps that they make us work and produce for them to spend![33]

Things did not go well in England, sadly.

The poor, as the saying goes, have always been with us. What seems to be novel in the earlier part of the large historical panorama depicted by Cohn is the emergence of the urban poor in the rapidly industrializing textile-producing cities of Flanders and Brabant from the eleventh century onwards. Thus, it is not simply that millenarian belief arises amongst the poor, but specifically amongst those groups whose traditional ways of life have broken down. Millenarian belief arises amongst the socially dislocated, recently urbanized poor who had moved from the country to the city for economic reasons. Although Cohn says nothing much on this topic, it is interesting to note that the socio-economic condition of possibility for revolutionary eschatology is dislocation, the category that best describes the formation of the industrial proletariat during the industrial revolution in the opening pages of Marx and Engels's *The Communist Manifesto*.[34]

Perhaps a similar hypothesis could be used to explain the formation of millenarian sects in the United States from the time of settlement onwards. I am thinking in particular of the explosion of millenarian faith in areas like the "burned-over district" of upstate New York during the late eighteenth century and the first decades of the nineteenth.[35] It is hardly difficult to find the living inheritances of such millenarian religious belief all across the contemporary United States. There seems to be a powerful correlation between evangelism, social dislocation, and poverty. Yet, what is sorely missing from contemporary American millenarianism is the radical anarcho-communism of groups like the Shakers, for whom all property was held in common, without mine and thine. An ethos of manual labor was combined with spiritual purification achieved through taking the vow of chastity. With hands at work and hearts set to God, the Shakers attempted to recover the communistic equality of Eden without the sins of the flesh. The founder of the Shakers, Ann Lee or Mother Ann (1736–84), emigrated from Manchester to New York in 1774 with a select band of persecuted Shakers—more properly, the Church of Believers in Christ—and set up communities in upstate New York and western Massachusetts. Various divine visitations led Mother Ann to declare her celibacy and the imminent second coming of Christ. She was seen by some as the female equivalent of God, the female complement to the divine male principle. For the Shakers, to be a believer in Christ was to participate in the dual nature of divinity, both male and female.[36]

Medieval revolutionary millenarianism drew its strength and found its energy amongst the marginal and the dispossessed. It often arose against a background of disaster, plague, and famine. As Cohn notes: "The greatest wave of millenarian excitement, one that swept through the whole of society, was precipitated by the most universal natural disaster of the Middle Ages, the Black Death."[37]

It was amongst the lowest social strata that millenarian enthusiasm lasted longest and expressed itself most violently. The flagellant movement first appeared in the Italian city of Perugia in 1260, as an apparent consequence of the famine of 1250 and the plague of 1259. By the fourteenth century, the movement had swept from Italy into the Rhine Valley, where great crowds of itinerant flagellants went from town to town like a scourging insurgency becoming God-like through acts of collective *imitatio Christi*. Such extreme self-punishment was deemed heretical because it threatened the Church's authority over the economy of punishment, penitence, and consolation: the poor were not meant to take the whip into their own hands. But the centerpiece of Cohn's book is its description and analysis of the dominant form of revolutionary millenarianism: the so-called heresy of the Free Spirit. It is to this that I would now like to turn.

THE MOVEMENT OF THE FREE SPIRIT

We know very little about the Movement of the Free Spirit, and some medieval historians, like Robert Lerner, have expressed significant doubts about the scope of Cohn's conclusions in *The Pursuit of the Millennium*, viewing them as something of a shaggy dog story.[38] Everything appears to turn on the interpretation of Paul's words from Second Corinthians, "Now the Lord is the Spirit, and where the Lord's Spirit is, there is freedom" (2 Cor. 3:17). There are two hermeneutic possibilities here: either the Lord's Spirit is outside the self or within it.

If the Lord's Spirit is outside the self, because the soul languishes in sin and perdition, then freedom can only come through submitting oneself to divine will and awaiting the saving activity of grace. Such is the standard Christian teaching, which explains the necessity for the authority of the Church as that terrestrial location or, better, portal to the Lord's Spirit.

But if—and here is the key to the heresy—the Lord's Spirit is within the self, then the soul is free and has no need of the Church's mediation with God. Indeed, if the Lord's Spirit is within the self, then essentially there is no difference between the soul and God. The heretical Adamites, who moved to Bohemia after being expelled from Picardy in the early fifteenth century, are reported as beginning the Lord's Prayer with the words, "Our Father, who art within us."[39] If a community participates in the Spirit of God, then it is free and has no need of the agencies of the Catholic Church, the state, law, or police. These are the institutions of the unfree world that a community based on the Free Spirit rejects. It is not difficult to grasp the anarchistic consequences of such a belief.

The apparently abundant and widespread doctrinal literature of the Movement of the Free Spirit was repeatedly seized and destroyed by the Inquisition. Very few texts remain, but one, apocryphally attributed to Meister Eckhart and bearing the inscription "That is Sister Katrei, Meister Eckhart's Daughter from Strasbourg," tells the story of the relationship between Sister Catherine and Eckhart, her confessor.[40] Although this is a huge topic that I do not want to broach here, the relation between Eckhart's thinking, deemed heretical posthumously by the pope at Avignon in 1327, and the Movement of the Free Spirit is hugely suggestive. I will focus on another of the handful of extant documents related to the Free Spirit, Marguerite Porete's *The Mirror of Simple and Annihilated Souls and Who Remain Only in Wanting and Desire of Love*—to give the text its full and grammatically ambiguous title. It is unclear whether the genitive article in the title is objective or possessive. As Amy Hollywood observes: "Does the text promise to be a reflection or representation of the two kinds of souls named in the title (objective genitive), or is it a mirror or representation of some other entity that has been given to these souls (possessive genitive)?"[41]

The attribution of *The Mirror* to Porete, a native of Hainault in northern France, was only established in 1946 by an Italian scholar, Romana Guarnieri, and the text was published as a journal article nearly twenty years later.[42] Like many texts in the Middle Ages, *The Mirror* seems to have circulated in multiple manuscripts and translations, and Porete appears to have had many followers from as far away as England and Italy. Eckhart seemingly knew Porete's *The Mirror* which he responded to implicitly in his texts and sermons. When Eckhart returned to Paris in 1311, a year after Porete's execution, he stayed at the same Dominican house as William Humbert, Porete's inquisitor.[43] One can only wonder at the content of their conversations. Indeed, it has been claimed by Edmund Colledge and J.C. Marler that Eckhart's presentation of the true "poverty of spirit" in one of his most radical sermons, *Beati pauperes spiritu*, has been identified nowhere else but in Porete's *Mirror*.[44] Thus, rather than the learned master theologian instructing the young woman, as in the pseudo-Eckhartian literature, the relation of influence is exactly the reverse: Porete is one of the sources for Eckhart's alleged heresy of identification of the soul with God. As Eckhart writes, "In the same way we are transformed into God so that we may know him as he is."[45]

We know relatively little with certainty about Porete, although there is a surprising amount of documentation related to her trial and execution for heresy.[46] She was a learned Beguine, a term used to describe semi-religious women who lived alone or in *Beguinages*, Beguine houses. These houses, which began to appear in the southern Low Countries in the late twelfth and early thirteenth centuries, were effectively communes or experimental associations for the sisters of the Free Spirit and their brothers, the Beghards, from which we derive the English word "beggar." Marguerite seems to have led an itinerant life of poverty accompanied by a guardian Beghard and referred to herself as a *"mendicant creature."* Her book on *fin amor*, refined love, was condemned, seized, and publicly burned in her presence at her home town, Valenciennes, by the Bishop of Cambrai. But Porete refused to retract her views. When she came to the attention of the Inquisition in Paris, she was imprisoned for eighteen months, but did not seek absolution or offer recantation. She was burnt at the stake on the last day of May, 1310, at the Place de Grève.

The fact that she was not immediately executed, but tried over a long period of time and persistently asked to recant her views, has led some to suggest that Porete was from the upper strata of society in Valenciennes—then an affluent city—and that she had some powerful friends. Although it is not my topic here, it is truly fascinating how many women were associated with the Movement of the Free Spirit, and their relatively high social status. Scholars of mysticism like Amy Hollywood and poets like Anne Carson have rightly identified Porete and the Beguine movement as vital precursors to modern feminism.[47] It is revealing that, in the proceedings of her trial, Porete's work is not just referred to as being "filled with errors and heresies," but as the work of a *"pseudo-mulier,"* a fake or fraudulent woman.[48]

The Mirror is an extraordinary text. On the one hand, it is a dialogue between the Soul and the divine in the guise of Love on the model of Boethius's *Consolation of Philosophy*. On the other hand, it is a romance in the medieval tradition of courtly love and *fin amor*. The dullard Reason acts as a comic foil for the principal characters of the Soul and Love, and various personified virtues also appear, such as Discretion, Divine Justice, Pure Graciousness, and The Exalted Damsel of Peace. God the Father also makes a brief cameo appearance. Porete consistently stresses the opposition between Holy Church the Less, governed by Reason, and Holy Church the Greater, which follows Porete's practice of self-annihilation in relation to what Porete oxymoronically calls "the Far-Near."[49] This idea of God seems to draw on Hadewijch of Antwerp's "Far-Off, Close at Hand," *Verre-Bi* in her medieval Dutch. Porete repeatedly describes this Far-Near as "lightning," or "an opening swift as a lightning flash" that takes place when the soul is brought to nothing.[50] This opening of divine rapture is followed by "rapid closing," which leads to the experience of distress and dereliction of distance from God that is common to much medieval mystical practice.

BECOMING GOD

The Mirror is didactic: an instruction manual of sorts, which was meant to be read aloud (Porete refers on several occasions to her "hearers"), and which details the seven stages that the soul must pass through in order to overcome original sin and recover the perfection that belonged to human beings prior to their corruption by the Fall. I'd like to identify the metaphysical kernel of the Movement of the Free Spirit by recounting the seven stages of what Porete calls "the devout soul" outlined in Chapter 118 of *The Mirror* (the book contains 139 Chapters). What is described is nothing other than the process of self-deification or auto-theism: becoming God.[51]

(i)   The first state occurs when the Soul is touched by God's grace and assumes the intention of following all God's commandments, of being obedient to divine law.

(ii) The second state mounts yet higher and the Soul becomes a lover of God over and above commandments and laws. Regardless of any command, the Soul wants to do all it can to please its beloved. In this second state, and one thinks of Saint Paul's argument in the Epistles to the Romans and to the Galatians here, the external becomes internal and law is overcome by love.

(iii) In the third state, consumed by love for divine perfection, the Soul attaches itself to making "works of goodness." These can be images, representations, projects, and objects that give us delight in glorifying God. But Porete insists, and this is another Pauline theme that Eckhart will take up in his German sermons, the Soul "renounces those works in which she has this delight, and puts to death the will which had its life from this."[52] The Soul no longer wills, but undergoes a detachment from the will by obeying the will of another, namely God. The Soul must become a "martyr"; that is, a witness and victim to God by abstaining from works and destroying the will. Porete's language here is extremely violent: "One must crush oneself, hacking and hewing away at oneself to widen the place in which Love will want to be."[53] Such metaphysical masochism is the beginning of the painful process of the annihilation of the Soul, where suffering is necessary in order to bore open a space that is wide enough for love to enter. Anne Carson rightly compares this process of annihilation with Simone Weil's idea of *decreation*, "To undo the creature in us."[54]

(iv) In the fourth state, when I have renounced my will and hewn
      away at myself, when I have begun to decreate and annihi-
      late myself, I am filled with God's love and exalted "into
      delight."[55] Porete's wording here is extraordinary: the Soul
      "does not believe that God has any greater gift to bestow on
      any soul here below than this love which Love for love has
      poured forth within her."[56] In the fourth state, the Soul is in
      love with love as such and becomes intoxicated, "Gracious
      Love makes her wholly *drunken*."[57]

Excursus: In his wonderfully capacious and open-minded investigation of mysticism in *The Varieties of Religious Experience*, William
James discusses the relation between mystical states and drunken-
ness.[58] This relation is summarized in what he calls the idea of
"anaesthetic revelation," which he links to his own experiences
with nitrous oxide or laughing gas, the drug of choice amongst
scientists, poets, and intellectuals throughout the nineteenth
century. Nitrous oxide, James recounts from personal experience,
induces a feeling of reconciliation or oneness at a level deeper
than that of ordinary waking consciousness with its separation
of subjects and objects. Indeed, James goes further and compares
this mystical experience of reconciliation, or cosmic consciousness, with what he sees as Hegel's pantheism. This is, for James,
the "monistic insight, in which the OTHER in its various forms
appears absorbed into the One."[59] On this reading of Hegel (and,
of course, other readings are possible and probably more plausible),
the key to dialectical thinking is the unity of the Same and the
Other, where what Hegel calls the Concept would be that movement of thinking which grasps both itself and its opposite. James
adds that "this is a dark saying," but he insists that "the living sense
of the reality" of Hegel's philosophy "only comes in the artificial
mystic state of mind."[60] In other words, Hegel can only be understood when one is drunk on laughing gas.
    Drunkenness is always followed by a hangover. Such is the
condition of what Porete calls "dismay," namely the distress and

distance from God mentioned above. The error of the fourth state—and by implication James's analysis of mysticism—is to believe that the progress of the Soul is complete with its beatific union with God. Such a conception of *unio mystica* is common to many mystics and was tolerated and even encouraged by the Church, when and where it could be controlled (again, as we will see below, this goes back to Paul). Porete, however, is engaged in a much more radical enterprise, namely the Soul's annihilation. This brings us to the fifth state.

(v)   The dismay and dereliction of the fifth state arises from the following sober consideration: on the one hand, the Soul considers God as the source of things that are, that is, of all goodness. But, on the other hand, the Soul then turns to consider itself, from which all things are not. The free will that God put into the Soul has been corrupted by the Fall. Insofar as the Soul wills anything, that thing is evil, for it is nothing but the expression of original sin and the separation from the divine source of goodness. As Porete puts it, "The Soul's Will sees … that it cannot progress by itself if it does not separate itself from her own willing, for her nature is evil by that inclination towards nothingness to which nature tends."[61] How, then, can I will not to will? I cannot, for every act of will—even the will not to will—is the expression of separation from divine goodness and therefore evil. As we saw in the third state, the Soul has tried to cut away at itself, to bore a hole in itself that will allow love to enter. But the momentary exaltation of the fourth state, drunk with divinity, was illusory and transitory. The fifth state, Porete writes, "has subdued her [i.e. the Soul] in showing to the Soul her own self."[62] It is here that we face what Porete repeatedly calls an "abyss," "deep beyond all depths," "without compass or end."[63] This abyss is the gap between the willful and errant nature of the Soul and divine goodness. It cannot be bridged by any action. In the fifth state, two natures are at war within

me: the divine goodness that I love and the evil that I am
by virtue of original sin. As Paul puts it: "The Good that
I would I do not, but the Evil that I would not that I do"
(Rom. 7:19). Faced with this abyss, in the fifth state I become
a paradox. The Soul wants to annihilate itself and unify with
God. But how? How are we to byss the abyss? How can an
abyss become a byss?[64]

(vi)   This is the work of the sixth state, which is the highest that
can be attained during earthly life. In the sobriety of the
fifth state, the Soul knows two things: divine goodness and
the errant activity of the will. In making "her look at herself
again," in such painful self-scrutiny, Porete adds, "These two
things that she sees take away from her will and longing and
works of goodness, and so she is wholly at rest, and put in
possession of her own state of free being, the high excellence
of which gives her repose from every thing."[65] Having gone
through the ordeal of the fifth state, the Soul finds repose
and rest, what Eckhart will call an experience of releasement
(*gelâzenheit*).[66]

The reasoning here is delicate: the abyss that separates the
Soul from God cannot be byssed or bridged through an act
of will. On the contrary, it is only through the extinction of
the will and the annihilation of the Soul that the sixth state
can be attained. The Soul itself becomes an abyss, that is, it
becomes emptied and excoriated, entering a condition of
absolute poverty. It is only in such poverty that the wealth
of God can be poured into the Soul. In the fifth state, the
Soul looked at herself and experienced dereliction. But in
the sixth state, "the Soul does not see herself at all."[67] Not
only that, but the Soul also does not see God. Rather, and
these words are extraordinary, "God of his divine majesty
sees himself in her, and by him this Soul is so illumined that
she cannot see that anyone exists, except only God himself,
from whom all things are."[68]

When the Soul has become annihilated and "free of all

things," then it can be illumined by the presence of God. It is only by reducing myself to nothing that I can join with that divine something. As Porete insists, in this sixth state the Soul is not yet glorified, a direct participant in the glory of God. This only happens after our death, in the seventh state. But what happens in the sixth state is perhaps even more extraordinary than glory:

> This Soul, thus pure and illumined, sees neither God nor herself, but God sees himself of himself in her, for her, without her, who—that is, God—shows to her that there is nothing except him. And therefore this Soul knows nothing except him, and loves nothing except him, and praises nothing except him, for there is nothing but he.[69]

Which means the following: the annihilated Soul becomes the place for God's infinite self-reflection. The logic here is impeccable: if the Soul has become nothing, then it can obviously see neither itself nor God. On the contrary, God enters into the place that I created by hewing and hacking away at myself. But that place is no longer my self. What the Soul has created is the space of its own nihilation. This *nihil* is the "place"—or better what Augustine would call the "no place"—where God reflects on himself, where "God sees himself of himself in her." God's love fills the annihilated Soul, in a movement of reflection that is at once both "for her" and "without her." The only way in which the Soul can become for God is by becoming without itself. In its nihilation, the no-place of the Soul becomes the place of God's reflection on himself, in-himself and for-himself.

As Anne Carson asks in her inquiry into how it is that women like Sappho, Simone Weil, and Marguerite Porete speak to God, "What is it that love dares the self to do?" She answers that, "Love dares the self to leave itself behind, to enter into poverty."[70] Love is, thus, the audacity of impoverishment, of complete submission, an economy of masochism. It is an act of absolute spiritual daring that induces a passivity whereby the self becomes annihilated. It is a subjective act in which the subject extinguishes itself. Become a husk or empty vessel through this act of daring, the fullness of love enters in. It is through the act of annihilation that the Soul knows nothing but God, "and loves nothing except him." Once the Soul is not, God is the only being that is.

(vii) As I already indicated, the seventh state is only attained after our death. It is the condition of "everlasting glory" of which we shall have no knowledge until our souls have left our bodies.

COMMUNISTIC CONSEQUENCES

Why was *The Mirror* condemned as heresy? For the simple reason that once the Soul is annihilated, there is nothing to prevent its identity with God. By following the itinerary of the seven states described in *The Mirror*, the Soul is annihilated and I become nothing. In becoming nothing, God enters the place where my Soul was. At that point, *I*—whatever sense the first-person pronoun might still have here—become *God*. When I become nothing, I become God. Such is the logic of auto-theism.

Varieties of this claim can be found in the mystical tradition. But—and we will ponder the possible meanings of these words in the next chapter—everything goes back to Paul's words in Galatians: "I live, yet not I, but Christ liveth in me" (Gal. 2:20). When I annihilate myself, when I crucify myself in an *imitatio Christi*, then Christ lives within me. In other words, the I that lives is not I but God. As Henry Suso, a student of Eckhart, observes: "The spirit dies, and yet it is alive in the marvels of the Godhead."[71] Or indeed, we could make a connection to the differenceless point of the Godhead at the heart of Eckhart's mystical theology, which seeks to attain an intensity of releasement in which God is no longer God and the creature is no longer the creature. This is what he calls "the breakthrough" (*durchbruch*), "Where I stand devoid of my own will and of the will of God and of all his works and of God himself, there I am above all created kind and am neither God nor creature."[72]

Yet Porete is more radical still. The heart of the heresy of the Free Spirit is not some Plotinian idea of the contemplative union of the intellect with the One as the source of an emanation: God, the bliss of contact with the divine. Rather, as Cohn writes, the heresy "was a passionate desire of certain human beings to surpass the condition of humanity and to become God."[73] What Porete is describing is a painful and passionate process of decreation: boring a hole in oneself so that love might enter. It is closer to Teresa of Avila's piercing of the heart that takes place when she is on fire with the love of God, "The pain was so great, it made me moan."[74] This desire for annihilation unleashes the most extreme violence against the self. For example, the thirteenth-century mystic Angela of Foligno writes: "There are times when such great anger ensues that I am scarcely able to stop from totally tearing myself apart. There are also times when I can't hold myself back from striking myself in a horrible way, and sometimes my head and limbs are swollen."[75]

As Caroline Walker Bynum has convincingly shown, the bodily access to the sacred is much more characteristic of women than men. "Despite the fame of Francis of Assisi's stigmata," Bynum writes, "he and the modern figure Padre Pio are the only males in history who have claimed all five visible wounds."[76] There are a huge number of such claims for medieval women, from stigmata, trances, levitations, and bodily seizures to "Miraculous elongation or enlargement of parts of the body, swellings of sweet mucus in the throat (sometimes known as the 'globus hystericus') and ecstatic nosebleeds."[77]

If the male mystic aspires to a contemplative peaceful union with the divine, then the female mystic wants something else, a kind of marriage with Christ, which is not simply corporeal, but is not at all disembodied. The greatest English mystic, Julian of Norwich, says of Christ, "I longed to be shown him in the flesh."[78] As Elizabeth Spearing convincingly argues, the mutilation of Christ's body in the Passion seems to inspire an echo among female mystics at the level of the body.[79]

Although this economy of masochism finds a high and subtle level of spiritual expression in the "shewings" or visions of Julian of Norwich, it becomes much wilder in the extraordinary antics of Margery Kempe, Mary of Oignies, Elizabeth of Spaalbeek and—most astonishing of all—Christina the Astonishing. Margery Kempe is described as persistently weeping, Mary of Oignies starved herself to death, until "her spine was stuck to her stomach and the bones of her back showed through the scant skin of her belly as through a linen cloth."[80] Elizabeth of Spaalbeek is described in various fugue states of bodily rigidity after which she often grew angry:

> She immediately strikes herself on the cheek so hard that her whole body sways down towards the ground with the force of her stroke; then she strikes herself on the back of her head— between her shoulders—on her neck—and she falls face-down, bending her body in an amazing way and dashing her head on the ground.[81]

Yet these antics are surpassed by Christina the Astonishing. While mass was being said for her at her funeral, her body suddenly revived, rose into the air and soared into the rafters of the church and remained there until mass was over. Christine felt such loathing for people that she fled into the wilderness and survived for nine weeks by drinking milk from her own breasts. She threw herself into burning-hot baking ovens, ate foul garbage and leftovers, immersed herself in the waters of the river Meuse for six days when it was frozen, and even hanged herself at the gallows for two days.[82]

The aim of this intensely physical relation to the sacred is metaphysical access to the divine through the power of love. In Porete's case, the consequence of the seven stages of self-deification is the overcoming of the condition of original sin and the return to the freedom that human beings enjoyed before the Fall. As the founder of the Quakers, George Fox, has it in his visions: "I was come up to the state of Adam in which he was before he fell."[83] It is not difficult to see why the Movement of the Free Spirit posed such a profound threat to the authority of the Catholic Church and the governmental and legislative authority of the various states in which it manifested itself. If it was possible, through a personal mystical itinerary, to overcome original sin and regain the Edenic state of intimacy with the divine, then what possible function might be served by the Catholic Church, whose authority as a mediator between the human and the divine is only justified insofar as human beings live and travail in the wake of original sin? As we have seen in regard to Schmitt, all forms of ecclesiastical and governmental authoritarianism require a belief in original sin. It is only because human beings are defective and imperfect that church and state become necessary. If human beings become free—that is, perfected by overcoming the sin and death that define the postlapsarian human condition—then this has dramatic political consequences.

To begin with—as we saw in John Ball's words of 1381—if the spirit is free then all conceptions of mine and thine vanish. In the annihilation of the Soul, mine becomes thine, I become thou, and the no-place of the Soul becomes the space of the activity of divine self-reflection. Such an experience of divinity, of course, is not an individual's private property, but is the commonwealth of those who are free in spirit. Private property is just the consequence of our fallen state. The Soul's recovery of its natural freedom entails commonality of ownership. The only true owner of property is God, and his wealth is held in common by all creatures without hierarchy or distinctions of class and hereditary privilege. The political form of the Movement of the Free Spirit is communism.

Furthermore, it is a communism whose social bond is love. We have seen how Porete describes the work of love as the audacity of the Soul's annihilation. Clearly, there can be no higher authority than divine love, which entails that communism would be a political form higher than law (Marx repeats many of these ideas, imagining communism as a society without law[84]). We might say that law is the juridical form that structures a social order. As such, it is based on the repression of the moment of community. Law is the external constraint on society that allows authority to be exercised, all the way to its dictatorial suspension. From the perspective of the communism of the Free Spirit, law loses its legitimacy because it is a form of heteronomous authority as opposed to an autonomously chosen work of love.

Furthermore—and perhaps this is what was most dangerous in the Movement of the Free Spirit—if human beings are free of original sin, where God is manifested as the spirit of commonality, then there is no longer any legitimacy to moral constraints on human behavior that do not directly flow from our freedom. The demands of the state and the church can simply be ignored if they are not consistent with the experience of freedom. To be clear, this is not at all to say that the Movement of the Free Spirit implies immoralism. On the contrary, it is to claim that morality has to flow from freedom by being consistent with a principle that is located not in the individual but in its divine source: the Free Spirit that is held in common.

The Movement of the Free Spirit has habitually been seen as encouraging both moral and sexual libertinage. One cannot exaggerate the extent to which the alleged sexual excesses of the adepts of the Free Spirit obsessed the Inquisition that investigated and condemned the Movement, destroying its literature and executing or incarcerating its members. Most of what we know of the Movement is mediated through the agency of the Church that outlawed it. Such evidence is clearly difficult to trust. In particular, the various inquisitors seem utterly preoccupied with cataloging instances of nakedness, as if this were evidence of the most depraved morals. But what are clothes for, apart from keeping the body warm? They are a consequence of the Fall, when we learned for the first time to cover our bodies for shame. If that shame is lifted with the overcoming of original sin, then why wear clothing at all? Furthermore, this tendency to prurience is continued by the Movement's modern inquisitors—like Cohn, who takes great pleasure in describing what he calls the "anarchic eroticism" of the adepts of the Free Spirit. For example, he takes evident delight in describing the excesses of the nuns of Schweidnitz in Silesia in 1330s, who claimed that they had such command over the Holy Trinity that they could "ride it as in a saddle."[85] On this view, the Movement of the Free Spirit allows and even encourages a sexual licentiousness in which adepts throw off the moral prudery of the Church and run amok in some sort of huge orgy.

It is, of course, impossible to assess these claims of erotic libertinage. After all, the accusations are made by the accusers and it would be somewhat odd to trust them entirely. Cohn's curiosity about the sexual antics of the Free Spirit's adepts is perhaps explained in part by the zeitgeist in which he was writing: in the conclusion to the 1970 revised edition of *The Pursuit of the Millennium*, Cohn argues for a continuity between medieval practices of self-deification and "the ideal of a total emancipation of the individual from society, even from external reality itself … with the help of psychedelic drugs."[86]

I see little evidence for the suggestion of such narcotic or erotic license amongst adepts of the Free Spirit. On the contrary, what one finds in Porete and in many other mystical texts from the period and later is not some wild unleashing of repressed sexual energy, but rather its subtle transformation. I agree with Robert Lerner who claims that "Free Spirits were motivated by pious desires for a truly apostolic life and communion with divinity."[87] Texts like *The Mirror* testify to a passion transformed from the physical to the metaphysical, to a certain spiritualization of desire. Some might call this sublimation. What is most striking in the writing of the mystics—especially the female mystics—is the elevation of the discourse of desire in relation to the object cause of that desire, which is the beloved: God, usually in the person of Christ. What the female mystic wants is to love and desire in the same place, and this requires both the articulation of desire and its transmutation into love. To reduce mystical passion to some pent-up sexual energy is to miss the point entirely. It is to mistake sublimation for repression. If anything, what seems to mark texts like *The Mirror* is the cultivation of an experience of passivity and an *askesis* of submission—which, of course, led to the Church's accusation of quietism and ignorance of the Sacraments. But the point is that the Movement of the Free Spirit is not about doing what you want. On the contrary, it is about the training and submission of free will in order to recover a condition of commonality that overcomes it, namely love.

Indeed, the emphasis on submission and sublimation that one finds in Porete and others seems more likely to lead to chastity than license. Unrestrained erotic exuberance would simply be the false exercise of the will. The point of Porete's seven-state itinerary is the *disciplining* of the self all the way to its extinction in an experience of love that annihilates it. To my mind, the Movement of the Free Spirit finds a greater echo in the chastity of groups like the Shakers than in the exhaustive and exhausting cataloging of the sexual excesses that took place in the Chateau de Silling in the Marquis de Sade's *120 Days of Sodom* or Pasolini's *Salò*.[88]

MYSTICISM IS NOT ABOUT THE BUSINESS OF FUCKING

There is no doubt that the Movement of the Free Spirit is deeply antinomian, refusing the metaphysical, moral, legislative, and political authority of both church and state. As such, it constituted a clandestine and subversive movement of resistance. The earliest mention of the many alleged heresies linked to the Free Spirit comes from an investigation held in Germany in the 1260s. The first of the accusations is revealing: "To make small assemblies and to teach in secret is not contrary to faith but is contrary to the evangelical way of life."[89] Note the emphasis on size and secrecy here. The great threat of the Movement of the Free Spirit was a secret network of small activist groups linked together by powerful bonds of solidarity and love. It was also a highly mobile network and what seems to have constantly worried the Church was the itinerant nature of the Beguines and Beghards and the way in which they moved from town to town and state to state. In addition, the rallying cry of these mendicants was "*Brod durch Gott*," (Bread for the sake of God), and they preached, as did the Franciscan Spirituals in Italy, a doctrine of Christ's radical poverty. As William Cornelius is reported to have said in the mid-thirteenth century, "No rich man can be saved, and all the rich are miserly."[90] The point is not lost on Cohn who writes that, at its height, the Movement of the Free Spirit "had become an invisible empire" held together by powerful emotional bonds.[91] Devoted to undermining the power of church and state, abolishing private property and establishing what can only be described as an anarcho-communist micro-politics based on the annihilation of the self in the experience of the divine, the ruthlessness with which the Movement was repeatedly crushed should come as no surprise.

It is in this context that Michel Foucault discusses Porete during his 1978 course at the Collège de France, *Security, Territory, Population*. Foucault mentions Porete during a discussion of what he calls "revolts of conduct"—forms of resistance that are not reducible to socio-economic factors like class. The questions at stake in such revolts are as follows: "To whom do we consent or are we directed to be conducted? How do we want to be conducted? Towards what do we want to be led?"[92] The most powerful of these revolts is obviously that associated with the name of Luther, although Foucault constructs a fascinating historical itinerary that begins in the twelfth century and extends through the late Middle Ages until the English Revolution and beyond. Foucault adds that these revolts of conduct are often linked to the "crucial problem of the status of women in society" and arise in convents or in relation to "women prophets" like Porete.

What kind of assessment can we make of the Movement of the Free Spirit? Cohn sees millenarianism as a constantly recurring and dangerous threat that is still very much with us. What finds expression with the heresy of the Free Spirit is, he writes, "an affirmation of freedom so reckless and unqualified that it amounted to a total denial of every kind of restraint and limitation."[93] As such, the Free Spirit is a precursor of what Cohn calls "that bohemian intelligentsia" that has plagued the twentieth century and which has been living from the ideas expressed by Bakunin and Nietzsche "in their wilder moments." The Free Spirit was "the most ambitious essay in total social revolution," which finds its continuation on the extreme left and right alike.[94] "Nietzsche's Superman," Cohn continues, "certainly obsessed the imagination of many of the 'armed bohemians' who made the National-Socialist revolution; and many a present-day exponent of world revolution owes more to Bakunin than to Marx."[95]

This is not the place to show either the erroneousness of such readings of Nietzsche and Bakunin, or the chronic limitation of pernicious arguments by insinuation that connect the Free Spirit to Nazism via Nietzsche. Let's just note that, as we saw with Porete, the Free Spirit is not a "reckless and unqualified" assertion of freedom that denies all "restraint and limitation." On the contrary, Porete is arguing for a rigorous and demanding *askesis* of the self, in which individual acts of willfulness are overcome by being directed outside themselves towards a divine source which is the basis for commonality. To say it once again, the Free Spirit is not about doing what you want. Neither is it amoral—rather, it is a stringent and demanding ethical disciplining of the self all the way to its nihilation.

Cohn uses the standard "depth psychology" talk of the 1950s and '60s to diagnose the alleged malady that drives the desire for mystical anarchism. He explains mysticism etiologically as a "profound introversion" of "gigantic parental images." This is both a defense against reality and "a reactivation of the distorting images of infancy." Thereafter, two possibilities emerge: either the mystic emerges from the process of introversion successfully, "as a more integrated personality," or he "introjects" these images unsuccessfully and "emerges as a nihilistic megalomaniac."[96] Cohn catalogs the repeated occurrence of such megalomaniacs with great power and historical detail and there is no denying the existence of forms of sophism, obscurantism, and charlatanry that are allied to the Movement of the Free Spirit.

However, I am not only suspicious of the validity of such etiological explanations, but I also want to interrogate the normative presuppositions that such explanations invoke for the emergence of phenomena like mysticism. Cohn simply assumes that an "integrated personality" is an unquestioned good, along with related ideas of reinforcing the ego and encouraging it to adapt to reality. In opposition to such an ego-psychological approach, what Porete is describing is what we might call a creative disintegration of the ego, an undermining of its authority that allows a new form of subjectivity to stand in the place inhabited by the old self. Rather than seeing Porete as a regression to some illusory infantile state, we might view the process of the Soul's annihilation as the self's maturation and mutation where it is no longer organized around individual identity and its self-regarding acts of will, but is rather orientated towards that which is unconscious in the life of desire. In my view, what Porete is describing is a transformation of the self through the act of love.

Here, I have Jacques Lacan in mind, in particular the way in which he stumbles upon Beguine mysticism in the course of Seminar XX, as he attempts to get close to what takes place in the experience of feminine enjoyment or *jouissance* and its relation to love.[97] For Lacan, mysticism is "something serious" and "mystical jaculations are neither idle chatter nor empty verbiage."[98] Most importantly, and keeping Cohn's sexual innuendos in mind, Lacan claims that to reduce mysticism to the "business of fucking (*affaires de foutre*)" is to miss the point entirely. He then goes on—and he is thinking explicitly of Hadewijch of Antwerp and Teresa of Avila—to state that "I believe in the jouissance of woman insofar as it is an extra (*en plus*)."[99] Female mystics are on the path of an experience of the *en plus* that exceeds knowledge, the order of what Lacan elsewhere calls truth, by which he means the truth of the subject. This dimension of an excessive *jouissance* that articulates something that is more (*en plus*) of what Lacan sees as the essentially phallic function of knowledge is what he calls, with a nod to Heidegger, "ex-sistence." It is this dimension of ecstasy, following the line of a transgressive desire into its *askesis*, that we can call love. To be clear, this is not something confined to women. Lacan adds, thinking of Kierkegaard (and this will be on my mind in the Conclusion to this book), "there are men who are just as good as women," namely those who "get the idea or sense that there must be a jouissance that is beyond. Those are the ones that we call mystics."[100]

DO NOT KILL OTHERS, ONLY YOURSELF

John Gray makes explicit what is implicit in Cohn's approach. Gray extends the condemnation of groups like the Free Spirit to any and all utopian movements. The burden of a book like *Black Mass* is to show the continued malign presence of millenarian, apocalyptic politics in the contemporary world. What is particularly powerful in Gray's approach is the manner in which he extends Cohn's diagnosis to the neo-conservative millenarianism of the George W. Bush administration, gleefully embraced by then British Prime Minister Tony Blair, for whom "the clichés of the hour have always been eternal verities."[101] However, as I have shown, Gray's critique of utopianism does not vindicate his call for political realism, which draws on his naturalization of the concept of original sin. Incidentally, one imagines that Carl Schmitt would have been out of sympathy with both the theology and politics of mystical anarchism. I'm sure Schmitt would have happily served as Porete's inquisitor and personally lit the fire that consumed her and her books.

A very different take on these matters can be found in Raoul Vaneigem's 1986 *The Movement of the Free Spirit*. In it, Vaneigem unwittingly confirms all of Cohn's worst fears: he offers a vigorous defense of the Movement of the Free Spirit as a precursor to the insurrectional movements of the 1960s such as the Situationist International, in which Vaneigem's writings played such a hugely influential role. He writes of the Free Spirit: "The spring has never dried up; it gushes from the fissures of history, bursting through the earth at the slightest shift of the mercantile terrain."[102]

In Debord's dystopian vision of the society of the spectacle, in which all human relations are governed by exchange—the dictatorship of a commodity system that Vaneigem always compares to the negativity of death—the Free Spirit is an emancipatory movement that operates in the name of life, bodily pleasures, and untrammeled freedom. Vaneigem reinterprets the Free Spirit's insistence on poverty of spirit as the basis for a critique of the market system, in which life is reduced to purposeless productivity and life-denying work.

The most radical element in the Movement of the Free Spirit, for Vaneigem, was "an alchemy of individual fulfilment," in which the cultivation of a state of perfection allowed the creation of a space where the "economy's hold over individuals" was relinquished.[103] The Free Spirit's emphasis on love is "the sole alternative to market society."[104] Wrapped around a compelling and extended documentation of the Movement of the Free Spirit, Vaneigem argues for what he calls an "alchemy of the self," based on unfettered enjoyment and bodily pleasures. He cites favorably the proposition of Hippolytus of Rome: "The promiscuity of men and women, that is the true communion."[105]

Vaneigem, however, advances an opposition between the Free Spirit and the Holy Spirit, identifying the latter with God and the former with his denial. Vaneigem is therefore skeptical of

Porete's position in *The Mirror*, arguing that self-deification is too dependent on a repressive, authoritarian idea of God.[106] Although Vaneigem borrows Porete's idea of the refinement of love, *fin amor*, he finds her approach too ascetic and intellectualized. Vaneigem defends an individualistic hedonism based not on intellect but on "a flux of passions,"[107] which has a stronger affinity with Fourier's utopianism of passionate attraction filled with *phalansteries* of free love and leisure than the sort of self-annihilation found in Porete. In this connection, we might consider Vaneigem's poetic rewriting of the declaration of human rights. Article 17 reads: "Every human being has the right to feel the movements of affection and disaffection which are inherent in the flux of passions and the freedoms of love."[108]

To my mind, a much more compelling line of argument than Vaneigem's can be found in Gustav Landauer, the German anarcho-socialist who exerted such influence over Buber, Scholem, and the young Benjamin.[109] In his 1901 essay "Anarchic Thoughts on Anarchism," Landauer is writing in the heated context of the anarchist politics of assassination that had seen the killing of US President William McKinley in 1901, itself patterned on the murder of King Umberto I of Italy the previous year.[110] Both perpetrators identified themselves as anarchists. Landauer asks rhetorically: "What has the killing of people to do with anarchism, a theory striving for a society without government and authoritarian coercion, a movement against the state and legalized violence?" The answer is clear, "Nothing at all."[111]

Landauer argues that all forms of violence are despotic and that anarchism entails nonviolence. If anarchists resort to violence, then they are no better than the tyrants whom they claim to oppose. Anarchism is not a matter of armed revolt or military attack; "it is a matter of how one lives."[112] Its concern is with "a new people arising from humble beginnings in small communities that form in the midst of the old."[113] This is what Landauer intriguingly calls "inward colonization."

Yet how is such an inward colonization possible? Landauer's

response is singular and draws us back to the idea of self-annihilation. He writes, "Whoever kills, dies. Those who want to create life must also embrace it and be reborn from within."[114] But how can such a rebirth take place? It can only happen by killing oneself "in the mystical sense, in order to be reborn after having descended into the depths of their soul." He goes on: "Only those who have journeyed through their own selves and waded deep in their own blood can help to create the new world without interfering in the lives of others."[115]

Landauer insists that such a position does not imply quietism or resignation. On the contrary, he writes, "one acts with others," but adds that "none of this will really bring us forward if it is not based on a new spirit won by conquest of one's inner self."[116] He goes on:

> It is not enough for us to reject conditions and institutions; we have to reject ourselves. "Do not kill others, only yourself": such will be the maxim of those who accept the challenge to create their own chaos in order to discover their most authentic and precious inner being and to become mystically one with the world.[117]

Although talk of authenticity and "precious inner being" leaves me somewhat cold, what I find significant here is the connection between the idea of self-annihilation and anarchism. The condition of possibility for a life of cooperation and solidarity with others is a subjective transformation, a self-killing that renounces the killing of others. For Landauer, it is not a matter of anarchism participating in the usual party politics, systemic violence, and cold rationalism of the state. It is, rather, a question of individuals breaking with the state's authority and uniting together in new forms of life. Talk of inward colonization gives a new twist to Cohn's idea of the Movement of the Free Spirit as an "invisible empire." What is at stake here is the creation of new forms of life at a distance from the order of the state—which is the order of visibility—and cultivating largely invisible commonalities, what Landauer calls anarchy's "dark deep dream."[118]

This killing of the self in an ecstatic mystical experience is close to what Bataille called "sovereignty," and which for him was constantly linked with his experimentation with different forms of small-scale, communal group collaborations, particularly in the 1930s and '40s, from Contre Attaque, the Collège de Sociologie and the Collège Socratique, through to the more mysterious Acéphale.[119]

SOME PERHAPSES: INSURRECTION AND THE RISK OF ABSTRACTION

We are living through a long anti-1960s. The various anti-capitalist experiments in communal living and collective existence that defined that period seem to us either quaintly passé, laughably unrealistic, or dangerously misguided. Having grown up and thrown off such seemingly childish ways, we now think we know better than to try to bring heaven crashing down to earth and construct concrete utopias. To that extent, despite our occasional and transient enthusiasms and Obamaisms, we are all political realists; indeed, most of us are passive nihilists and cynics. This is why we still require a belief in something like original sin, namely, that there is something ontologically defective about what it means to be human. As I suggested above, the Judeo-Christian conception of original sin finds its modern analogues in Freud's variation on the Schopenhauerian disjunction between desire and civilization, Heidegger's ideas of facticity and fallenness, and the Hobbesian anthropology that drives Schmitt's defense of authoritarianism and dictatorship (which has seduced significant sectors of the left hungry for what they see as Realpolitik). Without the conviction that the human condition is essentially flawed and dangerously rapacious, we would have no way of justifying our disappointment, and nothing gives us a greater thrill than satiating our sense of exhaustion and ennui by polishing the bars of our prison cell by reading a little John Gray. Gray provides a very persuasive Darwinian variant on the idea of original sin: it is the theory of evolution that explains the fact that we are *Homo rapiens*. Nothing can be done about it. Humanity is a plague.

It is indeed true that those utopian political movements of the 1960s, in which an echo of utopian millenarian movements like the Free Spirit could be heard—such as the Situationist International—led to various forms of disillusionment, disintegration, and, in extreme cases, disaster. Experiments in the collective ownership of property, or in communal living based on sexual freedom without the repressive institution of the family—or indeed R.D. Laing's experimental communal asylums with no distinction between the so-called mad and the sane—seem like distant whimsical cultural memories captured in dog-eared, yellowed paperbacks and grainy, poor-quality film. As a child of punk, economic collapse, and the widespread social violence in the United Kingdom in the late 1970s, it is a world that I have always struggled to understand. Perhaps such communal experiments tried to be too pure and were overfull of righteous conviction. Perhaps they were, in a word, too *moralistic* to ever endure. Perhaps such experiments were doomed because of what we might call a politics of abstraction, in the sense of being overly attached to an idea at the expense of a frontal denial of reality. Perhaps, indeed.

At their most extreme—say in the activities of the Weather Underground, the Red Army Faction, and the Red Brigades in the 1970s—the moral certitude of the closed and pure community becomes fatally linked to redemptive, cleansing violence. Terror becomes the means to bring about the end of virtue. Such is the logic of Jacobinism. The death of individuals is but a speck on the vast heroic canvas of the class struggle. Such thinking culminated in a heroic politics of violence, where acts of abduction, kidnapping, hijacking, and assassination were justified through an attachment to a set of ideas. As a character in Jean-Luc Godard's *Notre Musique* remarks, "To kill a human being in order to defend an idea is not to defend an idea, it is to kill a human being."[120]

Perhaps such groups were too attached to the idea of imme-diacy, the propaganda of the violent deed as the impatient attempt to storm the heavens. Perhaps such experiments lacked an under-standing of politics as a constant and concrete process of mediation. That is, the mediation between a subjective ethical commitment based on a general principle—for example the equality of all, friendship, or, as I would say, an infinite ethical demand—and the experience of local organization that builds fronts and alli-ances between disparate groups with often conflicting sets of interests, what Gramsci called the activity of "hegemony." By definition, such a process of mediation is never pure and never complete.

Are these utopian experiments in community—where we find an echo of the Free Spirit—dead, or do they live on in some form? I'd like to make two suggestions for areas in which this utopian impulse might live on, two experiments, if you will: one from contemporary art, one from contemporary radical politics. These two areas can be interestingly linked. Indeed, if a tendency marks our time, then it is the increasing difficulty in separating forms of collaborative art from experimental politics.

Perhaps such utopian experiments in community live on in the institutionally sanctioned spaces of the contemporary art world. One thinks of projects like *L'Association des Temps Libérés* (1995) or *Utopia Station* (2003), as well as many other examples gathered together in a show at the Guggenheim Museum in New York in Fall 2008, *Theanyspacewhatever*.[121] In the work of artists like Philippe Parreno and Liam Gillick, or curators like Hans-Ulrich Obrist and Maria Lind, there is a deeply felt Situationist nostalgia for ideas of collectivity, action, self-management, collaboration, and indeed the idea of the group as such. In such art practice, which Nicolas Bourriaud has successfully branded as "relational," art is the acting out of a situation in order to see if, in Obrist's words, "some-thing like a collective intelligence might exist."[122] As Gillick notes, "Maybe it would be better if we worked in groups of three."[123] So much contemporary art and politics is obsessed with the figure of the group and of work as collaboration, perhaps all the way to the refusal of work and the cultivation of anonymity.

Of course, the problem with such contemporary utopian art experiments is twofold. On the one hand, they are only enabled and legitimated through the cultural institutions of the art world and thus utterly enmeshed in the circuits of commodification and spectacle that they seek to subvert; and, on the other hand, the dominant mode for approaching an experience of the communal is through the strategy of reenactment. One doesn't engage in a bank heist, one reenacts Patty Hearst's adventures with the Symbionese Liberation Army in a warehouse in Brooklyn, or whatever. Situationist *détournement* is replayed as obsessively planned reenactment. The category of reenactment has become hegemonic in contemporary art, specifically as a way of thinking the relation between art and politics—perhaps radical politics has also become reenactment. Fascinating as I find such experiments and the work of the artists involved, I suspect here what we might call a "mannerist Situationism," where the old problem of recuperation does not even apply because such art is completely co-opted by the socio-economic system which provides its lifeblood.

To turn to politics, perhaps we witnessed another communal experiment with the events in France surrounding the arrest and detention of the so-called Tarnac Nine on November 11, 2008, and the work of groups that go under different names: Tiqqun, the Invisible Committee, the Imaginary Party.[124] As part of Nicolas Sarkozy's reactionary politics of fear—itself based on an overwhelming fear of disorder and a desire to erase definitively the memory of 1968—a number of activists who had been formerly associated with Tiqqun were arrested in rural, central France by a force of 150 anti-terrorist police, helicopters, and attendant media. They were living communally in the small village of Tarnac in the Corrèze district of the Massif Central. Apparently a number of the group's members had bought a small farmhouse and ran a cooperative grocery store, besides which they were engaged in such dangerous activities as running a local film club, planting carrots, and delivering food to the elderly. With surprising juridical imagination, they were charged with "pre-terrorism," an accusation linked to acts of sabotage on France's TGV rail system.

The basis for this thought-crime was a passage from a book published in 2007 called *L'insurrection qui vient*.[125] It is a wonderfully dystopian diagnosis of contemporary society—seven circles of hell in seven chapters—and a compelling strategy to resist it. The final pages of *L'insurrection* advocate acts of sabotage against the transport networks of "the social machine" and ask the question, "How could a TGV line or an electrical network be rendered useless?"[126] Two of the alleged pre-terrorists, Julien Coupat and Yldune Lévy, were detained in jail and charged with "a terrorist undertaking" that carried a prison sentence of 20 years. The last of the group to be held in custody, Coupat, was released without having faced prosecution on May 28, 2009, on bail of 16,000 Euros, and was forbidden to travel outside the greater Parisian area.[127] Late that year, fresh arrests were made in connection with the Tarnac affair.[128] Such is the repressive and reactionary force of the state— just in case anyone had forgotten. As the authors of *L'insurrection* remind us, "Governing has never been anything but pushing back by a thousand subterfuges the moment when the crowd will hang you."[129]

L'insurrection qui vient has powerful echoes of the Situationist International. Yet — revealingly — the Hegelian-Marxism of Debord's analysis of the spectacle and commodification is replaced with very strong echoes of Agamben, in particular the question of community in Agamben as that which would survive the separation of law and life.[130] As we will see in detail in the next chapter, matters turn here on an understanding of the relation between law and life, and the possibility of a nonrelation between those two terms. If law is essentially violence, which in the age of bio-politics taps deeper and deeper into the reservoir of life, then the separation of law and life is the space of what Agamben calls politics. It is what leads to his anomic misreading of Paul.

The authorship of *L'insurrection* is attributed to La Comité

Invisible and the insurrectional strategy of the group turns around the question of invisibility. It is a question of "learning how to become imperceptible," of regaining "the taste for anonymity," and of not exposing and losing oneself in the order of visibility, which is always controlled by the police and the state. The authors of *L'insurrection* argue for the proliferation of zones of opacity, anonymous spaces in which communes might be formed. The book ends with the slogan, "All power to the communes (*Tout le pouvoir aux communes*). In a nod to Maurice Blanchot, these communes are described as "inoperative" or "*désœuvrée*," as refusing the capitalist tyranny of work. In a related text simply entitled *Call*, they seek to establish a "series of foci of desertion, of secession poles, of rallying points. For the runaways. For those who leave. A set of places to take shelter from the control of a civilization that is headed for the abyss."[131]

A strategy of sabotage, blockade, and what is called "the human strike" is proposed in order to weaken still further our doomed civilization. As the Tiqqun group write in a 1999 text called "Oh Good, the War!": "Abandon ship. Not because it's sinking, but to make it sink." Or again: "When a civilization is ruined, one declares it bankrupt. One does not tidy up in a home falling off a cliff."[132] An opposition between the city and the country is constantly reiterated, and it is clear that the construction of zones of opacity is better suited to rural life than the policed space of surveillance of the modern metropolis. The city is much better suited to what we might call "designer resistance," where people wear Ramones T-shirts and sit in coffee shops saying "capitalism sucks," before going back to their jobs as graphic designers.

L'insurrection is a compelling, exhilarating, funny, and deeply lyrical text that sets off all sorts of historical echoes with movements like the Free Spirit and the Franciscan Spirituals in the Middle Ages, through to the proto-anarchist Diggers in the English Revolution and different strands of nineteenth-century utopian communism. We should note the emphasis on secrecy, invisibility, and itinerancy, on small-scale communal experiments in living, on the politicization of poverty that recalls medieval practices of mendicancy and the refusal of work. What is at stake is the affirmation of a life no longer exhausted by work, cowed by law and the police. These are the core political elements of mystical anarchism.

This double program of sabotage, on the one hand, and secession from civilization on the other, risks, I think, remaining trapped within the politics of abstraction identified above. In this fascinatingly creative reenactment of the Situationist gesture—which is why I stressed the connection with contemporary art practice —what is missing is a thinking of political mediation, where groups like the Invisible Committee would be able to link up and become concretized in relation to multiple and conflicting sites of struggle, workers, the unemployed, even the designer resisters and—perhaps most importantly—more or less disenfranchised ethnic groups. We need a richer political cartography than the opposition between the city and the country. Tempting as it is, sabotage combined with secession from civilization smells of the moralism we detected above: an ultimately antipolitical purism.

That said, I understand the desire for secession: it is the desire to escape a seemingly doomed civilization that is headed for the abyss. As we will see in detail in the next chapter, the proper theological name for such secessionism is Marcionism, which turns on the separation of law from life, the order of creation from that of redemption, the Old and New Testaments. In the face of a globalizing, atomizing, bio-political legal regime of violence and domination that threatens to drain dry the reservoir of life, secession is withdrawal, the establishment of a space where another form of life and collective intelligence are possible. Secession offers the possibility of an antinomian separation of law from life, a retreat from the old order through experiments with free human sociability: in other words, communism, understood as the "Sharing of a sensibility *and* elaboration of sharing. The uncovering of what is common *and* the building of a force."[133]

It is also the case that something has changed and is changing in the nature of tactics of political resistance. With the fading away of the so-called anti-globalization movement, groups like the Invisible Committee offer a consistency of thought and action that possesses great diagnostic power and tactical awareness. They provide a new and compelling vocabulary of insurrectionary politics that has both described and unleashed a series of political actions in numerous locations, some closer to home, some further away. The latter is performed by what the Invisible Committee calls—in an interesting choice of word—"resonance."[134] A resonating body in one location—like glasses on a table—begins to make another body shake, and suddenly the whole floor is covered with glass. Politics is perhaps no longer, as it was in the so-called anti-globalization movement, a struggle for and with visibility. Resistance is about the cultivation of invisibility, opacity, anonymity, and resonance.

THE POLITICS OF LOVE

I have my doubts about the politics of abstraction that haunts groups like the Invisible Committee. But if we reject such political experiments, what then follows from this? Are we to conclude that the utopian impulse in political thinking is simply the residue of a dangerous political theology that we are much better off without? Is the upshot of the critique of mystical anarchism that we should be resigned in the face of the world's violent inequality and update a belief in original sin with a reassuringly miserabilistic Darwinism? Should we reconcile ourselves to the options of political realism, authoritarianism, or liberalism, John Gray, Carl Schmitt, or Barack Obama? Should we simply renounce the utopian impulse in our personal and political thinking?

If so, then the consequence is clear: we are stuck with the way things are, or possibly with something even worse than the way things are. To abandon the utopian impulse in thinking and acting is to imprison ourselves within the world as it is and to give up once and for all the prospect that another world is possible, however small, fleeting, and compromised such a world might be. In the political circumstances that presently surround us in the West, to abandon the utopian impulse in political thinking is to resign ourselves to liberal democracy. As we showed above, liberal democracy is the rule of the rule, the reign of law that renders impotent anything that would break with law: the miraculous, the moment of the event, the break with the situation in the name of the common. It is a political deism governed by the hidden and divine hand of the market.

Let me return to mystical anarchism and to the question of self-deification or auto-theism. Defending the idea of becoming God might understandably be seen as going a little far, I agree. To embrace such mysticism would be to fall prey to what Badiou calls in his book on Paul the obscurantist discourse of glorification.[135] In terms of the schema of the four discourses that Badiou borrows from Lacan (master, university, hysteric, analyst), the mystic is identified with the discourse of the hysteric and contrasted with the anti-obscurantist Christian position that Badiou identifies with the discourse of the analyst. Badiou draws a line between Paul's declaration of the Christ-event, what he calls "an ethical dimension of anti-obscurantism," and the mystical discourse of identity with the divine, the ravished subjectivity of someone like Porete.[136]

Yet to acquiesce in such a conclusion would be to miss something vital about mystical anarchism, what I want to call its *politics of love*. What I find most compelling in Porete is the idea of love as an act of absolute spiritual daring that eviscerates the old self in order that something new can come into being. In Anne Carson's words, cited above, love dares the self to leave itself behind, to enter into poverty and engage with its own annihilation: to hew and hack away at oneself in order to make a space that is large enough for love to enter. What is being attempted by Porete—and perhaps it is *only* the attempt which matters here, not some theophanic outcome—is an act of absolute daring that opens onto what might be called the immortal dimension of the subject.

The only proof of immortality is the act of love, the daring that attempts to extend beyond oneself by annihilating oneself, to project onto something that exceeds one's powers of projection. To love is to give what one does not have and to receive that over which one has no power. As we saw in Landauer, the point is not to kill others, but to kill oneself in order that a transformed relation to others becomes possible, some new way of conceiving the common and being with others. Anarchism can only begin with an act of inward colonization, the act of love that demands a transformation of the self. Finally—and very simply—anarchism is not a question for the future, it is a matter of how one lives now. The question is: how are we to behave?

4

You Are Not Your Own:
On the Nature of Faith

Saint Paul is trouble. It is simply a fact about the history of Christian dogma that a return to Paul is usually very bad news for the established church. As the great German Protestant theologian Adolph von Harnack pointed out more than a century ago: "One might write the history of dogma as the history of the Pauline reactions in the Church, and in doing so would touch on all the turning points of the history."[1] This is true of Marcion's opposition to the Apostolic Fathers, Augustine after the Church Fathers through to Luther after the Scholastics and Jansenism after the Council of Trent. Harnack continues, "Everywhere it has been Paul ... who produced the Reformation."[2]

So, the spirit of Paul is the movement of reformation. It is the attempt to clear away the corruption, secularism, and intellectual sophistry of the established church and to return to the religious core of Christianity that is tightly bound up with its oldest extant documents, Paul's Epistles. The Pauline motivation for religious reformation is also true of Kierkegaard, Karl Barth, and Rudolf Bultmann. Perverse as it might sound, I think it is equally true of Nietzsche—even and perhaps especially when he dresses himself in the tragicomic garb of the Anti-Christ. Giorgio Agamben rightly sees Nietzsche's adoption of the figure of the Anti-Christ from Second Thessalonians as a kind of parody of Pauline Messianism.[3] Nietzsche's call for a revaluation of values is based on a sheer jealousy of Paul's achievement in bringing about such a revaluation. But also, Nietzsche's revelation of the intuition into Eternal Return, "6000 feet above man and time," is a kind of mimicry of Paul's road to Damascus experience. As Jacob Taubes writes, "Paul haunts Nietzsche all the way to the deepest intimacies."[4]

To begin to turn towards my angle of entry into Paul, what goes for Nietzsche also goes for Heidegger's passionate interest in *Urchristentum*, primal or primordial Christianity, in his lectures on Paul's Epistles in the crisis years that followed World War I. I will show below how the basic intuition of Heidegger's reformation of thinking is deeply Pauline. The very gesture of attempting to recover a primordial Christianity is the desire for a repetition of the Pauline moment. We must slough off the sediment of tradition—what Heidegger called in his famous 1919 letter to his priest, Father Engelbert Krebs, "The system of Catholicism"—and reactivate the traditions' sources in the name of an originary experience.[5] The return to Paul is the attempt, and this is Heidegger's word, at the *destruction* (*Destruktion*) or dismantling of a deadening tradition in the name of a proclamation of life.

As Wayne Meeks points out, Paul is both "the most holy apostle" and "the apostle of the heretics."[6] Since the times of his quarrel with Peter and the Jewish Christians, Paul has been the zealot foe of tradition's authority and the opponent of any and all forms of authoritarianism. Paul is the proper name of a ferment in the history of Christianity. Indeed, it is a ferment that places even the specificity of Christianity in question. For example, what the books by Daniel Boyarin, Taubes, and Agamben share is the desire to show that Paul is much better understood as a radical Jew. As Boyarin notes, "Paul lived and died convinced he was a Jew living out Judaism."[7] Taubes goes even further, claiming that "Paul is a fanatic, a Jewish zealot,"[8] and "more Jewish than any reform rabbi."[9] Agamben's governing hypothesis is to restore Paul's Epistles to their rightful place within the tradition of Jewish Messianism, a tradition reactivated through Scholem and Benjamin.[10]

If Paul's essence consists in anything, then it is surely activism. This spells trouble for any and every church that sees itself as founded, funded, and well-defended. What usually happens when Paul is invoked is that the established church is declared to be the Whore of Babylon and its hierarchy the Anti-Christ. The fact that there is so much interest in Paul at present shouldn't therefore be seen as a conservative gesture or some sort of return to traditional religion. On the contrary, the return to Paul is the demand for reformation. It is the demand for a new figure of activism, or what Alain Badiou calls a new militancy for the universal in an age defined by moral relativism, a communitarian politics of identity, and global capitalism.[11] What is being glimpsed and groped towards in the return to Paul is a vision of faith and existential commitment that might begin to face and face down the demotivated slackening of existence under conditions of liberal democracy. The return to Paul is motivated by political disappointment.[12]

PAUL'S ADDRESS

Written with an overwhelming sense of urgency, over a very brief period—ten years or so (51–62? AD)—in a context that, at the very least, could have been described as critical and crisis-ridden, Paul's Epistles have shown themselves to be susceptible to the widest and wildest interpretations, simplifications, and distortions. From the time of the subsequent writing of the Gospels, through to the Acts of the Apostles and the so-called heresy of Marcion onwards, there has seemed to be something infinitely malleable about the subtle antithetical complexities of Paul's thinking, what Luther called "an unheard-of speech."[13] To call Paul protean is to risk utter understatement.

Obviously, the most widespread and egregious distortion is that Paul was the "Founder of Christianity." As any reader of Paul will

know, the words "Christian" and "Christianity" were not employed
by Paul. He spoke rather of being "in Christ," a phrase which can
be understood in at least two ways:

(i)   Mystically, as a claim for the immanence of Christ in the
       soul, as when Paul says, "It is no longer I who live, but Christ
       who lives in me" (Gal. 2:19).[14]
(ii)   Politically, as what Martin Dibelius calls "membership in the
       waiting community."[15] I will turn below to the subtlety of
       Paul's critique of mysticism.

However much subsequent Christian doctrine might have tried
to transform him into a more Peter-like foundation stone or
pierre angulaire, Paul certainly didn't see himself as a founder of an
organized institutional religion, whether Orthodox or Catholic,
let alone Anglican.

Paul simply proclaimed the Messiah (*Mashiah, Christos*), whose
name was Jesus, the historical *Yeshu ben Yosef.* As we will see presently, Paul's faith is not the sort of abstract belief in God famously
criticized by Martin Buber, as much as a passionate commitment
to the Messiah.[16] The faith in Jesus as the anointed one or Messiah
was evidenced through the resurrection, and the absolute centrality
of the latter can be seen by reading any few pages of Paul. Without
resurrection, all faith is in vain. It cannot simply be dismissed as
a "fable," as Badiou does.[17] But with his faith in the resurrection,
Paul sought to build up communities that, in his words, would be
a "remnant, chosen by grace" (Rom. 10:5). As Taubes shows, Paul
constructs a negative political theology based on the single commandment of love that is against both the Jews and the Romans.
Paul writes to an illicit, secret, subterranean community, "a little
Jewish, a little Gentile,"[18] a bunch of rejects and *refuseniks*, the very
filth of the world: "We have become, and are now as the refuse of
the world (*perikatharmata tou kosmou*), the offscouring (*peripsiema*)
of all things" (1 Cor. 4:12).

What is being imagined here is a political theology of the

wretched of the earth, as Frantz Fanon would say, or the scum of the earth, which is the New International Version translation of *perikatharmata tou kosmou*. Paul's politics is a building-up of an unwanted offscouring that belongs neither to the world of the Romans nor of the Jews: an unclean husk, peel, or skin scale, that which is sloughed off and thrown away, the human dregs and nail clippings of the world—the shit of the earth.[19] I think Agamben is therefore justified in his critique of Badiou that what is at stake in Paul is not the simple assertion of universalism against communitarianism.[20] Paulinism is not Kantianism. What is at stake is a politics of the remnant, where the off-cuttings of humanity are the basis for a new political articulation.

The task of these scoured-off communities was to bear the message of the Messiah through the end times in which Paul believed he was living, "For the form of this world is passing away" (1 Cor. 7:31). As Agamben shows, Paul's concern is with the time that remains, *il tempo che resta;* that is, the remaining time between now and *parousia*, between the now that is defined by the historicity of the resurrection and the futurity of Jesus's return.[21] Pauline time—which can be described as Messianic or indeed ecstatic—is stretched between the "already" of the resurrection and the "not-yet" of *parousia*, a historicity and futurity that are marked in the now, the *kairos*, of Paul's address. The urgency of the address shows that he didn't think there was much time left.

It is the nature of the address in Paul that is so fascinating. Firstly, he writes letters that are addressed to a specific community—the Thessalonians, the Galatians—or, in at least one case, to a specific person: Philemon. But, secondly, and more importantly, Paul writes these letters because he was addressed, because he was called. So, Paul addresses letters because he was addressed. Paul never speaks of a conversion experience. The closest we get to conversion is the questionable passage in Acts when Jesus says, "Saul, Saul, why do you persecute me?," the scales fall from Saul's eyes, and he becomes Paul (Acts 9:4). Paul speaks rather of being called, *kletos*, or of a calling, *klesis*. As he writes at the beginning of Romans, Paul was called to be an apostle, a messenger (Rom. 1:1). In Corinthians 2, Paul speaks of himself in the third person: "I know a man in Christ who, fourteen years ago, was caught up to the third heaven" (2 Cor. 10:2). But whatever happens to Paul that transforms him from a persecutor of Jewish Christians into a preacher of Christ's gospel, he is the subject of a calling. Or, better, Paul's subjectivity is constituted through a call.

Who is Paul, we might ask? Paul is the called. Indeed, Paul is called Paul because he was called. Before the call, he was Saul or *Saulos*. Saul was a noble and kingly name, "of the tribe of Benjamin, a Hebrew born of Hebrews ... under the law blameless" (Phil. 3:5). Through his calling Paul writes, "I have suffered the loss of all things, and count them as refuse (*skubala*)" (Phil. 3:8). When Paul is called, he becomes trash, literally a piece of shit or dung as some of the earlier translations render *to skubalon*. As opposed to the nobility of Saul, a free Roman citizen, Paul becomes small. As Agamben reminds us, *paulus* in Latin means "small, of little significance."[22] It is linked to *pauper*, a man of poor, scanty, or meager means. The movement from Saul to Paul occasioned by the call is a switch from major to minor. *Paulos* is a diminutive, something like "Pauly" or "Paulinho." Crucially, Paul is a slave name and like all slave names it is a nickname—violently imposed—that superimposes itself in the place of the erased proper name. Once Paul is called, as he says at the beginning of Romans, he becomes a slave of the Messiah (*Paulos doulos Iesou Kristou*). The key to Paul's "unheard-of speech," his delight and brilliance in multiplying antitheses, is that slavery makes us free and weakness is strength: "For when I am weak, then I am strong" (2 Cor. 12:10). Christ was crucified in weakness to become powerful through the resurrection. Likewise, in becoming slaves of the Messiah, we are asked to abandon our secular, Roman life of freedom, and to assert our weakness. The power of being in Christ is a powerless power. It is constituted by a call that exceeds human strength. It gives subjects a potentiality for action through rendering them impotent. We shall return to the central theme of impotence below.

Furthermore, Paul insists, "This is my rule in all the churches" (1 Cor. 7:17): we should remain in the condition in which we were called. If you were a slave when called, then no matter: he who was called as a slave becomes free in Christ. Alternatively, if you were free when called, like Paul, then you become a slave of Christ. A similar oxymoronic logic governs Paul's approach to marriage: if you are bound to a wife, then "do not seek to be free." But if you are free of a wife, then "do not seek marriage" (1 Cor. 7:27). As Paul continues, "the appointed time has grown very short" and marriage will lead us into worldly troubles. Therefore, "let those who have wives live as if they had none" (1 Cor. 7:29). So much for so-called Christian family values. As Terry Eagleton reminds us, "Jesus's attitude to the family is one of implacable hostility."[23]

TROTH-PLIGHT: FAITH AS PROCLAMATION

My concern in this book is with the nature of faith. I'd like to address this issue directly by using Paul and some of his recent philosophical interlocutors as my guides. What kind of thing is faith and—more particularly—can someone who is nominally or denominationally faithless, such as myself, still have an experience of faith? Can one speak of a faith of the faithless?

The idea I want to propose here, and then develop more carefully through a reading of Heidegger, is that of faith as a declarative act, as an enactment, a performative that proclaims. To this extent, I want to tie the idea of the gospel and evangelical good tidings (*to euaggelion*) to the verbal sense of "to proclaim" or "to announce" (*euaggelixomai*). Faith is an announcement that enacts, a proclamation that brings the subject of faith into being.

To put it telegraphically, faith is an enactment in relation to a calling. It is proclaimed in the urgent and punctual literary form of the epistle. The letter, arising out of the address of a calling, is addressed to a specific community, usually at a critical moment in its existence. Faith announces itself in a situation of crisis where a decisive intervention is called for. In other words, faith takes place in a situation of struggle. At stake in the struggle is the meaning of the future and the exact extent of the shadow that the future casts across the present: eschatological struggle. So, faith is not an empty, fixed, or constant state with the distant pay-off of final bliss in the afterlife. It is, rather, an enactment in the present that is shot through both by the facticity of the past (for Paul, the fact of the resurrection) and the imminence of the future (*parousia*). The passion that defines Paul's proclamation in his letters concerns our relation to the futurity of a redemption that we anxiously await, but for which we must prepare ourselves.

Paul's conception of faith is not, then, the abstraction of a metaphysical belief in God. Nor is Christ some Hegelian mediation of the divine or a conduit to a transcendent beyond. Faith is rather a lived subjective commitment to what I have called elsewhere an infinite demand.[24] It is the infinite demand of the risen Christ that calls Paul to proclaim. It is in relation to that demand that the subject is constituted through an act of approval or fidelity. Crucially, and we will come back to this, the subject is not the equal of the infinite demand which is placed on it. If it were, the demand would not be infinite and the structure of faith would have the same shape as autonomy, namely the law that one gives oneself—as in Kant, for example. Rather, the infinite demand that calls Paul requires a faith in something that exceeds my power, the *Faktum* of Jesus Messiah. As we will see in the Conclusion, this infinite demand is a work of love in Kierkegaard's sense. This *Faktum* hetero-affectively constitutes the subject in a very specific way. Faith does not consist in the assertive strength of the subject that makes it the equal of the demand placed on it. Rather, the infinite demand confronts the strength of the subject with an essential weakness or state of wanting (*asthenia*). As Paul writes, and note the quasi-nihilistic logic of Paul's political theology: "God chose what is weak in the world to shame the strong. God chose what is low and despised in the world, even things which are not, to bring to nothing things that are" (1 Cor. 1:27–8).

As Agamben shows compellingly in his linking of Paul to Benjamin's "Theses on the Philosophy of History," Messianic power is always weak.[25] The adjective "weak" is not a qualification or diminution of Messianic power, as Derrida seems to believe in *Specters of Marx*.[26] As the Lord replies to Paul, "My grace is sufficient for you, for my power is made perfect in weakness" (2 Cor. 12:9). Faith—especially a faith of the faithless, since it lacks a transcendent, metaphysical guarantee—is a powerless power, a strength in weakness.

On "The Sixth Day" of his reading of the ten opening words of Paul's Letter to the Romans, Agamben turns to the question of faith in a way that finds an echo in the claim that I've just tried to make. In a gesture that one finds repeatedly in his writings, usually towards the ends of his books—sometimes, indeed, on the final page—Agamben tries to keep open a space between law and life.[27] His governing Benjaminian thesis is that history is the creeping juridification of all areas of human life, where the law is identified with violence. For Agamben, there is an essential decline in the experience of faith from Pauline *pistis* to the forms of sacramental faith that emerged in the centuries after Paul. The history of theology—and perhaps theology itself, the science of the divine—is the reduction of faith to creedal dogma or the articles of a catechism. When this happens, as Agamben lets slip in one his typically elliptical asides, "The law stiffens and atrophies and relations between men lose all sense of grace and vitality."[28] In what is essentially a repetition of the reformational gesture—Marcionite or Lutheran—that I noted at the beginning of this chapter, Agamben finds that vitality of faith in Paul.

Agamben links faith to the experience of making an oath, the domain of what he calls "*pré-droit*" (pre-law).[29] Such an oath is a kind of pledge or what I called above a proclamation. It is something that one swears. In this pre-creedal, pre-juridical experience of faith, there is no split between belief in God the Father and God the Son, as in the Nicene Creed—even if they are two aspects of the same Trinitarian ontological substance. Furthermore, and crucially for Agamben, faith is not ontological at all. It is not faith that "Jesus *is* the Messiah," where the latter is a predicate of the former. Rather, faith is expressed in the more compressed pledge of the *Faktum*: "Jesus Messiah." Being is not something that we can predicate of Christ through a constative proposition or even Hegel's speculative copula. Rather, Jesus Messiah is something otherwise than Being or beyond essence, to coin a phrase.

Similarly, Jesus Messiah is beyond existence, or rather he is not proven through the fact of the historical Jesus. As Paul makes clear in Galatians, when Jesus Christ was revealed to Paul in order that he might preach amongst the Gentiles, "I did not confer with flesh and blood, nor did I go up to Jerusalem to those who were apostles before me" (Gal. 1:16–17). Rather, he disappeared into "Arabia," which scholars suggest refers to somewhere in modern Syria or Jordan. Thus, the experience of faith cannot be explained with reference to the category of being, whether conceived as essence or existence. As Agamben makes clear, between the words "Jesus" and "Messiah" there is no elbow room into which the copula might squeeze its way. Faith, then, is the performative force of the words "Jesus Messiah"—nothing more, but nothing less. This is what Agamben calls "the effective experience of a pure power of saying."[30]

Faith is a word, a word whose force consists in the event of its proclamation. The proclamation finds no support within being, whether conceived as existence or essence. Agamben links this thought to Foucault's idea of *veridiction* or truth-telling, where the truth lies in the telling alone.[31] But the thought could equally be linked to Lacan's distinction, inherited from Benveniste, between the orders of *énonciation* (the subject's act of speaking) and the *énoncé* (the formulation of this speech-act into a statement or proposition). Indeed, there are significant echoes between this idea of faith as proclamation and Levinas's conception of the Saying (*le Dire*), which is the performative act of addressing and being addressed by an other, and the Said (*le Dit*), which is the formulation of that act into a proposition of the form "S is P." We are dealing here, as we saw in the Introduction, with a performative idea of truth as *troth*, an act of fidelity or "being true to," rather than a propositional or empirical idea of truth.[32] Truth is conceived as what, in a rather nicely antiquated English, can be called "troth-plight," the faithful act of pledging or proclaiming.

Truth as troth has to be underwritten by love: the proclamation of faith is an act of betrothal where one affiances oneself to another and where the other is one's fiancé. This recalls the famous line of thinking from 1 Corinthians 13, where Paul insists that if faith is not underwritten by love, then "I'm a noisy gong or a clanging cymbal" (1 Cor. 13:1). The context here, of course, is the polemic against *glossolalia* or speaking in tongues that had seemingly crept into the Corinthian congregation. But if faith is a troth-plight that proclaims the calling of an infinite demand, then the proclamation has to be supported by love, which "bears all things, believes all things, hopes all things, endures all things" (1 Cor. 13:7). Faith without love is a hollow clanging that lacks the subjective commitment to endure. As Paul puts it in Galatians, "For in Christ Jesus neither circumcision nor uncircumcision is of any avail, but faith working through love" (Gal. 5:6). This is a point that Badiou makes well in his reading of Paul. If faith is the coming forth (*le surgir*) of the subject in the proclamation of an infinite demand, then love is the labor (*labeur*) of the subject that has bound itself to its demand in faith. Love is what gives consistency to a subject and which allows it to persevere with what Badiou always calls "a process of truth." Love, like faith, does not allow for copulative predication; it does not assemble predicates of the beloved as reasons for love. As Agamben insists, in a curious example (given the name of Jesus's mother), the lover says, "I love beautiful-brunette-tender Mary," not "I love Mary because she is beautiful, brunette, tender."[33] Love has no reason and needs none. If it did, it wouldn't be love.[34]

HEIDEGGER ON PAUL

Agamben explicitly places his interpretation of Paul under the sign of Benjamin's Messianism and wants to see Paul, in Scholem's words, as "a revolutionary Jewish mystic."[35] Such is what we might identify as a new quasi-reformational orthodoxy in the reading of Paul that one also finds in Boyarin and Taubes. Given the long bloody history of Christian anti-Semitism that often sought its justification in an interpretation of Paul, the new turn towards the Epistles rightly returns Paul to a radical Judaism. However, as should become clear, Agamben owes much more to Heidegger's reading of Paul than to Benjamin. I do not know—although one may guess—the reason why Agamben tries to play down his debt to Heidegger.

A biographical remark might shed some light here. Although a defective physical constitution prevented Heidegger from active combat in World War I and he served his time behind the lines in the battle of Verdun with the Meteorological Service, involved with the dangerous business of weather forecasting, the experience of the war had a significant metaphysical impact on the young philosopher. Heidegger might not have written epistles to various congregations, but his recently published letters to his wife make fascinating reading in this regard. Although his early letters to Elfriede Petri, from 1915–17, betray a saccharine sentimentality buoyed up with a rather priggish Catholicism and a voracious academic ambition, something dramatically changes in Heidegger when he's deployed in the field in 1918. Ostensibly, the question at stake in the letters from this period is whether their recently born son, Jörg, should be given a Catholic upbringing—like his father—or a Protestant one, like his mother. Heidegger doesn't just concede to Elfriede's request for a Protestant upbringing, he writes, "The decision has already been taken."[36] It is at this point that the language of "elemental existence" and "primitiveness of existence" begins to enter the vocabulary of Heidegger's letters for the first time. He also criticizes "the Catholic system's inner lack of freedom" and incapacity for a "free inner decision."[37]

In the final month of the war, Heidegger writes a vivid series of letters in which he criticizes the German political leadership for "hollow-eyed aimlessness" and argues that "people have been systematically nauseated by pan-German pipe-dreams."[38] At the same moment, Heidegger's language becomes distinctly Pauline, writing, "Only the young will save us now—& creatively allow a new Spirit to be made flesh in the world."[39] Throughout these letters, Heidegger speaks of the necessity for a "birth of the spirit," one of the very philosophemes that, early on in *Being and Time*, he would explicitly say must be avoided.[40] Appearing to allude directly to Paul, Heidegger writes of a return "to the essence of personal spirit, which I conceive as a 'calling'."[41] In his final wartime letter, he writes, "only through radicalism—complete commitment of the human being as a whole—will we ourselves advance as real revolutionaries of the spirit."[42] He goes on to criticize his comrades in the military for "bourgeois mediocrity" and wanting to see a sign of the "radically new." He concludes, suggestively, that "our effect will at first be limited to just small circles."[43] There is perhaps much that we could say about the destiny of these remarks in relation to Heidegger's future political commitment to National Socialism.[44]

Less than two months after his return from the war, on January 9, 1919, Heidegger wrote a letter to his friend and priest Father Engelbert Krebs, the same Catholic priest who performed his simple wartime marriage to Elfriede in 1917. Heidegger writes that his philosophical research has made "the *system* of Catholicism problematic and unacceptable to me." But he goes on to add, significantly: "but not Christianity and metaphysics—these, though, in a new sense." It is this "new sense" that Heidegger sought to develop in what he called his "investigations in the phenomenology of religion."[45] This is important: Heidegger does not reject Christianity and turn, like Nietzsche, to "the angry and coarse polemics of an apostate."[46] Rather, it leads him, in the lectures that began in 1920—although he was making detailed plans and notes on religion and mysticism from summer 1919 onwards—back to what he calls primordial, primal, or originary Christianity, *Urchristentum*. It leads to *The Phenomenology of Religious Life*, in which the emphasis should be placed on the intimate connection between the terms "religion" and "life." Primordial Christianity expresses an original experience of life in what Heidegger was beginning to call in this period *facticity*.

Heidegger's break with Catholicism in 1919 leads him, the following year, to Paul. The first thing to note here is the essential Protestantism of Heidegger's turn to Paul. He writes, in the context of his reading of Galatians, "There are real connections of Protestantism with Paul."[47] The obvious reference here is Luther, as Galatians was the Luther's favorite Epistle. It is in his commentary on Galatians that Luther asserts, "The truth of the Gospel is, that our righteousness comes by faith alone."[48] In his notes for a lecture course, "The Philosophical Foundations of Medieval Mysticism"—a course Heidegger never gave—he writes, with some Husserlian throat-clearing: "Protestant faith and Catholic faith are *fundamentally different*. Noetically and noematically separate experiences. In Luther an *original* form of religiosity breaks out."[49]

Heidegger's rejection of the systematic and dogmatic character of Catholicism leads him, then, to Paul via Luther. But this has to be combined with what we might call the "crypto-Harnackianism" of Heidegger's suspicion of the philosophical character of Catholicism.[50] "It is," Heidegger writes, "a decrease of authentic understanding if God is grasped as an object of speculation ... Greek philosophy penetrated into Christianity. Only Luther made an advance in this direction."[51]

Slightly later, when Heidegger is trying to uncover the original meaning of eschatology, he writes that its meaning "was covered up in Christianity, from the end of the First Century ... following the penetration of Platonic-Aristotelian philosophy."[52] Although these remarks anticipate what Heidegger will call some years later the need for a destruction of the ontological tradition, at this point he is simply borrowing Harnack's constant polemic against the philosophical interpretation of religious experience. For example, the German epigraph from Goethe von Eckermann that appears in the first volume of the *History of Dogma* begins as follows: "*Die Christliche Religion hat nichts in der Philosophie zu thun*" (The Christian religion has nothing to do with philosophy).[53] In the course of his many volumes, Harnack shows the degeneration of Pauline Christianity into Catholic creed, on the one hand, and various forms of speculative heresy, like Gnosticism, on the other. Luther's critique of Catholicism returns Christianity to its Pauline roots in the experience of faith. Such is the Harnackian dogma. The insistence on the anti-philosophical purity of faith leads Harnack to Marcion, to whom we will soon turn: crypto-Harnackianism is crypto-Marcionism, the possible dangers of which will, I hope, become clear.

The effects of crypto-Harnackianism can be felt in Heidegger's insistence that we must approach Christianity "not through a historical tradition, but through an original experience."[54] The words "historical tradition" are an implicit reference to Catholicism. Surprising as it might sound, this suspicion of philosophy and dogmatic tradition leads Heidegger to a Messianic reading of Paul, one which has strong similarities with Agamben—particularly on the question of Messianic time, as we will see below. Heidegger notes how "In the synoptic gospels, Jesus announces the kingdom of God (*e basileia tou theou*). In Pauline gospel, the proper *object of the proclamation is already Jesus himself as Messiah.*"[55] The defining character of Pauline experience is the proclamation of Jesus Messiah. What is at stake is an experience of faith that takes place in and as a proclamation.

The central concept in Heidegger's reading of Paul is enactment (*Vollzug*) and his question is the following: how is Christian life enacted? The first thing one notices here is the presupposition that life is something to be enacted: "The enactment of life is decisive."[56] Thus, life is not a given or constant condition for a human being, like biological life; it is, rather, the consequence of a decision. How is that decision made? As we have already intimated, it is made in a proclamation (*Verkündigung*), where the latter has the meaning of *euaggelion*, announcement or gospel. This proclamation is made in an epistle, which is defined by a sense of urgency in a context of crisis. In a way that is surprising to find in the early Heidegger, he is very interested in the literary form of the epistle, not for any aesthetic reasons, but because the letter is, as he puts it in a marginal note (and notice the recurrence of the language of decision), "the How of explication, concern appropriation of the enactmental understanding—decision!"[57] The proclamation is what enacts life. And the proclamation doesn't occur in a treatise, but in a letter. This is because time is short and the situation is critical.

Another key term that pervades Heidegger's reading of Paul is "anguish" (*Not*), which obviously anticipates the concept of *Angst* in *Being and Time*. The basic Pauline subjective attitude is anguished waiting. This anguish has a range of senses: first and foremost, it is anguish in relation to a calling. As I tried to show above, what defines Paul as Paul is the fact that he is called. This is the experience of so-called conversion that he addresses elliptically in Galatians and Second Corinthians. If Christian life is enacted in a proclamation, then what is proclaimed is a calling. Such is the core experience of faith.

Furthermore—and this will become important when we turn to Marcion—anguish is the only proof (*endeigma*) of the calling. Faith is not knowledge, nor is it justified with reference to the orders of essence and existence. Rather, anguish becomes the subjective mark of the calling. Faith, it should be stressed again, is not some passive state of bovine tranquility or even the contentment of theoretical conviction—some Christian variant on Aristotelian *eudaimonia*. It is an anguished waiting, where anguish is both the "proof" of the calling and what Heidegger calls its "obstinate" character.[58] What Heidegger admires in Paul is the obstinacy of his faith—what Taubes calls his zealotry—the fact that he persists in the face of an often terrible and finally fatal adversity. It is anguish that leads Paul to act, to intervene again and again in the life of the churches. Finally, anguish not only describes the condition in which "each stands alone before God."[59] It is also the anguish that Paul wants to induce in the readers or listeners of his Epistles in order to bring them to the decision of faith. If the Epistles are rightly addressed and they reach their audience, then they will create communities of anguish.

PAUL AND MYSTICISM

This brings us to an important issue, which picks up on the theme of the previous chapter: the relation between Paul and mysticism. What concerns Heidegger is Paul's apostolic proclamation of a calling, the infinite demand in relation to which his subjectivity is enacted. But what is essential to Paul's calling is that he does not celebrate or even communicate directly the experience of being called. Thus, it is not Paul's rapture that interests him or should interest us. On the contrary, it is Paul's refusal of rapture that is essential: his insistence that faith in the Messiah can only be experienced in weakness. This weakness is interpreted by Heidegger as the weakness of life itself: "Not mystical absorption and special exertion, rather withstanding the weakness of life is decisive (*der Schwachheit des Lebens wird entscheidend*)."[60]

This can also be connected with the passage that concludes Heidegger's lectures on Paul, in which he writes, "There remains a deep opposition between the Mystics and the Christians."[61] By "Mystics," Heidegger refers to the passage in First Corinthians in which Paul talks about imparting a "secret and hidden wisdom (*sophia*)" amongst the "mature" or "perfect" (*teleios*) (1 Cor. 2:7). This would allow for the kind of glorification of the soul and identification with the divine that we saw in Marguerite Porete. In such a pneumatic state of spiritual ecstasy, Heidegger writes, "The human being becomes God himself."[62] Heidegger refuses such an interpretation of Christianity, which he sees as hermetic, and claims that the Christian knows no such "enthusiasm," nor is she lost in some drunken, enraptured state. Rather, the Christian says, "Let us be awake and sober."[63]

Of course, we are touching lightly here on a vast theme in Pauline scholarship. Was Paul a mystic? Adolf Deissmann and Albert Schweitzer both thought so.[64] However, I find Martin Dibelius's argument much more convincing. In "Mystic and Prophet," he claims that Paul's piety is prophetic rather than mystical—although I think "apostolic" would be preferable to "prophetic," as the latter refers to the search for signs of the future coming of the Messiah, whereas for Paul the Messiah has come.[65] Also, Dibelius insists that Paul is never concerned with a mystical proof of Christ, but rather rests his faith on salvational history, a soteriology rooted in the real, datable, historical event of Christ's resurrection. It is certainly true that Paul always emphasizes a distance between himself and Christ, and that there is never any talk of a deification of the soul. Furthermore—and here is Paul's real difference with the female mystics like Porete, Julian of Norwich, or Teresa of Avila—there is no *fruitio dei* in Paul, no bodily *jouissance* or enjoyment of God. Paul suffers Christ in anxiety, rather than enjoying him.

That said, Paul's relation to mysticism is fascinating. Everything turns here on Paul's relation to his calling in First and Second Corinthians, and what we might call the peculiar logic of boasting. Paul admonishes the Corinthians in a very curious way. With regard to glossolalia, ecstatic experiences, and reports of secret initiations, Paul doesn't simply refuse these phenomena. For example, he writes that "I thank God that I speak in tongues more than you all," but goes on: "Nevertheless in church I would rather speak five words with my mind, in order to instruct others, than ten thousand words in a tongue" (1 Cor. 14:18–19). Glossolalia and other ecstatic practices are, Paul seems to suggest, egotistical and have to be distinguished from preaching the gospel, which is altruistic and directed towards the community of the church. So, mystical experience tends towards selfish boasting; on the other hand the universality of the gospel, which is addressed to all, is subordinated to the piety and purity of the few.

Mystics, Paul says, are boasters and fools. With exquisite anti-thetical eloquence, he asks the Corinthians to accept him as a fool, "So that I too may boast a little" (2 Cor. 11:16). Paul says, "I am talking like a madman" (2 Cor. 11:23), and begins to list his achievements in a US curriculum vitae style: "Are they Hebrews? So am I. Are they Israelites? So am I. Are they descendents of Abraham? So am I. Are they servants or slaves of Christ? I am a better one" (2 Cor. 11:22–3).

Then we hear stories of lashings, stonings, three shipwrecks, being marooned at sea, hunger, thirst, toil, insomnia, and danger everywhere: "Danger from rivers, danger from robbers, danger from my own people, danger from Gentiles, danger in the city, danger in the wilderness, danger at sea, danger from false brethren" (2 Cor. 11:26). That's quite a lot of danger. Then Paul adds, in a theme we have already encountered, "apart from other things, there is a daily pressure upon me of my anxiety for all the churches." He concludes, "Who is weak, and I am not weak?" (2 Cor. 11:28–9).

Paul, therefore, will boast —but only of those things that show his weakness. He then turns to his "visions and revelations of the Lord," which are recounted indirectly in the third person: "I know a man in Christ who fourteen years ago was caught up to the third heaven" (2 Cor. 12:2). Paul has therefore known ecstasy and glorification more than any of the pneumatic infiltrators into the Corinthian community. Paul insists he will only boast of his weakness because "a thorn was given me in the flesh" (2 Cor. 12:7) to keep him from being too elated. When he inquired of the Lord the reason for this weakness, he replied, "My grace is sufficient for you, for my power is made perfect in weakness" (2 Cor. 12:9). In place of any *gnosis* of the divine, the proclamation of faith is not knowledge but an orientation of the subject towards the happening of grace. The thorn in the flesh is the constant presence of anxiety, the call of conscience that prevents Paul from complacency and drives him on in his preaching—that is, in his political work.

The ultimate difference between Paul and mysticism is that between the two possible meanings of the words "in Christ," which we noted above: (i) the immanence of Christ in the soul; and (ii) membership in the waiting community. Although Paul never excludes the reality of mystical experience, it risks resulting in what we called above a politics of secession and abstraction, an egotistical boasting that ignores the centrality of the apostolic mission, the urgency of preaching as the means to forge waiting communities of resistance.

PAROUSIA AND THE ANTI-CHRIST

What about that waiting community? What does it await? How does it await? This takes us directly to the question of temporality. Heidegger has two working theses with respect to Paul: first, that primordial Christian religiosity is bound up with an experience of the enactment of life in the way we have described above. Second, he claims that Christian religiosity "lives time itself" (*lebt die Zeit selbst*).[66] Everything turns here on the interpretation of *parousia*, which can be variously translated as presence, arrival, or, more commonly, the second coming. Heidegger tackles this issue in his interpretation of Second Thessalonians, which some scholars consider apocryphally ascribed to Paul. The sense of *parousia* as the literal return of Christ doesn't interest Heidegger much. His concern is rather with the way in which *parousia* suggests a temporality irreducible to an objective, ordinary, or what Heidegger will call in *Being and Time* "vulgar" sense of time. That is, a temporality "without its own order and demarcations," the simple demarcations into past, present, and future.[67] Rather, *parousia* refers back to the idea of life as enactment: namely, that what gets enacted in the proclamation of faith is a certain relation to temporality. More specifically, this is temporality as a relation with *parousia* as a futurity that induces a sense of urgency and anguish in the present. In short, what we see in the interpretation of Paul is a foreshadowing of ecstatic temporality in *Being and Time*, where the primordial phenomenon of time is the future.

But it is the key insight into the finitude of time in *Being and Time* that reflects back so suggestively onto the reading of Paul. If, in Heidegger's magnum opus, time is finite because it comes to an end with death, then the end of time in Paul turns on the concept of *parousia* as the *eschaton*, understood as the uttermost, furthermost, or ultimate. The person "in Christ" proclaims in the present a relation to an already (the historicity of resurrection) and a not-yet which is uttermost (the futurity of *parousia*). Temporality is not a sequential line, but a finite unity of three dimensions. In another crypto-Harnackian gesture, Heidegger claims that this Pauline experience of the eschatological was already "covered up in Christianity" by the end of the first century AD, "following the penetration of Platonic-Aristotelian philosophy into Christianity."[68] By contrast—and here we can note a further quasi-Messianic moment in Heidegger—the original sense of the eschatological is "late Judaic (*spätjüdisch*), the Christian consciousness [being] a peculiar transformation thereof."[69] This suggestive reading would allow for a bringing together of Messianic temporality, rooted in the *ho nun kairos*, the time of the now, which Agamben links to Benjamin's idea of *Jetztzeit*, now-time, and Heidegger's conception of the *Augenblick*, the moment of vision—which, of course, was Luther's translation of *kairos* in Paul.

Christian life, Heidegger insists, is lived without security. It is a "constant insecurity"[70] in which the temporality of factical life is enacted in relation to what is uttermost, the *eschaton*. It is this sense of insecurity and anguish that is at the heart of Second Thessalonians. This is where the figure of *parousia* has to be connected with "the son of perdition," namely the Anti-Christ. Paul writes: "Now concerning the coming (*parousia*) of our Lord Jesus Christ and our assembling to meet him ... Let no one deceive you in any way; for that day will not come unless the rebellion comes

first and the man of lawlessness is revealed, the son of perdition"
(2 Thess. 2:1, 3).

The figure of the Anti-Christ massively heightens the sense of
anguish and urgency among the waiting community of believers.
He is the figure who opposes all forms of worship and proclaims himself God. In one passage where Paul begins to sound
like Marcion, the Anti-Christ is declared "the god of this world"
(2 Cor. 4:4). Heidegger links the Anti-Christ to what would
become, in the years to follow, the theme of falling, *das Verfallen*:
"The appearance of the Anti-Christ in godly robes facilitates the
falling-tendency of life (*die abfallende Lebenstendenz*)."[71] What is
almost being envisaged here by Heidegger is a conflict between
two divine orders: Christ and Anti-Christ. For Heidegger, the
Anti-Christ reveals the fallen character of the world, in relationship to which "each must decide," and "in order not to fall prey
to it, one must stand ever ready for it."[72] Heidegger adds, "The
decision itself is *very* difficult."[73]

What the figures of *parousia* and the Anti-Christ reveal is the
falling tendency of life in the world. In a marginal note to the
lecture course, Heidegger writes telegraphically of the "Communal
world (*Mitwelt*) as 'receiving' world into which the gospel *strikes*";
and again, "this falling tendency of life and attitude in communal-
worldly tendencies (wisdom of the Greeks)."[74] Our everyday life
in the world—what Heidegger will later call *das Man*—is revealed
to be *abfallend*, in the sense of both falling, dropping, or melting
away, but also becoming *Abfall*, waste, rubbish, or trash. This discloses a peculiar double logic: in proclaiming faith and enacting
life, the world becomes trash and we become the trash of the
world. The waiting community becomes the unwanted offscouring that is seen as garbage by the lights of Greek wisdom and sees,
in turn, the existing communal world as garbage.

AS NOT: PAUL'S MEONTOLOGY

Paul has one fundamental rule for all his communities: remain in the condition in which you were called. That is, "Let everyone lead the life which the Lord has assigned to him, and in which God has called him" (1 Cor. 7:17). He continues in the following passage, given here in the Revised Standard version (note the five repetitions of the words, *hos me*, that Heidegger translates with "as if not (*als ob nicht*)," but can be more literally rendered "as not"):

> The appointed time has grown very short; from now on, let those who have wives live as though they had none (*hos me*), and those that mourn as though they were not mourning (*hos me*), and those who rejoice as though they were not rejoicing (*hos me*), and those who buy as though they had no goods (*hos me*), and those who deal with the world as though they had no dealings with the world (*hos me*). For the form of this world (*to skema tou kosmou*) is passing away. (1 Cor. 7:29–32)

To say that this is an over-determined passage in recently published interpretations of Paul is an understatement. It plays a crucial role in Heidegger's reading of Paul, as we will see presently. But it is an equally pivotal passage for the interpretations of Taubes, Badiou, and Agamben.

In a way that decisively influences Agamben, Taubes tries to make a connection between the above passage from Paul and Benjamin's Messianism, in particular as it is expressed in the "Theologico-Political Fragment" from 1921, the same year as many of Heidegger's lectures on Paul.[75] Following the fault line between the Messianic and the profane, Benjamin concludes this fragment by declaring that profane world politics is *nihilism*. Seen from the Messianic standpoint, the surrounding communal world must be seen "as not." In Paul and Benjamin, Taubes concludes, "We have a nihilistic view of the world, and concretely on the

Roman Empire."[76] When Paul writes that the form or schema of this world is passing away, he is asserting his negative political theology against imperial power, a power that is nihilizing itself and must be nihilized.

Paul is preaching a *meontology*, an account of things that are not. Furthermore, his is a double meontology: on the one hand, the form of this world is passing away or falling away and becoming nothing. This is the nihilism of world politics. But, on the other hand, what will take the place of the "god of this world" is at present nothing. It is simply the anguished vigilance of the Messianic standpoint defined by its relation to the futurity of *parousia*. We are close here to how Badiou reads Paul's words from 1 Corinthians: "God has chosen the things that are not (*ta me onta*) in order to bring to nought those that are (*ta onta*)" (1 Cor. 1:28).[77] What Paul is preaching is not something that *is*— conceived politically, being is completely determined by the reality of the Roman Empire, which is the "state of the situation" in Badiou's jargon. Rather, Paul is announcing something that, in Badiou's terms, breaks with the order of being in the name of an event which is *not*. The event is something *indiscernible* in the situation, which is how Badiou defines the central concept of his work: the generic God has chosen the weak things of the world to confound the strong and the powerless to confound power. This is the compressed form of the double meontology: *God has chosen the things that are not in order to bring to nothing the things that are.* This is why we must become the filth of the world, the scum of the earth. Badiou's word for trash or garbage is *déchet*, which he links to *déchéance*, which means fall, downfall, decay, and translates as Heidegger's *das Verfallen*, but which also has overtones of abasement.[78]

How does one live in a world that is trash when one has declared oneself the trash of the world? One lives in it as if it were not, *hos me*. A waiting community, an anguished community, an abased community, an *ecclesia* of the wretched of the earth, living in the world as if it were not by attending to a call or demand that is not of this world. This brings us to the central claim of Agamben's reading of Paul. As noted above, Agamben wishes to read Paul's letters as the "fundamental Messianic text for the Western tradition."[79] His question is, "What does it mean to live in the Messiah, and what is the Messianic life?"[80] The answer is already clear: the Messianic life is lived *hos me*, as not. Agamben cites the final words of the above passage from Corinthians, in his translation, "For passing away is the figure, the way of being of the world," and continues: "In pushing each thing toward itself through the *as not*, the Messianic does not simply cancel out this figure, but it makes it pass, it prepares its end. This is not another figure or another world: it is the passing of the figure of this world."[81]

It is at this point that Agamben's reading of Paul crosses Heidegger's 1920–21 lectures. I would like to track three slippages in Agamben's reading of Heidegger that might lead us to question the former's critique of the latter. The first, minor slippage is where Agamben claims that Heidegger "briefly commented"[82] on the above passage from Corinthians on the *hos me*, whereas in truth it is the climax and culmination of his argument of the entire 1920–21 lecture course. Let's immediately note a second slippage, the consequences of which will, I hope, become clearer as we proceed. That which calls in Paul is the Messiah, and Heidegger's reading of Paul does not seek to eliminate the Messianic, but acknowledges it. Once Christians have been called and have enacted their faith and indeed their life in the proclamation "Jesus himself as Messiah,"[83] how should they comport themselves to the surrounding world, what was named above by Heidegger the *Mitwelt*? Heidegger notes firstly and rightly that "one must remain in the position in which you were called," which means that one must find a "new fundamental comportment" to the world. Heidegger then goes on: "The indeed existing (*daseienden*) significances of real life are lived *hos me*, as if not."[84]

A key term in Heidegger's reading of Paul is *genesthai*, infinitive of *gignomai*, to become, to happen, or to be born. Paul writes in

1 Corinthians, "Were you called being a bondservant? Don't let that bother you, but if you get an opportunity to *become* (*genesthai*) free, use it" (1 Cor. 7:21, my emphasis). Heidegger seems to understand *genesthai* in the sense of becoming (*Werden*) or having become (*Gewordensein*).[85] Thus, in Heidegger's view, Christians should remain in the state in which they were called, i.e. in which they have become what they are. As Heidegger makes clear, the becoming of the Christian is a *douleuein*, slavery before God. As Paul says above, if one was called to Christ as a slave and one gets the opportunity to become free, then so much the better. But one is exchanging one form of bondage for another: one may no longer be the possession of any man—but one is the possession of God.

Heidegger interestingly claims in passing that Nietzsche misunderstands Paul as an ethical thinker when "he accuses Paul of *ressentiment*. *Ressentiment* in no way belongs to this realm."[86] Rather, Paul must be understood ontologically, or, better, meontologically. This brings us back to the *hos me*, which Heidegger defines in the following way: "all surrounding-world relations must pass through the complex of enactment of having become (*Vollzugzusammenhang des Gewordenseins*)."[87] What this means is that one has to look at the world from the standpoint of what one has become through the enactment and the proclamation of faith.

To push back in a proclamation against our tendency to fall towards the world and look at things *hos me* is to see the world in a Messianic light, from the standpoint of redemption. But—and this is both crucial to the argument I want to develop here and also the third and most important slippage in Agamben's reading of Heidegger—that which we orientate ourselves towards in our enactment, namely, the infinite demand or calling, is not in our power. It exceeds human strength. It is something that cannot be willed. It is, of course, the work of grace. Heidegger writes: "The Christian is conscious that this facticity cannot be won out of his own strength, but rather originates from God—the phenomenon of the effects of grace."[88]

For Heidegger, the proclamation seeks to proclaim and the

enactment seeks to enact what is out of our reach: "The enactment exceeds human strength. It is unthinkable out of one's own strength. Factical life, from out of its own resources, cannot provide the motives to attain even the *genesthai*."[89] Our becoming is not something that we can become. It is not a decision that we can take. As Paul puts it with much greater economy in 1 Corinthians, "You are not your own" (1 Cor. 6:19).

In Heidegger, crucially, we see an affirmation of weakness, *asthenia*, which has significant consequences for how we think about the nature of authenticity and its relation to the inauthentic. We can rejoin Agamben at this point, when he writes: "It is through his reading of the Pauline *hos me* that Heidegger seems to first develop his idea of the appropriation of the improper as the determining trait of human existence."[90]

Looking forward to *Being and Time*, this means that the authentic has no other content than the inauthentic. Authentic existence is not something which, as Heidegger puts it, "floats above falling everydayness."[91] It is not the attainment of some new, transformed, transcendent state. To be authentic is simply to look at the inauthentic under a new Messianic aspect: as if it were not. As Agamben writes in *The Coming Community*: "Ethics begins only when the good is revealed to consist in nothing other than a grasping of evil and when the authentic and the proper have no other content than the inauthentic and the improper."[92]

However, what Agamben criticizes in Heidegger is that although the content of the authentic is the inauthentic, and the former is only a modification of the latter, this is nonetheless the way in which "everydayness is seized upon." What Agamben objects to is Heidegger's claim that existence can be subject to such a "seizure," "*Ergreifen*."[93] This can be linked to a later passage in *Being and Time*, where Heidegger talks of the "moment of vision" as gaining momentary "mastery" over the everyday.[94] Agamben concludes that, for Paul, the Messianic subject is "unable to seize hold of himself as a whole, whether in the form of an authentic decision or in Being-towards-death."[95]

There is no doubt that *Being and Time* is decisively marked by an aspiration towards wholeness and autarchy. From beginning to end, "Being" or *Dasein* is defined in terms of its potentiality or ability to be (*Seinkönnen*), with the emphasis on the *können*. Heidegger's explicit concern is with trying to get Dasein into view as a whole. This means, concretely, getting the end of Dasein into our grasp. As the end of Dasein is death, the limit in relation to which Dasein's authenticity is measured in *Being and Time* is being-towards-death. Thus, authenticity consists in appropriating one's finitude in an act of potentialization—or what we could call, in a more vulgar register, an act of will. Death is essentially my death, and the call of conscience, which is the internalization of finitude, is Dasein calling to itself. Dasein, defined as potency, is its own equal.

What makes Heidegger's reading of Paul so suggestive, which is something that Agamben inadvertently—or perhaps not—misses, is his marking of a limit to human potency. In speaking of an "enactment that exceeds human strength," Heidegger embraces a logic of grace which entails that the project of how to become oneself is out of one's reach. The human being is essentially impotentialized in its relation to the Messiah. The decision about who I am is not in my power, but only becomes intelligible through a certain affirmation of weakness. Authenticity is not so much a "seizing hold" as the orientation of the self towards something that exceeds oneself, namely the hetero-affectivity of an infinite demand that calls me. Freedom is not something I can confer on myself in a virile assertion of autarchy. It is something that can only be received through the acknowledgement of an essential powerlessness, a constitutive impotence. Freedom can only be received back once one has decided to become a slave and attend in the endurance of love—for love endures all things.

In his lectures on Paul, one feels the freshness and fervor of Heidegger's insights into facticity and temporality communicated through the passionate urgency that he finds in the Epistles.

For once, the young Heidegger lets go of the banisters of his commitment to Husserlian phenomenology and doesn't encumber his discourse with Kantian transcendentalist throat-clearing—or indeed Aristotelian noises about the inquiry into the manifold meanings of being. Rather, what emerges is a compelling account of the formation of the self in relation to a calling that exceeds it. Life is enacted in a proclamation whose activity cannot eliminate passivity. Furthermore, seen in the light of the heroic logic of autarchy that threatens to dominate the way in which human existence is conceived in *Being and Time*, the interpretation of Paul allows us to glimpse a reading of Heidegger that would be rooted in an affirmation of weakness. It might even allow us to imagine a conception of conscience as the mark or imprint of what Taubes calls "a profound powerlessness" in the human being.[96] Might such an approach permit the possibility of a new interpretation of *Being and Time*? I think so. What I am dreaming of here is Heidegger with a thorn in his flesh; a little bit Gentile, admittedly, but also a little bit Jewish, to cite Taubes.[97] Keeping Heidegger's reading of Paul constantly in mind, I will now turn to *Being and Time* and analyze the logic of the call of conscience and its essential impotence.

THE POWERLESS POWER OF THE CALL OF CONSCIENCE

At times, reading a classical philosophical text is like watching a floe break up during global warming. The compacted cold assurance of a coherent system begins to become liquid and great pieces break off before your eyes and begin to float free. To be a reader is either to try to keep one's footing as the ice breaks up, or to fall in the icy water and drown. This is true of every page of Heidegger's *Being and Time*. But it is nowhere truer than in his discussion of conscience in Division 2, which to my mind is the most interesting moment in the book. I want to try to show where the floe of fundamental ontology begins to crack.

What Heidegger is seeking in Division 2 is an authentic potentiality for being a whole, which turns on the question of the self. If
Dasein's inauthentic selfhood is defined in terms of *das Man*—the
they—and this is something over which I exert no choice, then
what Heidegger is after in Chapter 2, Division 2, is a notion of
authentic selfhood defined in terms of choice. So, I either choose
to choose myself as authentic or I am lost in the choiceless pub-
licness of *das Man*. Heidegger's claim is that this potentiality for
being a whole—for being authentic—is attested in the voice of
conscience.

Ontologically, says Heidegger, conscience discloses something:
it discloses Dasein to itself:

> If we analyse conscience more penetratingly, it is revealed as a call
> (*Ruf*). Calling is a mode of *discourse*. The call of conscience has
> the character of an *appeal* to Dasein by calling it to its ownmost
> potentiality-for-Being-its-Self; and this is done by way of
> summoning it to its ownmost Being-guilty.[98]

Conscience is a *Ruf*, a call. The call is a mode of *Rede*, a silent call,
and has the character of an *Anruf*, an appeal that is a summons or
a convocation (*Aufruf*) of Dasein to its ownmost Being-guilty. We
will see below what Heidegger means by guilt, which is something closer to *lack* in the Lacanian sense, or indebtedness, than
moral guilt or culpability. Heidegger insists that our understanding
of this call, hearing this call, unveils itself as wanting-to-have-a-
conscience, *Gewissenhabenwollen*. Adopting this stance, making this
choice, choosing to choose, is the meaning of *Entschlossenheit*: resoluteness or decidedness or being determined or possessing fixity
of purpose. Such is the basic shape of the argument in Chapter 2,
Division 2, and the terminology employed in it.

Heidegger argues that the call of conscience calls one away
from one's listening to the they-self, which is always described as
listening away, *hinhören auf*, to the hubbub of ambiguity. Instead,
one listens to the call that pulls one away from this hubbub to

the silent and strange certainty of conscience: "The call is from afar unto afar. It reaches him who wants to be brought back."[99] Hearing the call, the self turns away from the sound of the crowd in a movement of *conversio* that is opposed to the *aversio* of inauthentic life.[100]

To what is one called in being appealed to in conscience? To one's *eigene Selbst*, to one's own self. Conscience calls Dasein to itself in the call. What gets said in the call of conscience? Heidegger is crystal clear: nothing is said.

> But how are we to determine *what is said in the talk* that belongs to this kind of discourse? *What* does the conscience call to him to whom it appeals? Taken strictly, nothing. The call asserts nothing, gives no information about world-events, has nothing to tell. Least of all does it try to set going a "soliloquy" in the Self to which it has appealed. "Nothing" gets called to (*zu-gerufen*) this Self, but it has been *summoned* (*aufgerufen*) to itself—that is, to its ownmost potentiality-for-Being.[101]

The call contains no information, nor is it a soliloquy, like that of the ever-indecisive Danish prince. It is the summoning of Dasein to itself that occurs silently: "Vocal utterance ... is not essential for discourse, and therefore not for the call either; this must not be overlooked."[102] So, conscience discourses in the mode of silence, in and as *Verschwiegenheit*, reticence, which is given an extraordinary privilege in the discussion of discourse in *Being and Time*. Reticence is the highest form of discourse. One says most in saying nothing.

The logic of the call is paradoxical. On the one hand, the call of conscience that pulls Dasein out of its immersion and groundless floating in the world of *das Man* is nothing else than Dasein calling to itself, calling to itself by saying nothing. It is not God or my genes calling to me, it is me, myself and I. As we will see, this logic will become more complex.

But is it at all necessary to keep raising explicitly the question of *who* does the calling? Is this not answered for Dasein just as une-quivocally as the question of to whom the call makes its appeal? *In conscience Dasein calls itself.* This understanding of the caller may be more or less awake in the factical hearing of the call. Ontologically, however, it is not enough to answer that Dasein is *at the same time* both the caller and the one to whom the appeal is made. When Dasein is appealed to, *is* it not "there" in a different way from that in which it does the calling? Shall we say that its ownmost potentiality-for-Being-its-Self functions as the caller?

Indeed the call is precisely something which *we ourselves* have neither planned nor prepared for nor voluntarily performed, nor have we ever done so. "It" calls, against our expectations and even against our will. On the other hand, the call undoubtedly does not come from someone else who is with me in the world. The call comes *from me* and yet *beyond* me.[103] ("*Der Ruf kommt aus mir und doch über mich.*") It is this "über *mich*" (in which we find an unwit-ting echo of Freud's *Über-Ich* or super-ego, baptized into being in 1923, a few years prior to *Being and Time*) which is so uncanny, which happens against my will and is something that I do not voluntarily perform. Dasein is both the caller and the called, and there is no immediate identity between these two sides or faces of the call. How do we explain this? How do we explain this divi-sion at the heart of the call of conscience, "which *everyone* agrees that he hears,"[104] as Heidegger rather question-beggingly insists? Does everyone hear the call? A vast question. The least we can say is that those who do not hear the call are not truly Dasein, and beings that are non-Dasein might be defined by the inability to hear the call.

In order to explain the division within the call, Heidegger folds the analysis of the call structure back into the structure of care, which is the being of Dasein. The situation of Dasein being both the caller and called corresponds to the structure of Dasein as both authentic and inauthentic, as anxious potentiality-for-Being or freedom and thrown lostness in *das Man*; that is, Dasein is both in the truth and in untruth. So, insofar as I am a thrown project, I am both called and the caller. This takes Heidegger back to the theme of uncanniness that first appears in the discussion of anxiety earlier in *Being and Time*. Heidegger asks: what if this Dasein that finds itself, *sich befindet*, in the very depths of its uncanniness should be the caller of the call of conscience? This leads us to the idea of the alien or stranger voice, *die fremde Stimme*:

> In its "who," the caller is definable in a "worldly" way by *nothing* at all. The caller is Dasein in its uncanniness: primordial, thrown Being-in-the-world as the "not-at-home"—the bare "that-it-is" in *the nothing of the world* [my emphasis]. The caller is unfamiliar to the everyday they-self; it is something like an *alien* voice. What could be more alien to the "they," lost in the manifold world of its concern, than the Self which has been individualized down to itself in uncanniness and been thrown into the "nothing."[105]

What should be noted here is the repeated emphasis of the word "nothing" and the general strangeness of the claim that Heidegger is making. The call of conscience is the anxious *Unheimlichkeit* of not being at home in the *Heimlichkeit* of domesticity, but then this "not at home" is claimed to be the *nothing* of the world (the word "nothing" mistakenly appears in quotation marks in the Macquarrie and Robinson translation). The self is thrown into the nothing of the world, and into that nothing I hear the silent call that strikes me as alien. The situation is thus acutely Pauline: once I have heard the call, I look at everything as if it were not and I look at everything that is from the standpoint of that which is not—such is Paul's double meontology.

Strictly speaking—and this is the thought that I want to get at—the self is divided between two nothings: on the one hand, the nothing of the world; and, on the other, the nothingness of pure possibility revealed in being-towards-death. It is akin to Lacan's idea of being "between two deaths" in *The Ethics of Psychoanalysis*, but perhaps even more radical.[106] The self is nothing but the movement between two nothings, the nothing of thrownness and the nothing of projection. Which is to say that the uncanniness of being human, being a stranger to oneself, consists in a double *impotentialization*.

Heidegger insists that the uncanny call calls silently:

> The call does not report events; it calls without uttering anything. The call discourses in the uncanny mode of *keeping silent*. And it does this only because, in calling the one to whom the appeal is made, it does not call him into the public idle talk of the "they," but *calls* him *back* from this *into the reticence of his existent* potentiality-for-Being. When the caller reaches him to whom the appeal is made, it does so with a cold assurance which is uncanny but by no means obvious.[107]

Note the unsentimental quality of the appeal here, the uncanniness of cold assurance, *kalte Sicherheit*. Uncanniness pursues Dasein down into the lostness of its life in "the they," in which it has forgotten itself, and tries to arrest this lostness in a movement that Heidegger will call "repetition" (*Wiederholung*). It is only in the self's repetition to itself of itself that it can momentarily pull clear of the downward plunge of *das Man*. When the self ceases to repeat itself, it forgets and ceases to be itself.

THE NULL BASIS–BEING OF A NULLITY: DASEIN'S DOUBLE IMPOTENCE

What does the uncanny call give one to understand? Conscience's call can be reduced to one word: "Guilty!"[108] But what does Dasein's guilt really mean? It means that because Dasein's being is thrown projection, it always has its being to be. That is, Dasein's being is a lack: it is something *due* to Dasein, a debt that it strives to make up or to repay. This is the ontological meaning of *Schuld*, which means guilt, wrong or even sin, but can also mean debt. To be *schuldig* is to be guilty or blameworthy, but it also means to give someone their due, to be owing, to be in someone's debt. *Schulden* are debts, which have a material origin, as Nietzsche shows convincingly in the *Genealogy of Morals*.[109] Life is a series of repayments on a loan that you didn't agree to, with ever-increasing interest, and which will cost you your life—it's a death-pledge, a *mort*-gage. As Heidegger perhaps surprisingly writes, although it should be recalled that he was writing in extremely troubled economic times in Germany, "Life is a business, whether or not it covers its costs."[110] Debt is a way of being. It is, arguably, *the* way of being. This is why credit, and the credence in credit, its belief structure, is so important.

Heidegger runs through the various meanings of guilt, understood as having debts, being responsible for, or owing something to another. Although this would require separate analysis, it is fascinating to watch Heidegger try to separate his own conception of guilt from the usual concept of guilt as responsibility to others, or from any idea of guilt understood in relation to law or the *Sollen*, the Kantian "ought" that Hegel criticizes and whose critique Heidegger implicitly follows. Heidegger, of course, is trying to get at an ontological meaning of guilt and to avoid the usual legal or moralistic connotations of the word. What he is aiming for is a pre-ethical or pre-moral understanding of guilt—or perhaps an originary ethical understanding of guilt. It is at this point that we confront some of the most radical passages in *Being and Time*.

As Heidegger tirelessly insists, Dasein is a thrown basis (*ein geworfene Grund*). It projects forth on the basis of possibilities into which it has been thrown. This is also to say, as we will now see, that Dasein is a *null* basis. He writes, and the German is dense and difficult to render here:

In being a basis—that is, in existing as thrown—Dasein constantly lags behind its possibilities. It is never existent *before* its basis, but only *from* it and *as this basis*. Thus "Being-a-basis" means *never* to have power over one's ownmost Being from the ground up. This "not" belongs to the existential meaning of "thrownness." It itself, being a basis is a nullity of itself. "Nullity" does not signify anything like not-Being-present-at-hand or not-subsisting; what one has in view here is rather a "not" which is constitutive for this *Being* of Dasein—its thrownness. The character of this "not" as a "not" may be defined existentially: in being its *Self*, Dasein is, *as* a Self, the entity that has been thrown. It has been *released* from its basis, *not through* itself but *to* itself, so as to be *as this basis*. Dasein is not itself the basis of its Being, inasmuch as this basis first arises from its own projection; rather, as Being-its-Self, it is the *Being* of its basis.[111]

The claim is that Dasein is a nullity of itself. Dasein understood as being a basis means that it does not have power over itself. Dasein is the experience of nullity with regard to itself. The potentiality for being-a-whole which defines Dasein's power of projection is revealed to be an impotentialization, a limit against which it runs, and over which it has no power. It is the impotence of Dasein that most interests me. As we will see, it is a double impotence.

As a thrown basis, Dasein constantly lags behind its possibilities. As Heidegger writes above, "In being a basis (*Grund-seiend*)— that is, in existing as thrown [*als geworfenes existierend*—another of Heidegger's enigmatic formulae]—Dasein constantly lags behind its possibilities." The experience of guilt reveals the being of being human as a lack, as something wanting. The self is not just the ecstasy of a heroic leap towards authenticity energized by the experience of anxiety and being-towards-death. Such would be the heroic reading of the existential analytic—and I do not doubt that this may well have been Heidegger's intention—that sees its goal in a form of *autarchy*: self-sufficiency, self-mastery, or what Heidegger calls "self-constancy" (*Die Ständigkeit des Selbst*[112]). Rather, on my view, the self's fundamental self-relation is to an unmasterable thrownness, the burden of a facticity that weighs me down without my ever being able to fully pick it up. This is why

I seek to evade myself. I project or throw off a thrownness that catches me in its throw and inverts the movement of possibility by shattering it against impotence. I am always too late to meet my fate.

Dasein is a being suspended between two nothings, two nullities: the nullity of thrownness and the nullity of projection. This is where Heidegger's text is at its most extreme:

> Not only is the projection, as one that has been thrown, determined by the nullity of Being-a-basis; as *projection* it is itself essentially *null*. This does not mean that it has the ontical property of "inconsequentiality" or "worthlessness"; what we have here is rather something existentially constitutive for the structure of the Being of projection. The nullity we have in mind belongs to Dasein's Being-free for its existentiell or worldly possibilities. Freedom, however, *is* only in the choice of one possibility—that is, in tolerating one's not having chosen the others and one's not being able to choose them.
>
> In the structure of thrownness, as in that of projection, there lies essentially a nullity. This nullity is the basis for the possibility of *in*authentic Dasein in its falling; and as falling, every inauthentic Dasein factically is. *Care itself, in its very essence, is permeated with nullity through and through.* Thus "care"—Dasein's Being—means, as thrown projection, Being-the-basis of a nullity (and this Being-the-basis is itself null). This means that *Dasein as such is guilty*, if our formal definition of "guilt" as "Being-the-basis of a nullity" is indeed correct.[113]

Dasein is a double nullity. It is simultaneously constituted and divided around this double nullity. This is the structure of thrown projection and the ontological meaning of guilt. That is, Dasein is guilty; it is indebted doubly; it is null at the heart of its being; it is essentially doubly lacking. Thrown projection means: *das nichtige Grund-Sein einer Nichtigkeit*, the null basis-being of a nullity. And this is nothing less than the *experience* of freedom. As Heidegger writes above, freedom is the choice of the one possibility of being: in choosing oneself and not the others. But what one is choosing in such a choice is the nullity of a projection that projects on the nullity of a thrown basis, over which one has no power. Freedom is the assumption of one's ontological guilt, of the double nullity that one is.

Heidegger goes on to show that this existential-ontological meaning of guilt is the basis for any traditional moral understanding of guilt. Heidegger's phenomenology of guilt—like Nietzsche's in the *Genealogy of Morals*—claims to uncover the deep structure of ethical subjectivity which cannot be defined by morality, since morality already presupposes it. Rejecting any notion of evil as *privatio boni*, Heidegger's claim is that guilt is the pre-moral source for any morality. It is beyond good and evil. Is guilt bad? No. But neither is it good. It is simply what we are. We *are* guilty. Such is Kafka's share of eternal truth.

Heidegger brings together a large number of the themes discussed above and returns to the question of uncanniness:

> In uncanniness Dasein stands together with itself primordially. Uncanniness brings this entity face to face with its undisguised nullity, which belongs to the possibility of its ownmost potentiality-for-Being. To the extent that for Dasein, as care, its Being is an issue, it summons itself as a "they" which is factically falling, and summons itself from its uncanniness towards its potentiality-for-Being. The appeal calls back by calling forth: it calls Dasein *forth* to the possibility of taking over, in existing, even that thrown entity which it is. It calls Dasein *back* to its thrownness so as to understand this thrownness as the null basis which it has to take up into existence. This calling-back in which conscience calls forth, gives Dasein to understand that Dasein itself—the null basis for its null projection, standing in the possibility of its Being—is to bring itself back to itself from its lostness in the "they"; and this means that it is *guilty*.[114]

Guilt has been shown to be the innermost meaning of Dasein's being, its very movement, its *kinesis*. Here and indeed elsewhere in his work, Heidegger is simply trying to think *kinesis* as the rhythm of existence and ultimately the rhythm of being itself. This movement, which is the movement of thrown projection—or what I prefer to call "thrown throwing off"—is the structure of the call, which "calls back by calling forth." It calls Dasein forth to take over its potentiality for being by taking it back to its thrownness and taking it over.

Look closely at Heidegger's words in the last quotation: Dasein is the *nichtiger Grund seines nichtigen Entwurfs*, the null basis for its null projection. That is, Dasein is a double nothing, a double zero. This is the meaning of thrown projection. Guilt is the kinesis of this nullity, a movement *vor und zurück*, back and forth—or to and fro, as Beckett might say. Such is the strangeness of what it means to be human, the uncanniness of being brought face to face with ourselves. As Heidegger writes in *Introduction to Metaphysics*, "Dasein is the happening of strangeness."[115] The human being is the utter strangeness of action between two nothings. The self is a potentiality for being whose sole basis, limit, and condition of possibility is a double nothing, a double impotentialization, which of course is to say that it is also its condition of impossibility, an existential quasi-transcendental. Impotence—finally—is what makes us human. We should wear it as a badge of honor. It is the signal of our weakness, and nothing is more important or impotent than that.

Heidegger insists that Dasein does not load guilt onto itself. It is in its being already guilty. Dasein is guilty, always already, but what changes in being-authentic is that Dasein *understands* the call or appeal of conscience and takes it into itself. Dasein as authentic comes to understand itself as guilty. Which means that Dasein as potent comes to understand itself as impotent. The human being is essentially marked by inauthenticity. All that changes in being authentic is that the way in which we experience the inauthentic is modified. But in undergoing such modification, Dasein has somehow chosen itself, *er hat sich selbst gewählt*, as Heidegger writes.[116] This means that what is chosen is not having a conscience, which Dasein already has *qua* Dasein, but what Heidegger calls *Gewissen-haben-wollen*, wanting to have a conscience. This is a second-order wanting, what we might describe as *wanting to want the want that one is.* This requires an ontic or existentiell decision:

> *Wanting to have a conscience is rather the most primordial existentiell presupposition for the possibility of factically coming to owe something.* In understanding the call, Dasein lets its ownmost Self *take action in itself* (*in sich handeln*) in terms of that potentiality-for-Being which it has chosen. Only so can it be answerable (*verantwortlich*).[117]

Thus, answerability or responsibility consists in hearing and assuming the call, in wanting to have a conscience. This choice, Dasein's choice of itself, is—in Heidegger's strange phrasing—taking action in itself. As Heidegger will remind us after World War II, "We are still far from pondering the essence of action decisively enough."[118] The word "action" is one that Heidegger uses in *Being and Time*, but one which he also continually reminds us that he wants to avoid. Such—as Derrida taught us—is the logic of Heidegger's avoidances.[119] But what might action mean as conceived in relation to the double nullity we have described? What might potentiality for being mean when its condition of possibility and impossibility is a double impotentialization? Mastery opens onto slavery, grasping gives way to receiving that over which one has no power. Action in the world requires an acknowledgement of weakness. Its strength *is* its weakness, as Paul might say. Such a conception of action might be called tragic, or better, tragicomic. As one of Beckett's gallery of moribunds, Molloy, asks himself, tongue firmly in his cheek, "From where did I get this access of vigour? From my weakness perhaps."[120]

CRYPTO-MARCIONISM

I would like now to return to the question of faith with which I began, and to turn the inquiry in a rather different direction. As noted above, in his commentary on Galatians, Luther famously writes: "The truth of the Gospel is, that our righteousness comes by faith alone."[121] The return to Paul that defines the movement of reformation is a return to the purity and authority of faith. As such, Luther draws the strongest of contrasts between faith and law: "Law only shows sin, terrifies and humbles; thus it prepares us for justification and drives us to Christ."[122] The effects of this radical distinction between faith and law in the constitution of Christian anti-Semitism, where the Jews are always identified with law, are well known and do not need to be rehearsed here.[123]

My question here concerns the relation between faith and law in Paul, and what is involved in the affirmation of a radical Paulinism that would be based on faith alone. In the history of Christian dogma, this is the risk of Marcionism, which I will unpack presently. It is, to quote Socrates, a fine risk, but one that ultimately has to be refused. My other concern is with the way in which a certain ultra-Paulinism asserts itself in figures like Agamben, Heidegger, and Badiou that might lead one to conclude that the contemporary return to Paul is really a return to Marcion.

As Taubes writes, there are two ways out of Paul:

(i)   The Christian church itself in its early centuries, the tradition of Peter; and,

(ii) Marcionism, which posed the greatest political threat to emergent Catholic Christianity, particularly in the latter half of the second century.

Marcion (c.85–160), like Paul, was a gifted organizer and a tenacious creator of churches. His followers were extremely numerous and lived in communities, in some cases whole villages, until the time of their persecution under Constantine in the fourth century. Marcionite communities reportedly endured as late as the tenth century. For Marcion, Paul was the only true apostle—and Marcion was his true follower. He called himself "Presbyteros," leader of the true followers of the true apostle. For Marcion, the core of Paul's proclamation is the separation between the orders of faith and law, grace and works, spirit and flesh. Marcion radicalizes the antithetical form of Paul's thought—his only known work is called *The Antitheses*, which is roughly dated to 140 AD—to the point of cutting the bond that ties creation to redemption. And Marcion is surely right here: creation plays a very small role in Paul and his constant preoccupation is redemption. Therefore, as Taubes notes: "The thread that links creation and redemption is a very thin one. A very, very thin one. And it can snap. And that is Marcion. He reads—and he knows how to read!—the father of Jesus Christ is *not* the creator of heaven and earth."[124]

As Harnack shows in his obsessive and oddly moving book— fifty years in the making—*Marcion: The Gospel of the Alien God*, Marcion cuts the ontological link that ties creation to redemption and establishes an ontological dualism.[125] The God of creation, whom Paul suggestively calls "the God of this world," is distinct from the God of redemption, the God who is revealed through and as Jesus Christ. In opposition to the known God of the Hebrew Bible, Christ is the unknown God, the radically new God. No word is more frequently used in Marcion's *Antitheses* than the epithet "new," and any critique of Marcion can be turned against the obsession with the figure of novelty in recent philosophical readings of Paul. The unknown God is the true God, but an alien God: apparently, in Marcionite churches, Christ was called "the Alien" or "the good Alien."[126] This means that God enters into the world as an outsider, a stranger to creation.

Marcion radicalizes the Pauline distinction between grace freely given and righteousness based on works, and attaches them to two divine principles: the righteous and wrathful God of the Old Testament, and the loving and merciful God of the Gospel. Of course, this sounds like Gnosticism, but crucially there is no *gnosis* for Marcion. In his *History of Dogma*, Harnack identifies *gnosis* with an "intellectual, philosophic element," namely some sort of intellectual intuition of the divine.[127] When Harnack calls something "philosophical," it is hardly a word of praise. It is rather to reduce religion to the categories of Hellenistic philosophy— and we have seen Heidegger echo this Harnackian gesture in his reading of Paul. In Harnack's view, Marcion cannot be numbered among the Gnostics because he places the entire emphasis on faith and not on any form of *gnosis*: "It was Marcion's purpose there-fore to give all value to faith alone, to make it dependent on its own convincing power, and avoid all philosophic paraphrase and argument."[128]

The consequence of this ontological dualism is dramatic: the alien God, being separate from the God of this world, frees human beings from the creator and his creation. For Marcion, as Harnack writes, "The God of the Jews, together with all his book, the Old Testament, had to become the actual enemy."[129] Marcion refused the syncretism of Old and New Testaments, as well as all allegorical forms of interpretation that understand the latter as the fulfillment of the former. Allegorically understood— and this is the core of Marcion's critique of the Apostolic Fathers like Clement of Rome and Ignatius of Antioch—Christianity is the fulfillment of Judaism.[130] By contrast, the two testaments need to be rigorously separated, and this is what Marcion did in what was the very first attempt, allegedly completed around 144 AD, to produce an authentic edition of the Old and New Testaments. The former was included in its entirety and treated as historical fact. The New Testament, on the other hand, included some expur-gated versions of Paul's Epistles and one Gospel, that of Luke: as Marcion stated, "One must not allegorize the Scripture."[131] For Marcion, the Christianity of the Apostolic Fathers was a Jewish Christianity—which is, of course, the criticism that Paul levels at Peter and at the Jerusalem Church. Emergent Christianity had, in Marcion's eyes, poured new wine into old wineskins. In so doing, the Catholic Church lost the radicality of the Gospel by seeing it continually in the rear-view mirror of the Old Testament. The formation of the Christian Biblical canon is a direct response to the text that Marcion created, and to that extent it is directly due to his alleged heresy. The very existence of the emergent Catholic Church depended on showing the concordance between the Old and New Testaments—hence the centrality of allegorical interpretation in Catholic doctrine.

There is a Marcionite saying: "One work is sufficient for our God; he has delivered man by his supreme and most excellent goodness, which is preferable to the creation of all the locusts."[132]

Once the thread connecting creation to redemption has been cut, therefore, the task of the Christian is no longer to love creation, but to separate oneself from it as radically as possible. The world is the prison cell of the creator God and it is full of vermin, locusts, and mosquitoes. There is a story of a 90-year-old Marcionite who washed himself each morning in his own saliva, in order to have nothing to do with the works of the evil, creator God.[133] In order to loosen the hold that the creator has upon us through the body, Marcion advocated a severe ascetic ethic, which forbade all marriage and sexual intercourse amongst his believers following baptism. In Harnack's words, for Marcion marriage was "filthy" and "shameful."[134] This is simply a radicalization of Paul when he says that because "form of this world is passing away," those who have wives should "act if it they had none," adding that "He who marries does well" but that "He who refrains from marriage will do better" (1 Cor. 7:29, 31, 38). Marriage, sex, and the whole business of the body are mere fleshly distractions from the urgency of the spiritual task at hand. Because "The appointed time has grown very short" (1 Cor. 7:29), the little time that remains should not be wasted on anything that draws the spirit back to the flesh of creation. Taubes writes of Marcionism: "It's a church with a radical mission that can't rest on its laurels as a people's church ... It's a church that practices, or executes, the end of the world."[135] The essence of Marcionism is constant activism: if followers are not permitted to reproduce, then the growth of the church can only be based on the continual winning of new converts.

Harnack—and this is the implicit agenda of his book—sees Marcion as a second-century Luther, a powerful intellect possessed of a prodigious reforming zeal. Marcion was the first Protestant. Cutting the bond between philosophical dogma and the religious experience of faith, he accused the existing church of heresy. In Marcion's eyes, Paulinism represented a great revolution that had, already at the beginning of the second century, been betrayed and that required reformation. The core of this reformation consisted in asserting the radicality of the Pauline distinction between law and faith, and asserting that grace alone was the purest essence of the Gospel. Taubes thinks that Marcion's adoption of dualism is an error, but an "ingenious" one that is consistent with a certain ambivalence in Paul as he conceives the relation between creation and redemption.[136] For Harnack to adapt Hegel's dying words—Marcion is the only one who understood Paul and he misunderstood him. But the conclusion that Harnack wants to draw from his study of Marcion is dramatic: that the Old Testament should be rejected. For Protestantism, Harnack insists, the Old Testament is "the consequence of a religious and ecclesiastical crippling."[137] Harnack wants to defend a radical fideism, where Christianity is nothing but faith in God's revelation in Christ.

Odd though it might sound, I think Agamben's reading of Paul is crypto-Marcionite in its emphasis on a radically antinomian conception of faith. For example, in the "Fifth Day" of his interpretation of Paul, Agamben focuses on the verb *katargeo*, which he wants to translate as "to render inoperative or inactive" or, most revealingly, "to suspend," which recalls our discussion above of *iustitium*.[138] Agamben implicitly links *katargeo* to the state of exception in Schmitt, where the sovereign is he who suspends the operation of the law. Agamben characterizes the Messianic as a lawlessness that, in a sovereign political act, suspends the legality and legitimacy of both Rome and Jerusalem. He backs this up with a willful reading of the idea of the figure of *anomia* or lawlessness in Second Thessalonians.[139] To my mind, it is more than simply arguable that Paul's reference to the "mystery of lawlessness" refers back to the "son of perdition," the Anti-Christ, who will appear prior to the *parousia* of the Messiah (2 Thess. 2:3–7). But Agamben wants to identify lawlessness with the Messianic in order to radicalize the distinction between law and life, a Benjaminian theme present throughout Agamben's writings: if law is violence and the history of law is the history of such violence—which has led to the present situation of what Agamben calls "global civil war"—then the Messianic occurs as the revolutionary suspension of law.[140] There are moments when Agamben seems to want to push Benjamin's Messianism towards a radical dualism of, on the one hand, the profane order of the created world and, on the other hand, the Messianic order of redemption. As we saw above, Agamben writes of "law in its nonrelation to life and life in its nonrelation to law."[141] But this is Marcion, not Paul.

Badiou gives a brief but compelling discussion of Marcion in his book on Paul. Although Badiou insists that Marcion's ontological dualism is "an instance of manipulation"[142] and cannot be based on any consistent reading of Paul, he nonetheless recognizes that "By pushing a little, one could arrive at Marcion's conception: the new gospel is an absolute beginning."[143] But isn't Badiou's position precisely that of Marcion? In opposition to Pascal's Old Testament reliance on "prophecies, which are solid and palpable proofs," Badiou asserts, "There is no proof of the event; nor is the event a proof."[144] For Paul there is only faith, and Badiou's basic claim is that fidelity to the event is what breaks with the order of being. Badiou continues: "For Paul, the event has not come to prove something; it is *pure beginning*."[145] What, though, is this "pure beginning" but the "absolute beginning" that Badiou attributes to Marcion? Might we not conclude that Badiou's ontological dualism of being and the event, where the latter is always described as the absolutely new and where Badiou sees his project as the attempt to conceptualize novelty, is a Marcionite radicalization of Paul? In his insistence on the Pauline figure of Christ as the experience of an event that provokes subjective fidelity, is there not an essential disavowal of law and the ineluctable character of the facticity of being-in-the-world?

There is also something Marcionite in Heidegger's reading of Paul. In the decades after Marcion's death, the splendidly reactionary Tertullian famously lambasted the Marcionite church for providing no proof for their views. But that is precisely Marcion's point: to avoid all reliance on Old Testament prophecy, philosophical argument, theological conceptualization, or even *gnosis*. Christianity must be based on faith alone. In a marginal note to his lecture course on Paul, Heidegger suggestively writes that proof (*Beweis*) lies "Not in having-had insight (*im Eingesehen-haben*); rather, the proclamation is 'showing' (*apodeixis*) of the 'spirit,' 'force' ('*Kraft*')."[146]

That is, the proof of faith lies only in the showing of the spirit in a proclamation which is a kind of force or power. To demand a proof for faith is to misunderstand faith's very nature. As I suggested above, there is an ultra-Protestantism at work in Heidegger's reading of Paul which is crypto-Harnackian in its refusal of the influence of Plato, Aristotle, and Hellenistic philosophy, and in its attempt to recover an *Urchristentum* against the dogmatic system of Catholicism.

However, although Heidegger wants to affirm what I have identified as a Messianic experience of faith as enactment in Paul, this has to be distinguished from Agamben's more radical antinomianism. As we have seen, authenticity for Heidegger culminates in an experience of *kairos*, but it consists in nothing else but seeing inauthentic, fallen everyday life in the world in a different light. Heidegger does not believe in the possibility of a radical faith that would absolutely break with the world. Law and life always remain in a relation of *modification* (*Modifikation*), which is in many ways the key concept in *Being and Time*.[147] The proclamation of faith always moves within the gravity of the inauthentic everydayness against which it pulls. The "nothing" of projection only projects from the "nothing" of a thrown basis that cannot be thrown off—the law of facticity is inexorable.

Marcionism has a great lure. Its ontological dualism and its separation of creation from redemption allows us to attribute all that is wrong with the world (locusts, mosquitoes, etc.) to the activity of the bad deity, rather than blaming ourselves through the standard Christian narrative of the fall, death, and original sin. The idea that religion consists in faith alone—as a subjective feature that is not based in any *gnosis* or intellectual intuition, and for which there can be no proof—has an undeniable power. It is the power of radical novelty, of an absolute or pure beginning. On the one hand it fosters a conception of faith as a testing self-responsibility, while on the other hand holding out the possibility that we might be entirely remade, renewed, and redeemed: born again.

Yet Marcionism has to be refused. Its dualism leads to a rejection of the world and a conception of religion as a retreat from creation. At its most extreme it encourages a politics of secession from a terminally corrupt world, of the kind that we saw above in variants of mystical anarchism, the heresy of the Free Spirit and the neo-insurrectionism of the Invisible Committee. Marcionism becomes a theology of alien abduction. As Harnack writes—half-longingly—in the final pages of his book, Marcion "calls us, not out of an alien existence in which we have gone astray and into our true home, but out of the dreadful homeland to which we belong into a blessed alien land."[148]

Much as we might sometimes desire it—and this desire fills so much of our cultural void, from science fiction to Hollywood's constant obsession with aliens which finds its most consummate ideological expression in James Cameron's 2009 *Avatar*—it is precisely the desire for a blessed alien land that has to be rejected.

FAITH AND LAW

For Paul, we don't escape from the law. This is also why Paul's Jewishness is essential. If the law was not fully within me, as the awareness of my fallenness and consciousness of sin, then faith as the overcoming of the law would mean nothing. If, with Marcion and Harnack, we throw out the Old Testament, then we attempt to throw away our thrownness and imagine that we can distance ourselves from the constitutive flaw of the law, from our onto-logical defectiveness. If we throw out the Old Testament, then we imagine ourselves perfected, without stain or sin. If we were ever to attain such a state, faith would mean nothing. Faith is only pos-sible as the counter-movement to law and the two terms of the movement exist in a permanent dialectic. There is no absolute beginning and the idea of life without a relation to law is a purist and slightly puerile dream.

This, I think, is what Paul shows in the sinuous complexity of Romans 7 and 8. The question in Romans 7 concerns the nature of the relation between the law and sin. Paul writes: "If it had not been for the law, I should not have known sin" (Rom. 7:7). He gives the example of coveting, that we would never have known what it is to partake in the sin of coveting if the law had not said "Thou shalt not covet" (Rom. 7:7). There is only sin in relation to the law and without the law: "sin lies dead." Paul goes on: "I was once alive apart from the law," meaning that there was a time prior to the law when human beings lived in paradise without sin (Rom. 7:9). "But when the commandment came," namely the prohibition not to eat of the tree of knowledge of good and evil, we erred and fell. As Paul puts it, "sin revived and I died" (Rom. 7:9). Therefore, the very commandment which promised life proved to bring death. But is that to say—and this is where things begin to get nicely tangled—that the law, which is holy and by defini-tion good, as it comes from God, brings death? "By no means!" Paul adds. It is rather that the law reveals negatively the sinfulness of sin, in order that "sin might be shown to be sin" and "become

sinful beyond measure" (Rom. 7:12). For—and here we confront
the extent of the antithesis between flesh and spirit—"the law is
spiritual; but I am carnal, sold under sin" (Rom. 7:14).

This dialectic between law and sin has the dramatic consequence
that "I do not understand my own actions" (Rom. 7:15). That is,
I do not do the thing that I want, to follow the law. Rather I do
the thing that I hate, namely sin. But if I do not do the thing that I
want, but do the thing that I hate, then what can we say of this "I"?
How might we characterize such a self? Such a self is a "dividual,"
radically divided over against itself in relation to the law. Sin is the
effect of the law and my being is split between the law and sin. As
Paul puts it at his oxymoronic best: "For I do not do the good I
want, but the evil I do not want is what I do" (Rom. 7:19). That
part of the self that does what I do not want is attributed to sin:
"It is no longer I that do it, but sin that dwells within me" (Rom.
7:17). The self is here radically divided between flesh and spirit.
On the one hand there is "my delight in the law of God," which
belongs to my "inmost self" (Rom. 7:22). But, on the other hand,
"I see another law at war with the law of my mind" (Rom. 7:23).
This outermost self "dwells in my members" (Rom. 7:23). But
inmost and outermost are not two selves, but two halves of the
same self, which is divided against itself: "*Talaiporos ego anthropos*,"
Paul exclaims, "Wretched man that I am!" (Rom. 7:24). The dialectic of law and sin is fatal and it divides the self from itself. How,
then, can this dialectic be broken? Or, as Paul puts it, "Who will
deliver me from this body of death?" (Rom. 7:24).

The answer, of course, is "Thanks be to God through Jesus
Christ our Lord!" (Rom. 7:25). But what does that mean? Of
course, what is stake here is salvation through grace, which is precisely what cannot be willed by the self. The self, by itself, cannot
be delivered from the body of death and the fatal dialectic of law
and sin. It is only through God sending his son in the likeness of
the flesh, and therefore in the likeness of sin and death, that sin
and death can be overcome. But—and this is crucial—it is not a
question, for Paul, of an Agambenian *anomia*, of lawlessness against

law. Rather, what is at stake is "the law of the Spirit (*nomos tou Pneumatos*)." It is the law of the Spirit that can set me free from "the law of sin and death" (Rom. 8:2). It is therefore a question of law against law. I think this is what Paul means when he writes later in Romans of love as the fulfillment of the law (Rom. 13:10). Fulfillment does not mean negation of the law, but its completion in the single commandment: "You shall love your neighbor as yourself" (Rom. 13:9). Fulfillment (*pleroma*) means filling up: it is a complement, not a replacement; a supplement.[149]

The key thought here is that redemption is not something that can be willed: "You are not your own." All that can be willed is the dialectic of law and sin. Redemption exceeds the limit of human potentiality and renders us impotent. The appearance of the law of the Spirit in the person of Jesus is the unwilled possibility of redemption, the possibility that, with the resurrection of Christ, we receive "the spirit of sonship" and might become "fellow heirs with Christ" (Rom. 8:15). If we suffer with Christ, Paul insists, then "we may also be glorified with him" (Rom. 8:16). But what is essential here is the subjunctive mood of Paul's discourse: we *may* be glorified with Christ. The realization of this possibility is something we may hope for and patiently await. But there is no certainty here. Otherwise hope would not be hope. This is the deep logic of groaning in Paul:

> We know that the whole creation has been groaning in travail together until now; and not only creation, but we ourselves, who have the first fruits of the Spirit, groan inwardly as we wait for adoption as sons, the redemption of our bodies. For in this hope we were saved. Now hope that is seen is not hope. For who hopes for what he sees? But if we hope for what we do not see, we wait for it with patience. (Rom. 8:22–4)

Corrupted by the fall but saved by the resurrection, creation groans in travail. That is, both human nature and external nature are pregnant and undergoing the pangs of childbirth. This is Paul's understanding of the present time: it is pregnant with the possibility of redemption and this gives us reason to hope. But hope requires patience and awaiting. This, I think, is the meaning of the phrase, "remain in this condition in which you were called." At the present moment, we patiently await: "For the night is far gone, the day is at hand" (Rom. 13:12). We look at all things *hos me*, as if they were not, in a Messianic light.

Finally, this is why the seduction of Marcion has to be refused and why contemporary crypto-Marcionist renderings of Paul are pernicious. If law and sin were not within me, then freedom would mean nothing. The self is broken, impotent and wretched, but its wretchedness is its greatness: we *know* that we are broken.[150] Furthermore, I can only hold out the hope for being put back together, the hope for "what we do not see," if I know I am broken. In other words, the Christian can only be Christian if he knows him or herself to be Jewish, at least on his father's side. In Paul's picture, the human condition is constitutively torn between faith and law or love and sin, and it is only in the strife that divides us that we are defined. It is only a being who is constitutively impotent that is capable of receiving that over which it has no power: love. As I've tried to show in this chapter, this is one way—the most persuasive, in my view—of thinking the relation in Heidegger between the authentic and the inauthentic, between the *kairos* of the moment of vision and the slide back into falling. It gives us, I think, a powerful picture of conscience, that most enigmatic aspect of what it means to be human: both our power and our constitutive powerlessness.

5

Nonviolent Violence

VIOLENT THOUGHTS ABOUT SLAVOJ ŽIŽEK

This book began with an attempt to triangulate the present around the three terms of politics, religion, and violence. The diagnostic claim was that religiously justified violence is increasingly employed as the means to a political end. Although the theme of violence has been continually implicit— and occasionally explicit—in the previous chapters, there is no doubt that the interconnection between politics and religion has been the primary focus. Now, I would like to turn to the theme of violence in order to reflect on the hugely difficult question of the nature and plausibility of a politics of nonviolence. In particular, I would like to focus on how such a politics has to negotiate the limits of nonviolence, and in what circumstances it might become necessary to transgress those limits. The complex necessity for such transgression is captured in Judith Butler's paradoxical formulation, "nonviolent violence."[1] I would like to explore the relation between violence and nonviolence by way of a running debate I've been having with Slavoj Žižek. It is something of an understatement to say that this dispute has become rather overheated at stages. For example, in a letter to the *London Review of Books*, Žižek accuses me of "the highest form of corruption"; elsewhere, he sees my response to his criticisms as

"One of the lowest points in today's intellectual debate."[2] Highs and lows aside, I don't want to dwell on the grisly details of our disagreement, but to use this dispute as a lever in order to open up a wider reflection on the relation between nonviolence and political action.[3]

Žižek enjoys a good joke. Here's one of my favorites: two men, having had a drink or two, go to the theatre, where they become thoroughly bored with the play. One of them feels a pressing need to urinate, so he tells his friend to mind his seat while he goes to find a toilet. "I think I saw one down the corridor outside," says his friend. The man wanders down the corridor, but finds no lavatory. Wandering ever further into the recesses of the theatre, he walks through a door and sees a plant pot. After copiously urinating into it, he returns to his seat and his friend says to him, "What a pity! You missed the best part. Some fellow just came on the stage and pissed in that plant pot."

This gag perfectly describes Žižek's position on the question of violence. Drunkenly watching the rather boring spectacle of the world stage, we might feel an overwhelming subjective need to follow the call of nature somewhere discreet. Yet, in our bladder-straining self-interest we lose sight of the objective reality of the play and our implication in its action. We are oblivious to the fact that we are pissing on stage for the whole world to see.

So it is with violence. Our subjective outrage at the facts of violence—a suicide bombing, a terrorist attack, the assassination of a seemingly innocent political figure, the subjugation of the resistance movement, or whatever—blinds us to the objective violence of the world, a violence where we are perpetrators and not just innocent bystanders. All we see are apparently inexplicable acts of violence that disturb the supposed peace and normal flow of everyday life. We consistently overlook the objective—or what Žižek calls "systemic"—violence that is endemic to our socio-economic order. Capitalism is the organization of the relations of production that violently produces inequality, alienation, and social dislocation.

Žižek constantly refers subjective violence to the objective violence that is its underside and enabling precondition. "Systemic violence is thus something like the notorious 'dark matter' of physics," Žižek writes.[4] He asks the good, tolerant multicultural Western liberal—the constant fall guy for Žižek's critique—to suspend his outraged and impassioned subjective response to acts of violence (what he later calls, with Nietzsche, a reactive rather than active force) and turn instead to the objective or systemic character of the global situation. In order to understand violence, we do not need liberal sentimentalism, Žižek would contend, but some good, old-fashioned, dispassionate Marxist materialist critique.

At the heart of Žižek's approach to violence is an argument about ideology that has been a powerful constant feature of his work since his 1989 *The Sublime Object of Ideology*, his first book in English.[5] Far from existing in some sort of post-ideological world at the end of history where all problems can be diagnosed with neo-liberal economics and self-serving assertions of human rights, our lived reality is completely structured by ideology. This ideology might be subjectively invisible, but it is objectively real. Although in our complacent intoxication we might realize what we are doing, each of us is onstage pissing in that plant pot. Ideology is not an illusion or a dream. It is that which structures or, better, *sutures* experience, masking what the early Žižek—at the time much, much closer to Laclau's neo-Gramscian theory of hegemony than now—saw as the basic antagonism, the *political* antagonism that structures social relations.

The nature of ideological fantasy is expressed in Marx's dictum, "they know not what they do, but they do it."[6] That is, ideology is not in a state of epistemic deficit or deception. We know very well that our lives are structured by fantasies, but we still believe in those fantasies. This is the deep, abiding truth of Marx's analysis of commodity fetishism: we know that there is nothing magical about commodities or indeed about the money that is needed to buy them, yet we act as if there were. To use an extreme but illuminating example, the punter knows that the dominatrix who is trampling his balls is doing it for the money, yet he believes in the fantasy nonetheless. We are fetishists in practice, not in theory. Reality is structured by belief, by a faith in fantasy that we know to be a fantasy yet we believe nonetheless. This is Žižek's compelling diagnostic insight. Yet my question is and always has been: what does one do with this insight? What consequences for action follow from this argument for the constitutive nature of ideological fantasy? Are we not eternally doomed to an unending plague of more fantasies that can in turn be criticized by Žižek and by generations of future Žižeks? Sometimes I wonder.

Be that as it may, the great ideological illusion of the present, which produces so much pseudo-activity, is that there is no time to reflect and that we have to act *now*. On the contrary, Žižek asks us to step back from the false reactive urgency of the present, with its multiple injunctions to intervene like good humanitarians. In the face of this fake urgency, he says, we should be more like Marx who, with a potential revolution at the gates in 1870, complained to Engels that the activists should wait a couple more years until he had finished *Das Kapital*. Žižek's diagnosis of this ideology produces counter-intuitive inversions that overturn what passes for common sense. In *Violence*, Žižek rages against the reduction of love to masturbatory self-interest, the multiple hypocrisies of the Israel/Palestine conflict, and the supposed liberal philanthropy of a Bill Gates or a George Soros. There is a fascinating analysis of the scenes of torture and humiliation of prisoners at Abu Ghraib—which display, Žižek rightly contends, nothing more than the obscene underside of American society: the politico-legal regime of incarceration.

But whither all this dialectical brio? Ay, there's the rub. Žižek concludes *Violence* with an apology for what he calls, following Walter Benjamin, "divine violence." Divine violence is understood theoretically as "the heroic assumption of the solitude of the sovereign decision."[7] Žižek illustrates this with the questionable examples of the radical Jacobin violence of Robespierre in France in the 1790s and the invasion of the Brazilian dispossessed in the 1990s, descending from the *favelas* in Rio de Janeiro to disturb the peace of the bourgeois neighborhoods which border them. But, in a final twist, Žižek counsels us to do *nothing* in the face of the objective, systemic violence of the world. We should "just sit and wait" and have the courage to do nothing. The book ends with the words, "Sometimes, doing nothing is the most violent thing to do."[8] True enough, but what can this possibly mean?

With this latter question in mind, let me briefly turn to a— arguably *the*—governing concept of Žižek's work, the *parallax*, which was the framing theme of what was purportedly his magnum opus, *The Parallax View*. The concept of parallax is a way of giving expression to, at its deepest, the radical non-coincidence of thinking and being. If Parmenides and the entire onto-theological tradition that follows him, famously recovered by Heidegger, claims that it is the same thing to think and to be, then Žižek disagrees. Between thinking and being—between, in his parlance, the ticklish subject and the tickling object—there exists a radical non-coincidence, a constitutive lack of identity. Žižek's basic metaphysical claim is that there is a gap at the heart of ontological difference. In Heideggerian terms, to which Žižek constantly refers (and his engagement with Heidegger on questions of ontology and politics is one of the most compelling aspects of the argument of *The Parallax View*), there is an irreducible break between the ontological and the ontic. It is precisely this gap that Heidegger sought to cover up in his political commitment to National Socialism and his pathetic attachment to life in the provinces by claiming to find an instantiation of the ontological in the ontic: of, say, being's historicity in the German people.

Žižek's methodological claim is that this non-coincidence between thought and being requires a *dialectical* articulation. To avoid misunderstandings, this dialectic is not positive—that is, it does not culminate in a higher positivity, synthesis, or reconciliation of opposites, as in Hegel's *Aufhebung*. It is rather characterized by what Žižek calls *Versagung*, a denial, privation, or failure: a *not* that expresses the *knot* at the core of that which *is*—its traumatic kernel. As Žižek insists, this "that which is" is materiality itself, and therefore his method is a dialectical materialism understood in a new sense. That is, not the ossified stupidities of Soviet-era *Diamat*, nor the aestheticized resignation of Adornian negative dialectics (although there are often unspoken proximities to Adorno and one sometimes wonders whether Adorno and Žižek have adjoining rooms in the same Grand Hotel Abyss), but something rather novel: namely, Lacan's teaching of the *pas-tout*, the not-all that circles around the traumatic kernel of the Real. It is a dialectic that forces us to face an insurmountable parallax gap at the heart of that which is.

In the conclusion to *The Parallax View*,[9] although it is suggested throughout the book, Žižek claims that the parallax view opens onto what he calls—echoing Badiou—a subtractive politics, expressed in the figure of Melville's Bartleby, who reappears as the hero in the closing pages of *Violence*.[10] What interests Žižek in Bartleby is his insistent "I would prefer not to." Žižek places the emphasis on the "not to" or the "not to do"; that is, on Bartleby's impassive, inert, and insistent being, which hovers uncertainly somewhere between passivity and the vague threat of violence. Žižek's closing fantasy in *The Parallax View* is a movie version of Bartleby, with a Norman Batesesque Anthony Perkins playing the psychotic lead.[11] So, at the level of politics, it is ultimately the politics of Bartleby's smile, of his "not," that Žižek wants to oppose to other forms of thinking about politics—for example, my own.

At the core of Žižek's relentless production of books, articles, and lectures is, I think, a very pure version of what psychoanalysts would call an obsessional fantasy. On the one hand, says Žižek, the only authentic stance to take in dark times is to do nothing, to refuse all commitment, to be paralyzed like Bartleby. On the other hand, Žižek dreams of a divine violence, a cataclysmic, purifying violence of the sovereign ethical deed, something like Sophocles's Antigone. But Shakespearean tragedy is a more illuminating guide here than its ancient Greek predecessor. For Žižek is, I think, a

Slovenian Hamlet: utterly paralyzed but dreaming of an avenging violent act for which, finally, he lacks the courage. In short, behind its shimmering dialectical inversions, Žižek's work leaves us in a fearful and fateful deadlock. A deadlock both metaphysical or philosophical, and practical or political: the only thing to do is to do nothing. We should just sit and wait. Don't act, never commit, and continue to dream of an absolute, cataclysmic revolutionary act of violence. Thus speaks the great obsessional.

As Hamlet says, "Readiness is all." But the truth is that Žižek is never ready. His work lingers in endless postponement and over-production. He ridicules others' attempts at thinking about commitment, resistance, and action while doing nothing himself. What sustains his work is a dream of divine violence, cruelty, and force.

VIOLENCE AND NONVIOLENCE IN BENJAMIN

Let me begin to try to deepen and depolemicize matters by going back to the source of Žižek's notion of divine violence in Benjamin's dense, difficult, and massively over-interpreted essay, "Critique of Violence." The thing to keep in mind is that Benjamin's essay is called "*Critique* of Violence," where the German *Gewalt* has a wide connotative range of meaning: violence, force, power, even sovereignty and dominion. I would like to think about what that critique might mean in relation to the theme of nonviolence. Benjamin's essay is a critique of the violence of the law, where, as he writes, "violence ... is the origin of the law."[12] This is exemplified in the death penalty as the violence over life and death, and embodied in the activity of the key executive institution of the modern state, the police. In the act of violence, then, the essence of the law is manifested, as well as—to use Hamlet's word—revealing something rotten, *etwas Morsches*, about the law.[13]

Benjamin advances three fascinating, but obscure, conceptual distinctions: between law-making and law-preserving violence;

between the political and the general strike; and between mythic and divine violence. Let's take them in turn and use them to unravel the argument of Benjamin's essay. The first distinction between a violence that is *rechtsetzend* and one that is *rechtserhaltend* is, for Benjamin, internal to the theory and practice of law. The claim is that all law is either law-making or law-preserving, and that both these forms are violent. Benjamin makes a fascinating aside about the violent origin of every contract,[14] which recalls Shylock's undermining of Antonio's idealization of law as mercy in *The Merchant of Venice* by returning legality to the brute materiality of the contract, of the bond, of the pound of flesh, cut from close to the heart. The same claim would also be applicable to constitutional law: it requires a violent cut, a moment of decision and the assertion of power, say, in a revolution or a period of dramatic social transformation.

What Žižek misses—and I suspect deliberately so—is the fact that the operation of both law-making and law-preserving violence raises a question. In Benjamin's words, "the question poses itself whether there are no other than violent means for regulating conflicting human interests." He then asks, "Is any non-violent (*gewaltlose*) resolution of conflict possible?"[15] His answer is that such a nonviolent resolution of conflict is indeed possible in what he calls "relationships among private persons," in courtesy, sympathy, peaceableness, and trust. This leads Benjamin to conclude that "there is a sphere of human agreement that is non-violent to the extent that it is wholly inaccessible to violence: the proper sphere of 'understanding,' language (*die Sprache*)."[16] Without wanting to get into the complexities of what Benjamin means by language, particularly his idea of a pure language (*reine Sprache*), we can already see that, unlike Žižek, he is not simply arguing that all human life is utterly determined at every level by systemic or objective violence, but that a sphere of nonviolence is available at the private or what Benjamin calls the "subjective" level. Against Žižek, I want to defend this sense of the subjective.

Turning to Georges Sorel's account of the general strike,

Benjamin makes a distinction between two forms of strike: the political strike and the proletarian general strike.[17] Whereas the political strike is law-making—that is, it simply reinforces state power—the general strike attempts to destroy state power, arguing for "a wholly transformed work, no longer enforced by the state." The proletarian general strike is, to use Benjamin's word, "anarchistic" (*anarchistisch*[18]): it is revolutionary rather than reformist, committed to nonviolence as a "pure means" rather than the violence of law, moral rather than governed by law and the state, and subjective rather than objective. Such anarchism does not require the violence of contracts or indeed constitutions, but aims at the extra-legal resolution of conflict, "Peacefully and without contracts," as Benjamin writes in the context of a discussion of diplomacy, "On the analogy of agreement between private persons."[19]

Given Žižek's understanding of violence and the shape of his overall philosophical position, it is not difficult to imagine why he chooses to avoid and suppress Benjamin's discussion of nonviolence. However, the question of the nature and possibility of nonviolence is the background against which Benjamin introduces the key concept of divine violence. God makes a sudden appearance in Benjamin's essay, in the context of a passing, but revealing, remark about the limited capacity of reason (*Vernunft*) to decide on the justification of means of action or the justness of ends: "For it is never reason that decides on the justification of means and the justness of ends: fateful violence (*schicksalhafte Gewalt*) decides on the former, and God on the latter."[20]

The justification of means is the realm of fateful violence, or what Benjamin will call mythic violence, and the justness of ends is the realm of God or divine violence. What is meant by this distinction?

Mythic violence is illustrated with reference to the Greek myth of Niobe's arrogance in mocking Leto for only having two children, Apollo and Artemis, as opposed to the fourteen she had herself. For such a seemingly mild indiscretion, Apollo slaughtered

Niobe's seven sons and Artemis her seven daughters; Niobe herself was turned into a stone statue that wept endless tears.[21] The concept of mythic violence establishes, for Benjamin, the violence that is essentially alloyed to the making of law. Law-making is power-making and to that extent necessarily a manifestation of violence. Arguably a better example of such mythic violence is Aeschylus's *Oresteia*. Here, the condition of possibility for Athena's institution of justice in Athenian democracy is the violent act that decides against the Furies and in favor of Orestes, for the simple reason that Athena honors the male principle in all things, having sprung directly from the head of Zeus without the mediation of the womb. The lesson of the *Oresteia*, and of Greek tragedy more generally, is that the traumatic cycle of revenge and family violence in the house of Atreus and of the palace of Thebes can only be suspended by Athena's violent institution of justice. Tragedy is mythic violence that attempts to break the repetitive cycle of family slaughter.

The only thing that can put a halt to the logic of mythic violence, Benjamin thinks, is divine violence, which is not law-making, but law-destroying, *rechtsvernichtend*.[22] If mythic violence is extremely bloody, then divine violence is, Benjamin says, "lethal but without spilling blood."[23] He gives the Biblical example of God's judgment against Korah for rebelling against him. Korah was not slaughtered by God; rather the earth opened up to engulf him with all his belongings—even the linen that was at the launderers and the needles borrowed by people living at some distance from him. Yahweh is nothing if not thorough. If mythic violence is bloody power over human affairs for the sake of state power, then divine violence is the bloodless power over life for the sake of the living, for the sake of life's sacredness, what Judith Butler calls its "sacred transience."[24]

DIVINE VIOLENCE AND THE PROHIBITION OF MURDER

Benjamin's argument in the closing paragraphs of "Critique of Violence" is compact, oracular, and indeed obscure. Divine violence is lethal and it annihilates, he says, but it also expiates: it is *entsühnend*, atoning or cleansing like the use of water in a religious ritual. Divine violence expiates for the guilt of "mere life" (*das bloße Leben*). Benjamin then draws a distinction between "mere life" and "natural life," while admitting in a parenthesis that the meaning of the latter "cannot be shown in detail here." He writes that, "blood is the symbol of mere life"; while "The dissolution of legal violence stems … from the guilt of more natural life." Divine violence, he adds, "'expiates' the guilt of mere life—and doubtless also purifies the guilty, not of guilt, however, but of law. For with mere life, the rule of law over the living ceases."[25] In her commentary on these difficult lines, Butler observes,

> The desire to release life from a guilt secured through legal contract with the state—this would be a desire that gives rise to a violence against violence, one that seeks to release life from a death contract with the law, a death of the living soul by the hardening force of guilt.[26]

Divine violence is violence against violence that releases the subject from its (de)formation by law. It expiates the guilt of mere life by purifying the latter from its determination by law. In striking without bloodshed, divine violence achieves the possibility of a separation of law and life. As Benjamin writes, "Divine violence is pure power over all life for the sake of the living."[27] If the problem of politics for Benjamin is its eclipse and determination by law, where the political field is determined and regulated by law-making mythic violence for the sake of state power—the experience of the *Oresteia*—then the alternative is an act that severs the connection between violence and law. This law-destroying act is divine violence: violence against violence. Such is the potentiality, but only the potentiality, of a transformation of the condition of mere life—or bare life in contemporary bio-politics —into a praxis of life's sacred transience, what we might call a provisional anarchism.

The question, of course, is how such a praxis might be realized, and more particularly what might be meant by a violence against violence as a way of achieving such a praxis? This brings us to a central issue that I would like to explore initially in Benjamin and which is pursued in an analogous register by Levinas. In the penultimate paragraph of "Critique of Violence," Benjamin gives an analysis of the Biblical commandment "Thou shalt not kill" (*Du sollst nicht töten*). The question at stake is as follows: does this commandment necessarily entail that in each and every instance I should not kill, that violence is absolutely prohibited? Matters turn here on how we understand the Biblical commandment, and indeed commands and demands in general. Is the commandment a criterion of judgment? Is it some sort of categorical imperative that must be followed in all cases? No, Benjamin insists: "Those who base a condemnation of *all* violent killing of one person by another on the commandment are therefore mistaken."[28] The divine commandment is not a principle, axiom, or categorical imperative, but what Benjamin calls a *Richtschnur des Handelns*, which can be translated as a guideline for the action of persons. But "guideline" doesn't quite render the provisional—indeed artisanal—idea of a plumb line or thumb-line suggested by *Richtschnur*, where the latter is that piece of string or *Schnur* used by a builder to mark out an intended direction or *Richtung* for construction. Such a *Richtschnur*—I take it this is Benjamin's point—is not an exact measure, but an approximation, a guess, a rule of thumb rather than an absolute, categorical law. Benjamin describes the prohibition against murder as such a rule or thumb for those who have "to wrestle with it in solitude (*in ihrer Einsamkeit sich auseinanderzusetzen*), and, in exceptional cases, to take on themselves the responsibility for ignoring it."[29]

This idea of wrestling in solitude may well originate in the story of Jacob's wrestling with an angel of God in Genesis 32 and, after he beats the angel, ending up with his name being changed to "Isra-el," or "he who struggles with God." The point is that the commandment arises in a situation of struggle. As Butler writes: "The commandment, 'thou shalt not kill,' functions not as a theological basis for revolutionary action, but as a non-teleological ground to the apprehension of life's value."[30]

The command, the first and last word of peace, does not exclude the possibility and the actuality of killing in exceptional circumstances. But, crucially, nor does it condone such killing. When we wrestle with the commandment in solitude and decide not to follow it, then the responsibility falls on us. The commandment "Thou shalt not kill" is not an impersonal or absolute prohibition. It is a fragile guideline for praxis outside the mythic violence of law whose performative force might arise in a situation where it is transgressed. The command or demand is non-coercive and addressed in the second person in a way that requires our assent.[31] To recall our discussion of Paul, the power of the call is a powerless power made manifest in and as weakness.

What is in question here is the complex relationship between violence and nonviolence, in which a commitment to the latter might still require the performance of the former. Paradoxically, an ethics and politics of nonviolence cannot exclude the possibility of acts of violence. If we are to break the cycle of bloody, mythic violence, if we are to aspire to what Benjamin anarchically calls in the final paragraph of the essay "the abolition of state power,"[32] if something like politics is to be conceivable outside of law and in relation to the sacredness of life, then what is required is the deployment of an economy of violence. Following Benjamin, the guideline for a true politics is nonviolence and its aim is anarchism, but this thumb-line cannot be a new categorical imperative of the Kantian kind. In the solitude of exceptional circumstances, the guideline of nonviolence might call for violence, for subjective violence against the objective violence of law, the police, and the state. In the essay's closing lines, Benjamin provocatively writes, "Divine violence may manifest itself in a true war."[33]

The point is that we are doubly bound: both to follow the thumb-line of the divine commandment and to accept responsibility for choosing not to follow it. We are bound both ways and doubly responsible. The commandment is not a decree that is to be followed once and for all, the moment it is made. On the contrary, the commandment is something we struggle with, that we wrestle with. The moral commandment is not an *a priori* moral law from which we derive the *a posteriori* consequences. In many ways, the situation is always the reverse: we find ourselves in a concrete socio-political-legal situation of violence, and all we have is a plumb line of nonviolence, of life's sacredness. There are no transcendental guarantees and no clean hands. We act, we invent.

What goes for the command also goes for the ethical demand, particularly the infinite ethical demand that I have elsewhere tried to describe and defend. It is a plumb line for action that we struggle with in our finitude and the concrete, finite demands which overwhelm us. On this view, let's ask: what is divine about divine violence? The name "God" is not the super-juridical source of the moral law. On the contrary, "God" is the first anarchist, calling us into a struggle with the mythic violence of law, the state, and politics by allowing us to glimpse the possibility of something that stands apart, an infinite demand that cannot be fulfilled, that divides the subjectivity that tries to follow it. To return to the example of the Sermon on the Mount discussed in the Introduction to this book, when Jesus proffers the infinite and unfulfillable ethical demand ("Love your enemies, bless them that curse you, do good to them that hate you, and pray for them which despitefully use you, and persecute you" [Matt. 5:44]), he is not stating something that might be simply followed or carried out. Jesus's ethical demand is a ridiculous demand. It puts the ethical subject into a situation of sheer ethical overload, as Habermas might say. But, in my view, ethics is all about overload. As noted in the Introduction, when Christ in the same sermon says, "Be ye therefore perfect, even as your Father which is in heaven is perfect" (Matt. 5:48), he does not imagine for a moment that such perfection is attainable, at least not in this life, as it would require the equality of the human and the divine. What such a demand does is expose our imperfection and failure and we wrestle with the force of the demand and the facts of the situation. As we will see below, it is precisely this dimension of imperfection that Žižek refuses in the name of divine violence as "the sign of our perfection."[34] Against this, to cite Wallace Stevens, I would insist that "the imperfect is our paradise."[35]

The logic of the relation between nonviolence and violence is close to that employed by Derrida in his late work.[36] For him, responsible political action can only consist in the negotiation between contradictory, irreconcilable, and yet indissociable demands. On the one hand, political action has to be related to—in our terms— a moment of the infinite demand or the Biblical command if it is not going to be reduced to the prudential, pragmatic needs of the moment. Action needs to be articulated in relation to a notion of the infinite that exceeds the finitude of any context. But, on the other hand, such an infinite demand cannot—or, for Derrida, *must* not—be permitted to *program* political action, where specific decisions would be algorithmically deduced from incontestable moral precepts. Action is guided by taking a decision in a situation that is strictly undecidable, and where responsibility consists in the acceptance of an ineluctable double bind. What should be avoided is the principled abstraction of the commitment to nonviolence, on the one hand, and the pragmatic instrumentality of the use of violence on the other.

THE RESISTANCE OF THAT WHICH HAS NO RESISTANCE: VIOLENCE IN LEVINAS

As I try to think through Benjamin's "Critique of Violence," I have Emmanuel Levinas in mind, in particular some of his opening thoughts in *Totality and Infinity*. Indeed, the two categories in the title of Levinas's book seem directly to echo those of Benjamin: mythic violence, for Levinas, would be the experience of totality, which is revealed in the experience of war or the generalized state of exception. *Totality and Infinity* begins with the declaration of a state of war: "The visage of being that shows itself in war is fixed in the concept of totality, which dominates Western philosophy."[37] Divine violence, by contrast, would be the surplus to totality, the surplus of being that Levinas seeks to express with the category of infinity, what he also calls "Messianic peace": "Morality will oppose politics in history … when the eschatology of Messianic peace will have come to superimpose itself upon the ontology of war."[38]

These are handsome words. The problem that Levinas faces is how categories like eschatology and Messianic peace might be expressed conceptually or philosophically without simply being explained away as dogma, blind faith, or opinion. Levinas's major claim in *Totality and Infinity* is that, without substituting Messianic eschatology for philosophy, it is possible to proceed from the experience of totality, violence, and war back to a situation where totality breaks up—a situation that is the very condition for that totality. Such is Levinas's fragile and provisional transcendental method. When for the first time he uses the key concept of the other in *Totality and Infinity*, he writes, "Such a situation is the gleam of exteriority or of transcendence in the face of the other (*autrui*)."[39]

The problem here is that just as the mythic violence of law, the state, and power always seems to nullify or annihilate that which opposes it, so too the experience of war and totality refutes and crushes all talk of peace understood either as life's sacredness or the infinity of the relation to the other. In a time of war, in dark times, as I suggested in Chapter 3, Carl Schmitt will always appear to be right. This is why Levinas must acknowledge violence in his attempt to give expression to the nonviolent relation to the other. Levinasian ethics is not pacifist. Rather, it walks a Benjaminian tightrope of nonviolent violence.

Levinas affirms that the very experience of welcoming the other is a violence for a mind committed to the ideal of autonomy.[40]

With the infinity of the ethical relation to the other, Levinas is suggesting that we are not and indeed should not be masters in our own house. To welcome the other is to unseat the archic assurance of our place in the world, our sovereignty. Thus, to open oneself to the experience of transcendence, to the pacific itself, is violence. It is what Levinas calls—and it is the word at the centre of my critique of Žižek—an *act*. Such an act is described by Levinas as a shattering of my capacities, as what he calls "a descent into the real" beyond the realm of thought and knowledge. "The notion of act involves a violence essentially," he writes, continuing: "What, in action, breaks forth as *essential violence* is the surplus of being over the thought that claims to contain it, the marvel of the idea of infinity."[41] Essential violence has the same structure as divine violence. It is a question of a disquieting surplus over the mythic violence of totality, whose ground is an experience of nonviolence.

For both Benjamin and Levinas, there is something beyond the spheres of mythic violence, totality, the state, law, land, and war. Both of them identify it with an experience of nonviolence, with the placelessness of a commandment, an infinite ethical demand, and both of them describe it as Messianic. In the "Theses on the Philosophy of History," Benjamin understands Messianic eschatology not as the end time or *eschaton*, but as the possibility at each moment that the homogeneous order of objective time might be interrupted. As he notes, during the July Revolution of 1830 insurgents turned their rifles on the clock towers to stop time and inaugurate another temporal order.[42] Both Levinas and Benjamin understand such a possibility as bound up with the experience of language and the realm of the subjective. Both see that which would break with mythic violence as anarchic; Levinas, though, sees the ethical relation to the neighbor as anarchic in the sense that it places the autarchy and autonomy of the subject in question, unbinding the subject by binding the self to the other. Anarchy is a radical disturbance of the state, a disruption of the state's attempt, as Levinas puts it, to set itself up as a Whole.[43] An anarchic subjective Messianism of nonviolence is the guideline that might give an orientation to action in a way that is outside law-making and law-preserving violence, and in the name of life. In this way, as I have tried to show elsewhere, we might even speak of an anarchic law.[44]

What must be emphasized is the fragility of what Levinas is describing in his work, its experimental character. As Butler rightly says of Levinas in relation to Kleinian psychoanalysis:

> The meaning of responsibility is bound up with an anxiety that remains open, one that does not settle an ambivalence through disavowal, but that gives rise to a practice, itself experimental, that seeks to preserve life better than it destroys it. It is not a principle of nonviolence, but a practice, itself fallible, of trying to attend to the precariousness of life, and not transmuting that life into non-life.[45]

Too often, Levinas is seen as the thinker of ethics as first philosophy as if he had some sort of *a priori*, axiomatic-deductive system that explained away all possible objections. Nothing could be further from the truth. Levinas's work is marked by utter fragility, and most profoundly in the experience of the commandment "You shall not commit murder" (*Tu ne tueras point*—which might be more directly translated without the "shall" as "You will not kill" or even "Don't kill!"), which stands at the centre of *Totality and Infinity*.[46]

For Levinas, the commandment is expressed in the face of the other, indeed as the face of the other. It is not expressed in a situation of peace, but in a life-and-death struggle where I am about to put the other to death, when "the sword or the bullet has touched the ventricles or auricles of his heart," as Levinas writes.[47] For Levinas, crucially, "the other is the sole being I can wish to kill,"[48] because he or she refuses my sovereign will in an act of defiance or resistance. At the point of killing the other, they can still resist me, still defy me, even when they die—perhaps especially when they die. Or again, as Levinas succinctly puts it in the 1984 essay, "Peace and Proximity": "The face of the other in its precariousness and defenselessness, is for me at once the temptation to kill and the call to peace, the 'You shall not kill.'"[49]

Note the words "at once" in these lines: the other's face is simultaneously that being that I am tempted to kill and which I cannot kill. It is this simultaneity that we struggle with in the actuality of a concrete encounter.

Again, this is where the fragility of Levinas's thinking needs to be emphasized. The commandment that prohibits murder arises in a murder scene where the face still resists. What, then, is ethical resistance? Levinas paradoxically asserts that it is "the resistance of what has no resistance."[50] This is an extraordinary thought. True resistance is the resistance of that which has no resistance: the powerless, the impoverished, the destitute, the hungry. My point here is that what Levinas is offering—again like Benjamin—is a plumb line, a guideline, a rule of thumb for action, nothing more. "For the little humanity that adorns the earth," as he puts it in the closing words of *Otherwise than Being or Beyond Essence*.[51] The nonviolent relation to the other is what Benjamin famously calls a weak Messianic power, nothing more. As I have shown, Messianic power is always weak—it is the power of powerlessness. As Levinas writes of the other, "In the contexture of the world, he is a quasi nothing (*quasi rien*)."[52]

This is why the most pacific ethics has to negotiate with violence and war. Levinas gives us an ethics with dirty hands, not some angelic abstraction from the political realm, as some contend. For Levinas, there is no pure realm of ethics or pure ethical Saying, to use the language of *Otherwise than Being or Beyond Essence*. It is always a question of its articulation within the Said of politics and law. Just as when Benjamin speaks of divine violence showing itself in a true war, so too Levinas, continuing the quotation begun above, writes: "For the little humanity that adorns the earth, a relaxation of essence to the second degree is necessary: *in the just war that is waged on war, to tremble—still to shudder—at each instant, because of this very justice.* This weakness is necessary (*Il faut cette faiblesse*)."[53]

Here, Levinas is not providing a theory of just war, or some ideological justification for military intervention. It is rather the description of an experimental and experiential praxis of a war waged on war—a nonviolent violence—that causes us at each instant to shudder and to tremble. Such shuddering, such trembling, is the visceral experience of justice understood as the prohibition of murder that finds itself in a situation of violence with its provisional plumb line of nonviolence. For this, all virile, heroic talk of justified violence and just war will not suffice. Rather, what is necessary is the acknowledgement of weakness.

Slightly earlier in the same text Levinas begins an amazing passage with a phrase in which I've never quite known where to place the emphasis: "we other Westerners" (*nous autres occidentaux*). Does this simply mean "we Westerners amongst others," or might it refer to those who are others to the West? It is unclear, to say the least. Levinas writes: "The true problem for us other Westerners is not so much to refuse violence as to question ourselves about a struggle against violence which—without blanching in the non-resistance to Evil—could avoid the institution of violence out of this very struggle."[54]

The question is: can a struggle against violence avoid becoming itself a violent struggle? The only honest answer is to acknowledge that we do not know, we cannot be certain. As is evidenced by Aeschylus's *Oresteia*, but also by the violence of colonization and decolonization and the multiple wars of the present and recent past, violence exerts a repetition effect from which subjects cannot seem to free themselves. We are caught ineluctably in a loop of violence and counter-violence, of justification and counter-justification. The world is cut in two by a violence that is in the very air we breathe and whose unforgiving political, mythic, and legal logic is cold, bloody, and irrefutable. In such a world, the platitudes of realpolitik will always appear reasonable. All that we have is the folly of a plumb line of nonviolence, a set of exceptional circumstances and a political struggle in which we wrestle with the infinite ethical demand. Such wrestling requires the virtues of tact, prudence, and a concrete understanding of the situation in which we find ourselves, combined with a stubborn—at times, indeed, belligerent—faith in what appears at each and every moment impossible: another, nonviolent way of conceiving the social relations amongst human beings.

RESISTANCE IS UTILE: AUTHORITARIANISM VERSUS ANARCHISM

Žižek's critique of my work casts light on an important, indeed perennial, political debate: the conflict between authoritarianism and anarchism that is focused historically in the polemics between Marx and Bakunin, or between Lenin and the anarchists. Žižek's initial article was entitled "Resistance Is Surrender."[55] Really, the title says it all: all forms of political resistance are simply surrender unless they seize hold of the state. Žižek criticizes those on the "postmodern left," such as myself (though, incidentally, I challenge anyone to find a positive usage of the word "postmodern" in anything I've written), who call for a "new politics of resistance" by withdrawing from the domain of state power in order to create "new spaces outside of its control." Žižek claims that such a "politics of resistance is nothing but the moralizing supplement to a Third Way Left." Such a politics of protest, he asserts, simply shows the symbiotic relation between the state and resistance: the latter is permitted and even encouraged by the former but poses no threat to the existence of the liberal democratic state. On the contrary, resistance greases the wheels of the state machine. This is how Žižek reads the anti-war protests of 2003, and by implication all forms of mass street protest and demonstration. He writes: "The protesters saved their beautiful souls: they made it clear that they don't agree with the government's policy in Iraq. Those in power calmly accepted it, even profited from it."[56] By contrast, real politics cannot simply waste its time in resisting state power: it should "grab" it and "ruthlessly" exploit it.

The logic of Žižek's position is Leninist, and recalls the argument of *State and Revolution*. One of the striking features of Lenin's text is the fact that his critique of liberals, social democrats, and the bourgeoisie pales in comparison to the venom he reserves for the true enemy: the anarchists. The key to Lenin's *State and Revolution* is the interpretation of two phrases from Marx and Engels: "the dictatorship of the proletariat" and "the withering away of the state." Let me begin with the second phrase. Lenin follows Engels closely in making a distinction between the withering away of the state, which he supports, and the abolition of the state, which is the view ascribed to the anarchists: "The state is not 'abolished': *it withers away*."[57] As Lenin makes clear, he does not disagree with the abolition of the state, "as an aim."[58] The question is how this aim is to be realized, and concerns in particular "the use of arm and organized violence" as a means of realization. Lenin piggybacks on Engels's critique of the Proudhonists, "who called themselves 'anti-authoritarians.'"[59] By contrast, in Engels's words, communist revolutionaries accept that "A revolution is certainly the most authoritarian thing that is possible" and it requires "extremely authoritarian means," namely, "rifles, bayonets and cannons."[60] On this view, anarchists—and here we see the source of Žižek's rhetoric—are anti-revolutionary, petit bourgeois cowards who simply will not face up to the reality of authority and the necessity for proletarian violence. This brings us to the question of the state.

Everything turns here on the interpretation of the Paris Commune in 1871, discussed above in connection with Badiou, as the prime historical example of the dictatorship of the proletariat. The question is: to whom does the memory and legacy of the Commune belong? Does the Commune's "storming of the heavens," as Marx puts it, belong to the anarchists or to the communists?[61] Is the Commune best understood, with Bakunin, as "A well articulated and daring rebuttal of the State"?[62] Or is the Commune the foreshadowing of Lenin's Bolshevism? Does the legacy of the Commune and the possibility of communism require a centralist, statist dictatorship of the kind that Lenin envisages, or the decentralized non-state federalism of anarchists like Proudhon, Bakunin, and Kropotkin, for whom "the state is a crock"?[63] Lenin insists, rightly, that "Marx is a centralist."[64] Although Marxists and anarchists seemingly agree about the aim of politics in the withering away of the state, Lenin asserts that "We maintain that, to achieve this aim, we must make *temporary* use of the instruments, resources and methods of state power."[65]

Lenin argues with an admirable sleight of hand. He appears to agree with the anarchists in saying that we should abolish the bourgeois state, but then asserts that a centralist workers' state should be implemented. The goal of such a state—and here's the trick—is purportedly faithful to Marx and Engels's idea of the withering away of the state in communism, but this can only be achieved through a transitional state. This state is somewhat laughably called "fullest democracy"[66] by Lenin; in one passage, indeed, he calls it "truly complete democracy."[67] Against what Lenin sees as the bourgeois complicity of the anarchists, an authoritarian interlude is necessary in order to realize the possibility of communism. In fact, as history has shown, this was a rather long interlude, one which gave no indication of coming to an end until state socialism began to collapse from within in the late 1980s. "Temporary" can clearly be interpreted in quite an elastic way.

In 1872, the year after the Paris Commune, Marx deliberately excommunicated Bakunin and his supporters at the meeting of the First International in The Hague. In response, Bakunin teasingly wrote that "Mr. Marx considers himself the continuation of Bismarck."[68] In a letter to a Brussels newspaper the same year, Bakunin wrote, "As befits good Germans, they [i.e., the Marxists] worship the power of the State," adding, "their International even flies, all too often, the colors of Pan-Germanism."[69] In Marx's defense, he ridicules the political pretentions of Bismarck in *The Civil War in France*, but Bakunin's question concerns the necessity of the state form and the idea of "the people's state."[70] In his

1873 *Statism and Anarchy* Bakunin takes the point further, pointing out the essential contradiction in the Marxist theory of the state. Bakunin writes, exposing *avant la lettre* the shallowness of Lenin's claim for a "temporary" state: "If their State is indeed 'a people's State,' on what grounds would it be abolished? And if, on the other hand, its abolition is necessary for real emancipation of the people, how could it be described as a 'people's State'?"[71]

Bakunin continues to his inevitable conclusion: "any State, their 'people's State' included, is a yoke, which means that, on the one hand, it fosters despotism and, on the other, slavery." Given the adventure of Marxist-Leninism in the twentieth century, these are remarkably prescient words.

The contradiction that Bakunin identified in the idea of the dictatorship of the proletariat as the justification for a centralized, authoritarian state was also observed by Errico Malatesta in the wake of the Bolshevik Revolution. In a 1919 letter to Luigi Fabbri, he argued that, logically, given that the proletariat is the party of humanity: "Dictatorship of the proletariat would signify the dictatorship of everybody, which is to say, it would be a dictatorship no longer, just as government by everybody is no longer a government in the authoritarian, historical and practical sense of the word."[72] The truth is that dictatorship of the proletariat is the dictatorship of one party, or rather of the leaders of that party, or rather of the party leader. It is a genuine dictatorship, with its state structures, its penal sanctions, its henchmen and, above all, its armed forces. These armed forces were initially employed in order to protect the revolutionary government against external enemies. But, Malatesta writes, predicting the rise of Stalin, these armed forces will "tomorrow be used to impose the dictators' will upon the workers," to put the brake on any genuine emancipation, and will simply produce a new ruling class that will exist in order to protect its own interests.[73] Through its insistence on the centralized state form, the first victim of revolution—following an inevitable Bonapartist logic—will be the revolution itself and those in whose name it claims to function, namely the proletariat.

The most eloquent and darkly comic testimony in this context is an incident reported in a letter from Voline, a.k.a. Vsevolod Mikhailovitch Eichenbaum. Voline was a Russian anarchist, active in the period following the 1917 revolution, who eventually joined forces with the Ukrainian anarchist guerrilla Nestor Makhno, until they were arrested and persecuted by the Bolsheviks in 1919. He tells the story of meeting Trotsky in New York in April 1917, where they both edited separate Russian-language newspapers. Naturally enough, conversation turned to the differences between Marxism and anarchism. Trotsky reportedly said, "what is the difference between us? A little question of methodology, quite secondary."[74] Trotsky accepted that both anarchists and Marxists were revolutionaries and wanted the same thing, saying "Like you, we are anarchists in the final analysis." The "small" difference is that whereas anarchists want to abolish the state right away, "we Marxists believe that one cannot 'leap' into the libertarian realm in a single bound."[75] Marxists propose a "transitional stage" whereby the path can be cleared for anarchist society, namely, "the dictatorship of the proletariat exercised by the proletarian party in power." He concluded that the difference between anarchism and Marxism was a difference of degree, nothing more: "Essentially, we are very close to one another. Brothers in arms." Two and a half years later, in December 1919, Voline was arrested by the Bolshevik authorities in Ukraine and deemed "a militant of some standing." The authorities sent a telegram to Trotsky asking how Voline should be handled. His answer arrived snappily, also by telegram: "Shoot out of hand—Trotsky." By sheer accident, Voline escaped.

We saw in Chapter 3 how, for Carl Schmitt, there are two main traditions on the non-parliamentary, non-liberal left: authoritarianism and anarchism, which draw on opposing evaluations of human nature. It should not be forgotten that Schmitt was a great admirer of Lenin, an admiration only exceeded by the praise he lavished on Mao.[76] If, with characteristic Leninist violence, Žižek attacks my position for advocating anarchism, then it is clear which party he supports. From Engels to Lenin to Žižek, the critique of anarchism has remained oddly constant: that it is marked by a lack of both realism and ruthlessness. In his June 1918 audience with Lenin, the anarchist Nestor Makhno reports the former as saying: "Have anarchists ever acknowledged their lack of realism in the 'here and now' of life? It doesn't even occur to them."[77] In *State and Revolution* Lenin writes, following Marx closely, that the tactics of the anarchists are those of despair in place of a "mercilessly bold revolutionary work."[78] What this masculinist rhetoric of merciless boldness and ruthless power-grabbing conceals is the elision between organization and authoritarianism, and the belief that the former entails the latter.

In Žižek's case, the identification of organization with authoritarianism leads to a defense of dictatorship and a centralized state defended with military power. But, as Malatesta eloquently showed already in the 1890s, anarchism is not opposed to organization. What it opposes, Malatesta explains, is the identification of organization with authority: "Organization is only the practice of cooperation and solidarity, the natural and necessary condition of social life."[79] In a similar way, it is a mistake to identify anarchism with disorder. Opposition to the fictions of state and government is advanced not in the name of disorder, but of another principle of order: free organization, self-determination, collaboration, cooperation, or, to use Rousseau's word, association. In Malatesta's words:

> Abolition of government does not and cannot signify destruction of the social bond. Quite the opposite: the cooperation which today is forced and which is today directly beneficial to a few, will be free, voluntary and direct, working to the advantage of all and will be all the more intense and effective for that.[80]

For crypto-Bismarckian authoritarians like Lenin and Žižek, the only choice in politics is all or nothing: state power or no power. I think this alternative should be refused. For me, politics is about the movement between no power and state power, and it takes place through the creation of what I call "interstitial distance" within the state.[81] Although Žižek misunderstands this point, these interstices are not given or existent. They are not something to which one can withdraw, as Žižek imagines.[82] Indeed, at the present moment, through the deployment of increasingly pervasive techniques of surveillance and security apparatuses, the state threatens to saturate totally the space of the social. The interstices are not given: they are to be created through political articulation. On my view, the activity of politics is working within the state against the state in an inventive movement, the forging of a common front, imagining and enacting a new social bond that opens a space of resistance and opposition to government. Politics is the invention of interstitial distance, the making of space where—to all appearances—no space exists.

I discuss elsewhere various examples of such political processes, such as the indigenous rights movements in Mexico and Australia, but I would now also mention Bolivia's Evo Morales, who was placed in power by, and remains answerable to, genuine social movements.[83] Other movements are significant in this connection: from actions around the *sans papiers* and the *sans abri* in France; to the movement for an alternative globalization and the anti-war movement (despised by Žižek for its complicity with power and complacency, but which I see as articulating the possibility of a new language of civil disobedience); through to various direct-action organizations, from civil society groups to NGOs. To this list I would add the struggle around the question of immigration in North America and Europe, which I see as a key political issue in the coming decades. With unstoppable and massive population transfers from the impoverished south to the rich north, the political task is the creative articulation of immigrant rights and the exerting of pressure on the state, such that extensive immigration reform becomes a reality. I am far from being an expert in the history and ethnography of such movements, but I have tried to listen and learn a little over the years.

This is all of no avail to Žižek. Such forms of resistance are, for him, simply surrender and complicity with established power. The concealed consequence of Žižek's dialectical inversions is captured with precision and sarcasm by late, great Chris Harman: "'Sit at home and watch the barbarity on television' seems to be Slavoj Žižek's new slogan for fighting capitalism." Harman continues, with withering irony:

> Žižek's brilliant dialectical insight allows us to see that all struggles that do not fully achieve their objectives sanctify the status quo. So, the events of May 1968 in France must have legitimized the Gaullist regime, the Cuban revolution continued US domination of Latin America, the independence of India the British Empire, the revolutions of 1848 European reaction, the civil rights movement American racism. The logic of dialectical inversion produces equivalences between revolution and reaction whose conclusion is political paralysis and the celebration of inactivity that we find in Žižek.[84]

Žižek betrays a nostalgia—which is macho and finally manneristic —for dictatorship, political violence, and ruthlessness. Again, he is true to Lenin, who acknowledges that the dictatorship of the proletariat calls for the bourgeoisie to be "crushed by force" or "definitively crushed."[85] It is almost as if Lenin were unwittingly attempting, a few years *avant la lettre*, a definition of Benjamin's mythic violence and its cycle of bloody retribution. In this connection, Žižek's defense of Hugo Chávez's limitation of democracy in Venezuela is very revealing. In a passage that Žižek edited out of the text when it appeared in *In Defense of Lost Causes*, he writes— and note his rhetoric of "grabbing" and "ruthlessness":

> Far from resisting state power, he [i.e. Chávez] *grabbed* it (first by an attempted coup, then democratically), *ruthlessly* using the Venezuelan state apparatuses to promote his goals. Furthermore, he is *militarizing* the barrios, and organizing the training of armed

units there. And, the ultimate scare: now that he is feeling the economic effects of capital's "resistance" to his rule (temporary shortages of some goods in the state-subsidized supermarkets), he has announced plans to consolidate the 24 parties that support him into a single party.[86]

We return, once again, to the basic obsessional fantasy of Žižek's position: do nothing, sit still, stay at home and watch TV, prefer not to, be Bartleby, and silently dream of a ruthless violence, a grabbing of power, a consolidation of state power into one man's hands: a sheer act of brutal physical force or punishment of which you are the object or the subject, or perhaps both at once. What Žižek seems to wish for—which is very odd for a Lacanian—is for someone to occupy the position of master. When Lacan was being heckled by Leninist students at Vincennes in December 1969, he concluded by saying that "What you aspire to as revolutionaries is a master. You will get one."[87]

In Žižek's response to an earlier version of my critique, entitled "What is Divine about Divine Violence?," he vigorously objected to my talk of obsessionality. Žižek claims that the best way to understand the obsessional attitude is through the notion of "*false activity*: you think you are active, but your true position, as embodied in the fetish, is passive."[88] In a tense group situation, the obsessional is "frantically active … talks incessantly, makes jokes, in order to defer that awkward moment of silence that would make the participants aware of the underlying tension."[89] Žižek then links this to a constant theme of his recent work that we have already discussed, namely that "The threat today is not passivity, but pseudo-activity." Žižek identifies the obsessional attitude with compulsive behavior. This is true, but it is only half the story. For the other side of obsessionality is cessation: doing nothing, impotence and inhibition. It is precisely this experience of obsessional cessation that Žižek celebrates with the figure of Bartleby, and which he even identifies with my talk of "nonviolent violence."[90] But the obsessional attitude is not simply to be identified with compulsive behavior, but more importantly with the cessation that flows from massive and paralyzing inhibition. What is at stake here is not an attack on Žižek's "personality,"[91] as he suggests, but the persistence of a general subjective structure that hold us captive.

In his critique of my political position, Žižek pulls out the most hackneyed and obvious trump card in all political games in the following terms: "And what would Critchley do if he were facing an adversary like Hitler? Surely in such a case one should 'mimic and mirror the archic violent sovereignty' one opposes?"[92]

Not at all. National Socialism is a powerful example, the most powerful twentieth-century example, of Benjamin's mythic violence. But should one confront mythic violence with a mythic counter-violence? No. Surely the lesson of Benjamin's essay is that there is a need for a distinction between the mythic violence of archic sovereignty and the anarchism of divine violence, which I have tried to describe as a nonviolent violence. What might this have meant concretely in the situation of Nazi Germany? First, it would have meant not treating National Socialism as some version of normal politics and seeking to appease it as, say, the British and French governments sought to do. Second, it would have meant that what National Socialism reveals is that the state of exception is no longer the exception, but the rule, and calls for an exceptional intervention. Third, and crucially, an opposition to National Socialism would not necessarily have limited itself to strategies of nonviolence, but would also have rendered violent resistance necessary. One thinks of Dietrich Bonhoeffer and the way he was eventually driven to drop the pacifism he adopted in the 1930s and participate in the attempted tyrannicide of Hitler and failed *coup d'état* against the National Socialist regime that led to his brutal execution in 1945, shortly before the end of the war. Bonhoeffer's ethics does not rest on absolute, law-like principles, but on a freely assumed responsibility that, in extreme situations and as a last resort, is willing to act violently. The extreme necessities of a critical situation, Bonhoeffer writes, "appeal directly to the free responsibility of the one who acts, a responsibility not bound by any law."[93] But such a conception of ethical action would not lead to the sort of celebration of violence endemic to fascism and National Socialism, but to an infinite responsibility for violence that, in exceptional circumstances, might lead us to break the commandment "Thou shalt not kill." Responsible action involves what Bonhoeffer calls a "willingness to become guilty" (*Bereitschaft zur Schuldübernahme*): this is the price one pays for freedom.[94] Would such a strategy of resistance have been successful? In Bonhoeffer's case, we know that the attempted tyrannicide failed. But the point here is that I am not preaching nonviolence in all political cases, and no more am I arguing for some easy "clean hands" retreat from the state. On the contrary.

THE PROBLEM WITH PRINCIPLED NONVIOLENCE

> *But ancient Violence longs to breed,*
> *new Violence comes,*
> *when its fatal hour comes.*
> Aeschylus, *Agamemnon*

> *In this sense, non-violence is not a peaceful state, but a social and political struggle to make rage articulate and effective—the carefully crafted "fuck you."*
> Judith Butler, *Frames of War*

Violence is not reducible to an act in the here and now which might or might not be justifiable in accordance with some or other conception of justice. On the contrary, violence is, as Robert Young reminds us, "a phenomenon that has a history."[95] It is never a question of a single act, but of one's insertion into a historical process saturated by a cycle of violence and counter-violence. Violence is always a double-act "between human subjects, subjects whose experience of violence interpolates them in a repetition effect from which they cannot free themselves."[96] Consider the overwhelming evidence of colonialism—as Young writes, "Violence is never an abstract concept for the colonized."[97] Historical amnesia and incuriousness about the violence of the past is the luxury of the oppressor. The colonized subject lives the historical violence of their expropriation viscerally, corporeally, all the way to psychosis, mental disorder, and phenomena like demonic possession, as Frantz Fanon shows in detail.[98] No word seems more often used in *The Wretched of the Earth* than the adjective "muscular."[99] Violence is the muscular assertion of the colonized against the colonist in the context of a national struggle for liberation. Violence is "the absolute praxis," "a cleansing force," driven by a "ravenous taste for the tangible."[100] It is through violence against the colonist that colonized subjects can rid themselves of their deformed inferiority and liberate or literally remake themselves. Fanon writes that "Decolonization is truly the creation of new men."[101]

I have deep suspicions about the idea of violence as a cleansing force: the heroic, virile assertion that violence is that healing, bloody crucible through which men are redeemed and remade, where the colonized "thing" becomes a free man through what Sartre calls "the patience of the knife."[102] Nor am I persuaded by Sartre's hyperbolic dialectic, in which "killing a European is killing two birds with one stone": in one violent act, the opposition of oppressor and oppressed is *aufgehoben* or sublated and the formerly colonized subject "for the first time ... feels a *national* soil under his feet."[103] This is a glorification of violence that wildly exceeds Marx, Sorel, or Lenin and is perhaps, as Arendt notes, caused by the "severe frustration of the faculty of action in the modern world."[104]

However, what remains irrefutable in Fanon is the understanding of violence as a lived, historical experience of expropriation, whose effects constitute the daily humiliation of the wretched of the earth. When violence is understood in this way, there is no doubt that principled assertions of nonviolence simply miss the point. Worse still, nonviolence can be an ideological tool introduced by those in power in order to ensure that their interests are not adversely affected by a violent overthrow of power. Nonviolence here becomes a negotiating strategy. As Fanon writes, with bitter distrust: "Nonviolence is an attempt to settle the colonial problem around the negotiating table before the irreparable is done, before any bloodshed or regrettable act is committed."[105]

As ever, Sartre makes the point more colorfully:

> Get this into your head: if violence were only a thing of the future, if exploitation and oppression never existed on earth, perhaps displays of nonviolence might relieve the conflict. But if the entire regime, even your nonviolent thoughts, is governed by a thousand-year-old oppression, your passiveness serves no other purpose but to put you on the side of the oppressors.[106]

History is a seemingly unending cycle of violence and counter-violence, and to refuse its overwhelming evidence in the name of some *a priori* conception of nonviolence is to disavow history in the name of an abstraction that, in the final analysis, is ideological. There are contexts where a tenacious politics of nonviolence, such as Gandhi's Kropotkinesque strategy of *Satyagraha*, can be highly effective. There are contexts where a *mimesis* of Gandhi's tactics might also prove successful, as was the case for several years in the civil rights movement in the United States in the 1960s and in the words and deeds of Martin Luther King. There are contexts where techniques of direct action that David Graeber calls "non-violent warfare" may prove effective and timely.[107] There are contexts where a difficult pacifism that negotiates the limits of violence might be enough. But—and this is the point gleaned from our reading of Benjamin—there are also contexts, multiple contexts, too depressingly many to mention, where nonviolent resistance is simply crushed by the forces of the state, the police, and the military. In such contexts, the line separating nonviolent warfare and violent action has to be crossed. Politics is always a question of local conditions, of local struggles and local victories. To judge the multiplicity of such struggles on the basis of an abstract conception of nonviolence is to risk dogmatic blindness.[108]

Does a commitment to nonviolence exclude the possibility of violence? That is the question. As Benjamin remarks: "Every conceivable solution to human problems, not to speak of deliverance from the confines of all the world-historical conditions of existence, obtaining hitherto, remains impossible if violence is totally excluded in principle."[109]

So, we cannot expect a radical change in the state of human beings in the world if we exclude violence as a matter of principle. Benjamin's is a crucial point: in the political sphere, it makes little sense to assert and hold to some abstract, principled, *a priori* conception of nonviolence. As is well known, the standard objection to anarchist uses of political violence always turns on this point. It will be said: how can you justify your use of violence? Shouldn't you be committed to nonviolence? If you resort to violence, don't you begin to resemble the enemy you are fighting against? Of course, nonviolence conceived as the domain of cooperation and mutual aid, the life of the social bond, Benjamin's realm of courtesy, peaceableness, and trust, is both the presupposition and aspiration of anarchist politics. But why should anarchists be the only political agents who have to decide beforehand that they will not be violent, when the specific circumstances of a political situation are still unknown? To this extent, the abstract question of violence versus nonviolence risks reducing anarchism to what we might call the politics of the spectator position, where nonviolence becomes a transcendent value, an abstraction, a principle or categorical imperative.[110] In specific political sequences, and it is always and only a case of such specifics—a locality, a series of actions, an evental site, as Badiou might say—the turn to violence is often entirely comprehensible. The violence of protesters, critics and opponents of a regime is usually, but not always, a response to the provocations of police or military violence.

To return to the debate with Žižek and conclude: my problem is not, then, so much with violence, as with armchair or writing-chair romantic glorifications of revolutionary violence of the kind that one finds in Žižek's manneristic Leninism, which is all the more bloody because all the more distanced from reality. In the words of Tiqqun, "classical virility demands an analgesic."[111] As we have seen, the basic—indeed recurrent—fantasy of Žižek's position is a combination of Bartleby with Norman Bates, refusal and violence.[112] Indeed, Žižek views the shower murder scene from Hitchcock's *Psycho* as "divine violence at its purest."[113] He responds to an earlier version of my critique by asking rhetorically, "Is, then, the Bartlebian gesture of 'preferring not to' precisely a case of 'nonviolent violence?'"[114] However, the response to the question is clearly negative, as nonviolent violence is not "preferring not to." It is not an act of refusal. It is, rather, engaging in a series of *preferred* actions, even violent actions, which are necessary but not justifiable. Žižek even has the audacity to compare his Bartlebian position to Gandhi's resistance to the British in India.[115] However, what defines Gandhi's nonviolent resistance is not inactivity or passivity, as Žižek suggests, but a stubbornly persistent and hugely imaginative activism.

This brings us back to the question of divine violence, which Žižek defines as "the counter-violence to the excess of violence that pertains to state power."[116] So far, so good. Referring back directly to *Violence*,[117] Žižek gives us a list of examples of divine violence, expanding it slightly: Leninist revolutionary fervor, necklace killings or *Père Lebrun* in Haiti, flash mobs, the murder scene in Hitchcock's *Psycho*, and even the murderous actions of the nameless monster in Mary Shelley's *Frankenstein*.[118] For Žižek—in what we might call his *jouissance*—these acts of divine violence are "beyond good and evil … in a kind of politico-religious suspension of the ethical."[119] Interestingly and revealingly, Žižek then translates divine violence into Kantian categories as "the direct intervention of the noumenal into the phenomenal."[120] Divine violence becomes equated with the Kantian sublime as the violent transgression of human finitude. For Kant, the sublime is an emotion that places human beings in the fundamental tension between infinity (*Unendlichkeit*) and finitude (*Endlichkeit*), between immanence and transcendence, between representation and that which exceeds it. On this view, divine violence is the sudden piercing of the finite by the infinite, of the phenomenal by the noumenal. Against a view that he attributes to me, Žižek insists that divine violence is not the "price we pay for our imperfection, it is the sign of our perfection, of our participation in the 'noumenal' divine dimension."[121] Or again, divine violence is "divine in itself, it manifests in itself the divine dimension."[122]

Here, we arrive at the basic fantasy of Žižek's thinking: the overcoming of imperfection, sin, and guilt through the intervention of the divine order into human experience, the miraculous incarnation of the sublime into the everyday. It is the fantasy of an act of cataclysmic, redeeming violence that does not emanate from us—we are but passive, Bartlebian spectators—but which transforms the situation without the intervention of the will. It is, finally, the fantasy of guilt-free perfection and clean hands. Now, if this is what Benjamin means by divine violence, then Žižek is right and I am wrong; I should apologize. Of course, this recalls an old joke, about Stalin standing on Lenin's Mausoleum in Red Square: "Comrades," he tells the crowd. "An historic event has occurred! I have received a telegram from Leon Trotsky!" The crowd hushes. Stalin reads: "Joseph Stalin. The Kremlin. Moscow. You were right and I was wrong. You are the true heir of Lenin. I should apologize. Leon Trotsky." The crowd roars. But in the front row a little Jewish tailor gestures to Stalin. Stalin leans over to hear what the tailor has to say. "Such a message," says the tailor. "But you didn't read it with the correct emphasis." Stalin raises his hand and stills the crowd. "Comrades," he says, "we have here a simple worker who says I read Trotsky's message without the right feeling. I am asking the worker to read it to us the way he think it should be read." He gives the telegram to the tailor, who gets up to read the telegram. He clears his throat and reads: "Joseph Stalin. The Kremlin. Moscow. "*You* were right and *I* was wrong? *You* are the true heir of Lenin? *I* should apologize?"

★   ★   ★

The focus of this chapter has been the link between divine violence and the commandment that prohibits murder. Benjamin understands this commandment as a thumb-line or plumb line for action that we "wrestle with in solitude," which I linked to Levinas's idea of the face as the precariousness of both the temptation to kill and the prohibition of killing. This is what I mean by the double bind of responsibility where subjects are bound to both the guideline of the divine commandment and "to take on themselves the responsibility of ignoring it."[123] Žižek sees this position as "a heroic compromise of dirtying one's hands for a higher goal."[124] He insists, "We do not tragically dirty our hands—the violence is divine, which means that our hands remain clean."[125] I believe, however, that when it comes to political action it is a question of dirty hands all the way down. If this is heroic, then so be it. It is the kind of guilty heroism that perhaps Benjamin has in mind. As he writes, divine violence "purifies the guilty, not of guilt, however, but of law."[126] It expiates the guilt that stems from law, but not guilt as such. What Žižek dreams of is a guilt-free perfection of sublime violence, where the infinite pierces the finite in a divine act. It sounds exciting. My view is different: politics is action that situates itself in the conflict between a commitment to nonviolence and the historical reality of violence into which one is inserted, and which requires an ever-compromised, ever-imperfect action that is guided by an infinite ethical demand. As we have seen, my view of the subject is defined by the constitutive character of guilt and original sin understood as the movement of existential indebtedness.

At the end of his critique of my political position, Žižek raises a criticism that seems initially powerful:

> The lesson here is that the truly subversive thing is not to insist on "infinite" demands we know those in power cannot fulfill (since they also know it that we know it, such an "infinitely demanding" attitude is easily acceptable to those in power: "so wonderful that, with your critical demands, you remind us

what kind of world we would all like to live in—unfortunately, however, we live in the real world, where we are just honestly doing what is possible"), but, on the contrary, to bombard those in power with strategically well-selected *precise, finite* demands which cannot allow for the same excuse.[127]

But Žižek gets it back to front. In political action, it is not a question of issuing infinite demands that cannot be fulfilled. By their very exorbitance, such demands can easily be accommodated by being ignored. What is infinitely demanding, rather, is the ethical disposition of being open and attentive to what exceeds the finite situation in which we find ourselves.[128] "Infinite" here does not consist in the demands that I make, but in finding something in the situation that exceeds its limits. Infinite demands are not issued by a subject, but are the mark of the subject's responsiveness to and responsibility for what is unlimited in a situation. In a concrete action—a wage dispute, say—we might indeed begin with a finite demand, a demand for a living wage or for the right to join a union. Such a demand will either be accommodated or not, and that might be the end of the matter. The problem with restricting struggles to "*precise, finite* demands" is that once those demands have been either met or ignored, then the struggle is at an end. Such is the politics of accommodation. But there can also be a politics that refuses to be satisfied with accommodation at the level of state or government. In such political actions, the finite demand around which a struggle organizes itself extends itself beyond the limits of the identity of the concerned group and becomes something more radical and far-reaching. In this way, the concrete struggles of particular groups and interested parties, defined by region or ethnic identity, say, can rapidly become radicalized and perhaps begin to place in question the entire governmental framework or socio-economic state of the situation. By limiting oneself to finite demands, one loses the radical potential of struggles to extend beyond their particularity, to link with other struggles in other locations and to become generalized. The key to any genuinely emancipatory politics consists in an openness to the possibility of a generalized struggle that exceeds any particularity or any claim to identity. What is infinitely demanding is that process by which specific, perhaps self-interested or defensive struggles become something else: they open onto something hitherto unknown about the situation in which one finds oneself. What is infinitely demanding, to reiterate, is this ethical commitment towards a possibility as yet unknown and inexistent in the situation, but still powerfully imagined: a supreme fiction.

As we saw above, the infinite demand is a double, meontological demand: to see what is in terms of what is not yet, and to see what is not yet in what is. Such is the implication of taking up the Messianic standpoint, seeing all things *hos me*, as not, for "the form of this world is passing away." This means embracing a double nihilism, an affirmative nihilism: both what we called above, with Benjamin, "the nihilism of world politics," and trying to focus attention on that which has no existence in such a world politics. Politically, the demand exerted on us by the finite context exceeds the content of any finite demand that might be accommodated at the level of government or state. Literally speaking, the infinite demand is nothing—but a massively creative nothing.

6

Conclusion

BE IT DONE FOR YOU, AS YOU BELIEVED

I'd like to finish this book as I began it, with a kind of parable. In the conclusion to *Works of Love*, Kierkegaard ponders the nature of the commandment of love that he has been wrestling with throughout the book. What is the status and force of the words "you shall love your neighbor"? Kierkegaard stresses the strenuousness and, in the word most repeated in these pages, the *rigor* (*Strenghed*) of love. As such, Christian love is not some sort of "coddling love," which spares believers any particular effort and which can be characterized as "pleasant days or delightful days without self-made cares."[1] This easy and fanciful idea of love reduces Christianity to "a second childhood" and renders faith infantile. Kierkegaard then introduces the concept of "the Christian like-for-like" (*det christelige Lige for Lige*), which is the central and decisive category of *Works of Love*. The latter is introduced by distinguishing it from what Kierkegaard calls "the Jewish like-for-like," by which he means "an eye for an eye, a tooth for a tooth": namely a conception of obligation based on the equality and reciprocity of self and other.[2] Although this is a stereotyped and limited picture of Judaism, as a cursory reading of Franz Rosenzweig's *The Star of Redemption* can easily show,[3] Kierkegaard's point is that Christian love cannot be reduced to what he calls the "worldly" conception of love where you do unto others what others do unto you and no more. The Christian like-for-like engages in a kind of transcendental *epoche* of what others owe to me, and instead "makes every relationship to other human beings into a God-relationship."[4] This move coincides with a shift from the external to the inward. Although the Christian, for Kierkegaard, "must remain in the world and the relationships of earthly life allotted to him," he or she views those relationships from the standpoint of inwardness, that is, mediated through the relationship to God. As Kierkegaard puts it emphatically in Part One of *Works of Love*: "Worldly wisdom thinks that love is a relationship between man and man. Christianity teaches that love is a relationship between: man-God-man, that is, that God is the middle term."[5]

The rigor of Christianity is a conception of love based on radical inequality, namely the absolute difference between the human and the divine. This is how Kierkegaard interprets Jesus's words from the Sermon on the Mount: "Why do you see the speck that is in your brother's eye, but do not notice the log that is in your own eye" (Matt. 7:3). The log in my own eye does not permit me to judge the speck in the other's. Rather, I should abstain from any judgment of what others might or might not do. To judge others is to view matters from the standpoint of externality rather than inwardness. It is arrogance and impertinence. What others owe to me is none of my business. In Kierkegaard's words: "Christianly understood you have absolutely nothing to do with what others do to you." "Essentially," he continues, "you have only to do with yourself before God." Once again, the move to inwardness does not turn human beings away from the world; it is rather "a new version of what other men call reality, this is reality (*Virkeligheden*)."[6]

The address of Kierkegaard's writing has a specific direction: the second-person singular, *you* (*Du*). He tells the story from the Gospels (the versions rendered in Matthew and Luke) of the Roman centurion in Capernaum, who approached Jesus and

asked him to cure his servant or boy—the sense is ambiguous—
"sick with the palsy, grievously tormented" (Matt. 8:6). After
Jesus said that he would visit the boy, the centurion confessed
that, as a representative of the occupying imperial authority with
soldiers under his command, he did not feel worthy that Jesus
should enter his house. When Jesus heard this he declared that
he had not experienced a person of such great faith in the whole
of Israel. He added, and this is the line that interests Kierkegaard,
"Be it done for you, as you believed" (*Dig skeer som Du troer*[7]). This
story reveals the essential insecurity of faith. Kierkegaard writes
that it does not belong to Christian doctrine to vouchsafe that
you—"precisely *you*"[8]—have faith. If someone were to say, "it is
absolutely certain that I have faith because I have been baptized in
the church and follow its rituals and ordinances," then the appro-
priate reply might be, "Be it done for you, as you believed." The
point of the story is that the centurion, although he was not baptized as a Christian, nonetheless believed. As Kierkegaard writes,
"in his faith, *the* Gospel is first *a* gospel."[9] As we saw above, it is
faith as a proclamation that enacts life. It is the decision that brings
the inward subject of faith into being over and against an external
everydayness. Such a proclamation is as true for the non-Christian
as for the Christian. Indeed, it is more true for the non-Christian,
because their faith is not supported by the supposed guarantee
of baptism, creedal dogma, regular church attendance, or some
notion that virtue will be rewarded with happiness if not here on
earth, then in the afterlife. Thus, paradoxically, non-Christian faith
reveals the true nature of the faith that Christ sought to proclaim.
Even—and indeed especially—those who are denominationally faithless can have an experience of faith. If faith needs to be
underpinned by some sort of doctrinal security, then inwardness
becomes externalized and the strenuous rigor of faith evaporates.

What sort of certainty, then, is the experience of faith?
Kierkegaard writes, and again the second-person singular direction of address should be noted: "It is eternally certain that it
will be done for you as you believe, but the certainty of faith,

or the certainty that *you, you in particular*, believe, you must win at every moment with God's help, consequently not in some external way."[10]

Kierkegaard insists—and one feels here the force of his polemic against the irreligious, essentially secular order of Christendom, in his local case the pseudo-Christianity of the Danish National Church—that no pastor or priest has the right to say that one has faith or not according to doctrines like baptism and the like. To proclaim faith is to abandon such external or worldly guarantees. Faith has the character of a continuous "striving (*Strid*) … in which you get occasion to be tried every day."[11] This is why faith and the commandment of love that it seeks to sustain is not law. It has no coercive, external force. As Rosenzweig writes, "The commandment of love can only proceed from the mouth of the lover."[12] He goes on to contrast this with law, "which reckons with times, with a future, with duration." By contrast, the commandment of love "knows only the moment (*Augenblick*); it awaits the result in the very moment of its promulgation (*Augenblick seines Lautwerdens*)."[13] The commandment of love is mild and merciful, but, as Kierkegaard insists, "there is rigor in it." As we saw in Porete, love is that disciplined act of absolute spiritual daring that eviscerates the old self of externality so that something new and inward can come into being—a process of decreation and impoverishment.

As Kierkegaard puts in *Works of Love*, citing Paul, "Owe no one anything, except to love one another."[14] It sounds simple, but what is implicit in this minimal-sounding command is a conception of love as an experience of infinite debt—a debt that it is impossible to repay: "When a man is gripped by love, he feels that this is like being in infinite debt."[15] We have looked, in relation to Heidegger, at the existential conception of guilt as ontological indebtedness. To be is to be in debt—I owe therefore I am. If original sin is the theological name for the essential ontological indebtedness of the self, then love is the experience of a counter-movement to sin that is orientated around an infinite demand that exceeds the projective potentiality of the self. Kierkegaard writes—and the double emphasis on the "moment" that finds an echo in Rosenzweig should be noted—"God's relationship to a human being is the infinitizing at every moment of that which at every moment is in a man."[16] Withdrawn into inwardness and an essential solitude ("If you have never been solitary, you have never discovered that God exists"[17]), each and every word and action of the self resounds through the infinite demand of God.

At this point, in the penultimate paragraph of *Works of Love*, Kierkegaard shifts to auditory imagery. God is a vast echo chamber in which each sound, "the slightest sound," is duplicated and resounds back loudly into the subject's ears. God is nothing more than the name for the repetition of each word that the subject utters. But it is a repetition that resounds with "the intensification of infinity." In what Kierkegaard calls "the urban confusion" of external life, it is nigh impossible to hear this repetitive echo of the infinite demand.[18] This is why the *epoche* of externality is essential: "externality is too dense a body for resonance, and the sensual ear is too hard-of-hearing to catch the eternal's repetition (*Gjentagelse*)."[19] We need to cultivate the inner or inward ear that infinitizes the words and actions of the self. As Kierkegaard makes clear, what he is counseling is not "to sit in the anxiety of death, day in and day out, listening for the repetition of the eternal."[20] What is rather being called for is a rigorous and activist conception of faith that proclaims itself into being at each instant without guarantee or security, and which abides with the infinite demand of love.

Faith is the enactment of the self in relation to a demand that exceeds my power, both in relation to my factical thrownness in the world and the projective movement of freedom achieved as responsibility. Faith is not a like-for-like relationship of equals, but the asymmetry of the like-to-unlike. This is what I have tried to describe in this book as a subjective strength that only finds its power to act through an admission of weakness: the powerless power of conscience. Conscience is the inward ear that listens for the repetition of the infinite demand. Its call is not heard in passive resignation from the world, but in the urgency of active engagement. It has been my contention in this book that such an experience of faith is not only shared by those who are faithless from a creedal or denominational perspective, but can be experienced by them in an exemplary manner. Like the Roman centurion of whom Kierkegaard writes, it is perhaps the faithless who can best sustain the rigor of faith without requiring security, guarantees, or rewards: "Be it done for you, as you believed."

Notes

INTRODUCTION

1   Oscar Wilde, *De Profundis and Other Writings* (Penguin, London, 1954), p. 153 (hereafter abbreviated as DP).
2   DP 155.
3   DP 154.
4   DP 154.
5   See Charles Taylor, *A Secular Age* (Harvard University Press, Cambridge MA and London, 2007), p. 6 et passim.
6   DP 154.
7   DP 52.
8   DP 161.
9   DP 171.
10 DP 154.
11 DP 179.
12 DP 178.
13 DP 179.
14 DP 179.
15 DP 19.
16 DP 20.
17 See Simon Critchley, *Infinitely Demanding* (Verso, London and New York, 2007), pp. 38–68.
18 Having said what I will do in this book, let me also say what I will not do. There has been a massive resurgence of interest in the

question of the religious-secular distinction, and about where and indeed whether one can make such a distinction. An indication of the broad philosophical, historical, sociological, political, and theological dimensions and stakes of this debate can be seen in summary form in the papers collected in "The Religious-Secular Divide: the US Case," *Social Research*, Vol. 76, No. 4 (Winter 2009). Obviously, these debates have found a focus in Charles Taylor's *A Secular Age*, alluded to above. For ongoing debates around the questions of secularism, religion, and the public sphere, I would recommend "The Immanent Frame," available at http://blogs.ssrc. org. Also fascinating in this regard is the flowering of research in the sociology of religion. Particularly influential here is the work of my former colleague, José Casanova; see his *Public Religions in the Modern World* (University of Chicago, Chicago, 1994). Although it was on my mind during the writing of this book, particularly in the early stages, I will also not engage directly with well-rehearsed debates around the legitimacy or otherwise of modernity in Hans Blumenberg's comprehensive critique of Karl Löwith's account of secularization. See H. Blumenberg, *The Legitimacy of the Modern Age*, trans. R. Wallace (MIT Press, Cambridge MA, 1983); and K. Löwith, *Meaning in History* (University of Chicago Press, Chicago, 1949). Let me make clear—if it is not clear enough already—that my interest in political theology does not arise from some conservative abuse of the secularization thesis that would want to argue, with Schmitt and Heidegger, for the illegitimacy of the modern age largely because it is a faint echo of its antecedent ancient Greek, Christian, or medieval worldviews. Similarly, I do not engage with Habermas's recent work on religion, notably his debate with Joseph Ratzinger, Pope Benedict XVI. See Jürgen Habermas, *Between Naturalism and Religion*, trans. C. Cronin (Polity, Cambridge, 2008). Habermas's debate with Ratzinger can be found in an extraordinary and highly useful compendium of writing on politics and religion, *Political Theologies: Public Religions in a Post-Secular World*, eds. H. de Vries and L. Sullivan (Fordham University Press, New York, 2006), see esp. pp. 251–68. The philosophical and political stakes of this debate are concisely expressed in Habermas's public debate with a group of Jesuit philosophers from 2007; see Jürgen Habermas et al., *An Awareness of What Is Missing: Faith and Reason in a Post-Secular*

Age (Polity, Cambridge, 2010). I will also not engage directly with debates surrounding either postmodern theology or radical orthodoxy, although, concerning the latter, I would like to thank John Milbank for his helpful and penetrating response to the argument of Chapter 4. Allow me a final, but necessary, confession: although I have had a longstanding fascination with (and an occasional aversion to) religion and questions of theology, I have no expert competence in this domain. I write, then, as an enthusiastic—albeit not en-thused—amateur.

19   See William Connolly, *Why I Am Not a Secularist* (University of Minnesota Press, Minneapolis, 1999), p. 3 et passim.

20   James Wood, "God in the Quad," *New Yorker*, August 31, 2009, p. 79.

21   Dietrich Bonhoeffer, *Letters and Papers From Prison*, new edition, ed. Eberhard Bethge (Simon & Schuster, New York, 1997), p. 279.

2. THE CATECHISM OF THE CITIZEN

1   Jean-Jacques Rousseau, *The Discourses and Other Early Political Writings*, ed. V. Gourevitch (Cambridge University Press, Cambridge, 1997), p. 245, emphasis mine (hereafter abbreviated as D).

2   D 246, emphasis mine.

3   Mikhail Bakunin, "Revolutionary Catechism," in *Bakunin on Anarchy*, ed. Sam Dolgoff (Knopf, New York, 1972), pp. 76–97. Sergei Nechaev, "Catechism of a Revolutionary," available at uoregon.edu.

4   D 108.

5   I am thinking in particular of Hannah Arendt's influential but misguided critique of Rousseau, in particular on the question of the general will. See Hannah Arendt, *On Revolution* (Viking, New York, 1963).

6   I owe this insight on the relation of politics to religion to conversations with Joe Tinguely.

7   Emilio Gentile, *Politics as Religion*, trans. G. Staunton (Princeton University Press, Princeton and Oxford, 2006).

8   See my "Barack Obama and the American Void," *Harper's Magazine*, No. 1902 (November 2008), pp. 17–20.

9   Quoted in Gentile, *Politics as Religion*, p. 31, emphasis mine.

10   Included in Louis Althusser, *Philosophy of the Encounter: Later Writings, 1978–1987*, ed. F. Matheron and O. Corpet (Verso, London and New York, 2006), pp. 163–207.

11   Norman Cohn, *The Pursuit of the Millennium* (Oxford University Press, Oxford, 1970, revised and enlarged edition [1957]), p. 76 (hereafter abbreviated as C).

12   Jean-Jacques Rousseau, *The Social Contract and Other Later Political Writings*, ed. V. Gourevitch (Cambridge University Press, Cambridge, 1997), pp. 296–7 (hereafter abbreviated as SC).

13   Jean-Jacques Rousseau, *Collected Writings*, Vol. 4, *The Social Contract, Discourse on the Virtue Most Necessary for a Hero, Political Fragments and Geneva Manuscript*, eds. R.D. Masters and C. Kelly (University Press of New England, Hanover and London, 1994), p. 77 (hereafter cited as CW).

14   CW 78.

15   SC 78, 155.

16   CW 79.

17   CW 82. On the attribution of the character of the "violent reasoner" to Diderot's article for the *Encyclopédie* on "Natural Right" from 1755, see CW 235–6.

18   CW 79.

19   CW 80.

20   CW 80.

21   CW 80, emphasis mine.

22   Thomas Hobbes, *Leviathan*, ed. R. Tuck (Cambridge University Press, Cambridge, 1991), p. 474.

23   Ibid., p. 117.

24   CW 80.

25   SC 159, CW 81–2, emphasis mine.

26   Hobbes, *Leviathan*, p. 10 and p. 491.

27   Ibid., p. 9.

28   CW 82.

29   SC xxxviii.

30   CW 70.

31   SC 41.

32   CW 82.

33   D 132.

34   Alain Badiou, *Being and Event*, trans. O. Feltham (Continuum, London and New York, 2005), pp. 353–54 (hereafter abbreviated as B).

35   SC 49–50.

36   SC 50.

37   SC 49.

38   Giorgio Agamben, *State of Exception*, trans. K. Attell (University of Chicago Press, Chicago and London, 2005), pp. 2–3; see also pp. 85–8.

39   Exactly what Rousseau might mean by "change of nature" would require a separate investigation and would take us into the significant Stoical influences on Rousseau's thought. For an excellent discussion of these issues, see two unpublished papers by Wayne Martin, "Conscience and Confession in Rousseau's Naturalistic Moral Psychology," and "Stoic Self-Consciousness," both available at essex.ac.uk/~wmartin.

40   Cf. Denis Guénoun, *L'Enlèvement de la politique* (Circé, Paris, 2002), p. 15.

41   SC 50.

42   SC 50.

43   Louis Althusser, "Rousseau: The Social Contract (The Discrepancies)", in *Montesquieu, Rousseau, Marx* (Verso, London and New York, 1972), p. 127 (hereafter abbreviated as A).

44   A 147.

45   D 173.

46   SC 54.

47   Jean Starobinski, *Jean-Jacques Rousseau: Transparency and Obstruction*, trans. A Goldhammer (University of Chicago Press, Chicago, 1988).

48   SC 10.

49   SC 13.

50   SC 16.

51   See Jürgen Habermas, *The Postnational Constellation: Political Essays*, trans. M. Pensky (MIT Press, Cambridge MA, 2001).

52   Barack Obama, *The Audacity of Hope* (Three Rivers, New York, 2006), pp. 71–100.

53   Sarah Palin, *Going Rogue* (Harper Collins, New York, 2009), p. 395.

54   SC 179.

55　SC 179.

56　SC 186.

57　See Jean-Jacques Rousseau, *Politics and the Arts*, trans. A. Bloom (Cornell University Press, Ithaca, 1960).

58　SC 186.

59　D 161.

60　The play can be found, together with Rousseau's Preface, in the *Œuvres Complètes*, Tome 2, ed. B. Gagnebin and M. Raymond (Gallimard [Pléiade], Paris, 1961), pp. 959–1018. I will be quoting from the 1767 English translation of Rousseau's *Narcisse*, available at emory.edu.

61　Jean-Jacques Rousseau, *The Confessions*, trans. J.M. Cohen (Penguin, London, 1953), p. 119.

62　Ibid., p. 361.

63　Quoted in Maurice Cranston, *Jean-Jacques: The Early Life and Work of Jean-Jacques Rousseau* (University of Chicago Press, Chicago, 1982), p. 228.

64　Rousseau, *Œuvres Complètes*, Tome 2, p. 972, my translation.

65　Ibid., p. 973, my translation.

66　Ibid., p. 126.

67　I follow Jacques Rancière here in his fascinating article, "Schiller et la promesse esthétique," *Europe. Revue littéraire mensuelle*, April 2004, pp. 7–21.

68　Rousseau, *Œuvres Complètes*, Tome 2, p. 967, my translation.

69　SC 66.

70　SC 67.

71　A 136.

72　SC 67.

73　SC 114.

74　In this connection, see Alain Badiou, *Logiques des Mondes* (Seuil, Paris, 2006), p. 575.

75　Rousseau, *Politics and the Arts*, p. 126.

76　B 347.

77　Rousseau, *Confessions*, p. 547.

78　SC 114.

79　Edmund Morgan, *Inventing the People: The Rise of Popular Sovereignty in England and America* (Norton, New York, 1988), pp. 38–54 (here-after abbreviated as M).

80 SC 115.
81 SC 117.
82 SC 117–18.
83 SC 179.
84 Such, of course, is the central issue in the critique of transcendental philosophy as nihilism in the 1790s in Jacobi's critique of Fichte. See F.H. Jacobi, "Open Letter to Fichte," trans. D. Behler, in *Philosophy of German Idealism*, ed. E Behler (Continuum, New York, 1987), pp. 119–41.
85 SC 68.
86 SC 68.
87 SC 53.
88 SC 69.
89 SC 69.
90 *The Confession of St. Augustine*, trans. J.K. Ryan (Doubleday, New York, 1960), p. 254.
91 SC 70.
92 SC 70.
93 SC 68–9.
94 SC 95.
95 SC 71.
96 SC 70–1.
97 SC 71.
98 SC 71.
99 SC 77.
100 SC 78.
101 SC 138.
102 See "Iustitium," in Agamben, *State of Exception*, pp. 41–51.
103 SC 138.
104 Benjamin quoted in Agamben, *State of Exception*, p. 6.
105 SC 147. On this point, see Gourevitch's helpful elucidation, "*Sacer estod* 'be accursed': the ancient Roman formula uttered upon delivering someone to public execration and the Gods" (SC 305–6).
106 Robert N. Bellah, *The Broken Covenant: American Civil Religion in Time of Trial* (University of Chicago Press, Chicago and London, 1992 [1975]).
107 Available at bartleby.com.

108   SC 147–8.
109   SC 149.
110   SC 146.
111   SC 142–6.
112   SC 146–9.
113   SC 149–51.
114   SC 144.
115   SC 146.
116   Hobbes, *Leviathan*, p. 405.
117   SC 146.
118   Quoted in Mark Silk, "Numa Pompilius and the Idea of Civil Religion in the West," *Journal of the American Academy of Religion*, Vol. 72, No. 4 (December 2004), p. 883.
119   SC 146, emphasis mine.
120   SC 181.
121   Silk, "Numa Pompilius and the Idea of Civil Religion in the West," pp. 871–4.
122   SC 147.
123   SC 147.
124   SC 147.
125   CW 122.
126   SC 149.
127   SC 150.
128   SC 150.
129   SC 150.
130   SC 151.
131   CW 124.
132   SC 147.
133   I borrow here from Gentile, *Politics as Religion*, pp. xi–xii et passim.
134   I owe the following remarks to conversations with my good friend Gido Berns. See his lecture, "Maria's Flag: Religion and Public Space in Europe," available at http://videolectures.net.
135   In this connection, see Paul Kahn, *Sacred Violence* (University of Michigan Press, Ann Arbor, 2008).
136   Paul Staniland and Gregory Treverton, *Analyzing Religious Politics and Violence* (Santa Monica, CA: RAND Corporation, forthcoming).

137   SC 8.

138   M 37.

139   Patrick Riley, *The General Will Before Rousseau* (Princeton University Press, Princeton, 1986).

140   Cited in ibid., p. 5.

141   Ibid., p. 258.

142   Immanuel Kant, *Critique of Pure Reason*, trans. N. Kemp Smith (Macmillan, London, 1929), p. 644, emphasis mine.

143   Ibid.

144   M 153.

145   SC 115–16.

146   Voltaire, *Miracles and Idolatry*, trans. T. Besterman (Penguin, London, 2005), p. 54.

147   David Hume, *Political Writings*, ed. S. D. Warner and D. W. Livingstone (Hackett, Indianapolis, 1994), pp. 240–52.

148   Ibid., p. 252.

149   Ibid., emphasis mine.

150   M 271.

151   SC 145.

152   David Hume, *Political Essays*, ed. Knud Haakonssen (Cambridge University Press, Cambridge, 1994), p. 16. See M 14.

153   See Gentile, *Politics as Religion*.

154   I wrote a book on Stevens a few years ago (*Things Merely Are* [Routledge, London and New York, 2005]) and, based on conversations with Alain Badiou, I have been pondering the possible political implications of poetry, which are notably absent from that book, whose concerns are epistemological.

155   Wallace Stevens, *Opus Posthumous*, ed. M.J. Bates (Knopf, New York, 1989), p. 189.

156   Wallace Stevens, *The Palm at the End of the Mind* (Vintage, New York, 1967), p. 187.

157   Ibid., p. 230. I'd like to thank Todd Kronan for showing me that the roots of Stevens's idea of the supreme fiction lie in his reading of Santayana.

158   In *Marx-Engels Werke*, Band 1 (Dietz, Berlin, 1988), p. 389; and *Marx's Early Political Writings*, ed. J. O'Malley (Cambridge University Press, Cambridge, 1994), p. 67.

159   Karl Marx, *Capital*, Vol. 1, trans. B. Fowkes (Penguin, London,

1990), p. 171; Daniel Guérin, *No Gods, No Masters: An Anthology of Anarchism* (AK Press, Oakland and Edinburgh, 2005), p. 535 (hereafter abbreviated as GM).

160   Alain Badiou, "Politics: A Non-expressive Dialectics," available at blog.urbanomic.com.

161   SC 245.

162   DP 34.

163   Alain Badiou, *Manifesto for Philosophy*, trans. N. Madarasz (State University of New York Press, Albany, 1999), p. 108.

164   Alain Badiou, *Polemics*, trans. S. Corcoran (Verso, London and New York, 2006), p. 9 (hereafter abbreviated as BP).

165   BP 35.

166   BP 21.

167   BP 10.

168   BP 99.

169   BP 114.

170   BP 85.

171   See Alain Badiou, *The Meaning of Sarkozy*, trans. D. Fernbach (Verso, London and New York, 2008).

172   BP 56.

173   BP 57.

174   B 175.

175   B 344.

176   B 346–54.

177   B 340.

178   BP 97.

179   This was on the occasion of a conference on Badiou's work at Cardozo Law School, New York, in November 2008. The proceedings were published as "Law and Event," *Cardozo Law Review*, Vol. 29, No. 5 (2008). See also Badiou's excellent response to my argument in *Infinitely Demanding*, "On Simon Critchley's Infinitely Demanding: Ethics of Commitment, Politics of Resistance," *Critical Horizons*, Vol. 10, No. 2 (2009), pp. 154–62.

180   BP 95.

181   BP 95.

182   BP 96.

183   BP 284.

184   BP 286.

185   BP 291–328.
186   See V.I. Lenin, *The State and Revolution*, trans. R. Service (Penguin, London, 1992), pp. 33–51 (hereafter abbreviated as SR).
187   BP 307.
188   BP 287.
189   BP 289.
190   BP 292.
191   B 201–11.
192   Arendt, *On Revolution*, p. 76 et passim; Jean-Paul Sartre, *Critique of Dialectical Reason*, Vol. 1, trans. A. Sheridan-Smith (Verso, London and New York, 2004 [new edition]), pp. 345–51.
193   B 110–11.
194   BP 321.

3. MYSTICAL ANARCHISM

1   I would like to thank Robert Sinnerbrink for his invaluable help with the editing and preparation of this chapter.
2   Carl Schmitt, *Political Theology: Four Chapters on the Concept of Sovereignty*, trans. G. Schwab (University of Chicago Press, Chicago and London, 1985), p. 36 (hereafter abbreviated as SP).
3   SP 36.
4   Available at whitehouse.gov.
5   SP 5.
6   SP 36.
7   SP 15.
8   SP 53–66.
9   Barack Obama, *The Audacity of Hope: Thoughts on Reclaiming the American Dream* (New York: Random House/Crown, 2006), p. 92.
10   SP 65.
11   Carl Schmitt, *The Concept of the Political*, trans. G. Schwab (University of Chicago Press, Chicago and London, 1996), p. 58.
12   SP 58.
13   See Sigmund Freud, "On the Universal Tendency to Debasement in the Sphere of Love," *On Sexuality* (Penguin, London, 1977), pp. 247–60, see esp. p. 259.

14   See Martin Heidegger, "The Problem of Sin in Luther," in *Supplements*, ed. J. van Buren (SUNY Press, Albany, 2002), pp. 105–10.

15   John Gray, *Straw Dogs* (Granta, London, 2002), p. 155.

16   John Gray, *Black Mass* (Penguin, London, 2007), p. 1 (hereafter abbreviated as GB).

17   C 15.

18   See Norman Cohn, *Cosmos, Chaos and the World to Come* (New Haven, CT: Yale University Press, 2001).

19   Ibid., Foreword.

20   Ernesto Laclau, "What do Empty Signifiers Matter to Politics?," in *The Lesser Evil and the Greater Good*, ed. J. Weeks (London: Rivers Oram Press, 1994).

21   C 61.

22   See Christopher Tyerman, *The Crusades* (Oxford University Press, Oxford, 2004).

23   GB 271–88.

24   B 263.

25   GB 206.

26   Martin Heidegger, "Overcoming Metaphysics," in *The End of Philosophy*, trans. J. Stambaugh (Harper & Row, New York, 1973), p. 110.

27   Martin Heidegger, "Only a God Can Save Us," the *Spiegel* interview, trans. W. J. Richardson, in *Heidegger: The Man and the Thinker* (Precedent Publishing, Chicago, 1981), pp. 477–95.

28   Friedrich Nietzsche, *The Will to Power*, trans. W. Kaufmann and R.J. Hollingdale (Vintage, New York, 1968), pp. 18, 36, 38.

29   See Terry Eagleton, *Reason, Faith and Revolution: Reflections on the God Debate* (Yale University Press, New Haven and London, 2009), p. 2 et passim.

30   Jean-Jacques Rousseau, *Reveries of the Solitary Walker*, trans. P. France (Penguin, London, 1979), p. 115.

31   See my *Infinitely Demanding*, pp. 119–32.

32   C 199.

33   Cited in Jean Froissart, "The Peasant Revolt in England," in *Chronicles*, trans. G. Brereton (Penguin, London, 1968), pp. 212–13.

34   Karl Marx and Friedrich Engels, *The Communist Manifesto*, in *Marx's*

Early Political Writings, ed. T. Carver (Cambridge University Press, Cambridge, 1996), pp. 1–12.

35 See Whitney R. Cross, *The Burned-Over District: The Social and Intellectual History of Enthusiastic Religion in Western New York, 1800–1850* (Harper & Row, New York, 1950).

36 Charles Noordhof, *The Communistic Societies of the United States: Harmony, Oneida, the Shakers and Others* (Red & Black, St. Petersburg FL, 2008); and *America's Communal Utopias*, ed. D.E. Pilzer (University of North Carolina Press, Chapel Hill, 1997).

37 C 282.

38 Robert E. Lerner, *The Heresy of the Free Spirit in the Later Middle Ages* (University of California Press, Berkeley, 1972), see esp. pp. 8–9.

39 Raoul Vaneigem, *The Movement of the Free Spirit*, trans. R. Cherry and I. Patterson (Zone Books, New York, 1998), p. 194 (hereafter abbreviated as FS).

40 See Franz Pfeiffer, *Deutsche Mystiker des Vierzehnten Jahrhunderts, Band 2: Meister Eckhart* (Leipzig, 1845–57); C. de B. Evans, *Meister Eckhart by Franz Pfeiffer* (London, 1924), pp. 312–34; see Lerner, *The Heresy of the Free Spirit*, pp. 208–21.

41 Amy Hollywood, *The Soul as Virgin Wife* (University of Notre Dame Press, Notre Dame and London, 1995), p. 87. We should also note an ambiguity in the spelling of Porete's name. Most scholars refer to her as "Marguerite Porete," although the English translation of *The Mirror of Simple Souls* attributes the book to "Margaret Porette."

42 *Archivio Italiano per la storia della pietà*, IV (1965), pp. 351–708.

43 See Michael Sells, "Porete and Eckhart: The Apophasis of Gender," in *Mystical Language of Unsaying* (University of Chicago Press, Chicago, 1994), pp. 180–205; see esp. p 180. On the relation between Porete and Eckhart, see Hollywood, *The Soul as Virgin Wife*, pp. 54–6 and pp. 173–206.

44 Edmund Colledge and J.C. Marler, "Poverty of the Will: Ruusbroec, Eckhart and *The Mirror of Simple Souls*," in *Jan van Ruusbroec: The Sources, Content and Sequels of his Mysticism*, ed. P. Mommaers and N. de Paepe (University of Louvain Press, Louvain, 1984). For Eckhart's sermon, see Reiner Schürmann, *Meister Eckhart: Mystic and Philosopher* (Indiana University Press, Bloomington, 1978), pp. 214–20.

45 Cited in Schürmann, *Meister Eckhart*, p. 104.

46 See the "Foreword" and long "Introductory Interpretative Essay" in Margaret Porette (Marguerite Porete), *The Mirror of Simple Souls*, trans. E. Colledge, J.C. Marler, and J. Grant (University of Notre Dame Press, Notre Dame, 1999), pp. vii–lxxxvii (hereafter abbreviated as P).

47 See Anne Carson, "Decreation: How Women like Sappho, Marguerite Porete and Simone Weil Tell God" and "Decreation (An Opera in Three Parts)," in *Decreation* (Knopf, New York, 2005), pp. 155–83 and pp. 187–240; Hollywood, *The Soul as Virgin Wife*; and Amy Hollywood, *Sensible Ecstasy: Mysticism, Sexual Difference and the Demands of History* (University of Chicago Press, Chicago, 2002).

48 Cited in Carson, *Decreation*, p. 203.

49 P 78.

50 P 77–9.

51 What follows is adapted from *The Mirror* (P 140–6).

52 P 142.

53 P 142.

54 Carson, *Decreation*, p. 179; see also Simone Weil, *Gravity and Grace*, trans. A. Wills (University of Nebraska Press, Lincoln, 1997), p. 81.

55 P 142.

56 P 143.

57 P 143, emphasis mine.

58 See William James, *The Varieties of Religious Experience: A Study in Human Nature* (BiblioBazaar, Charleston SC, 2007), pp. 332–70. See also James's essay, originally published in *Mind* in 1882, "Subjective Effects of Nitrous Oxide," available at ebooks.adelaide.edu.au.

59 James, *The Varieties of Religious Experience*, p. 340.

60 Ibid.

61 P 144.

62 P 148.

63 P 144.

64 In this connection, consider the sixteenth-century mystic, Jacob Boehme, when he writes "In one quarter of an hour I saw and knew more than if I had been many years together at an university. For I saw and knew the being of all things, the Byss and the Abyss, and the eternal generation of the holy Trinity, the descent and

original of the world and of all creatures through the divine wisdom" (cited in James, *The Varieties of Religious Experience*, pp. 359–60).

65 P 145.

66 For a compelling discussion of the relation between releasement in Eckhart and Heidegger's notion of *Gelassenheit*, see Schürmann, *Meister Eckhart*, pp. 192–213.

67 P 145.

68 P 145.

69 P 145–6.

70 Carson, *Decreation*, p. 162.

71 See *Life of Blessed Henry Suso by Himself*, Chapter LVI, "Of the Very Highest Flight of a Soul Experienced in the Ways of God" (cited in James, *The Varieties of Human Religious Experience*, p. 411).

72 Eckhart, from the sermon *Beati paupers spiritu*, cited in Schürmann, *Meister Eckhart*, p. 219.

73 C 174.

74 Teresa of Avila, *The Life of St. Teresa of Avila by Herself*, trans. J.M. Cohen (Penguin, London, 1988), Chapter 29, pp. 16–17.

75 Angela of Foligno, "The Memorial," in *The Essential Writings of Christian Mysticism*, ed. Bernard McGinn (Modern Library, New York, 2006), p. 376.

76 Caroline Walker Bynum, *Fragmentation and Redemption: Essays on Gender and the Human Body in Medieval Religion* (Zone Books, New York, 1992), pp. 186–7.

77 Ibid., p. 186.

78 Julian of Norwich, *Revelations of Divine Love*, in *Medieval Writings on Female Spirituality*, ed. E. Spearing (Penguin, London, 2002), p. 175.

79 Ibid., p. xi.

80 Ibid., p. 106.

81 Ibid., p. 109.

82 Ibid., pp. 75–86.

83 George Fox, *Journal*, quoted in Pink Dandelion, *The Creation of Quaker Theory: Insider Perspectives* (Ashgate, London, 2004), p. 161.

84 See Karl Marx, "Economic and Philosophical Manuscripts," in *Early Writings*, ed. L. Colletti (Penguin, London, 1975), p. 349. I owe this line of thought to conversations with Alain Badiou.

85 C 175.

86 C 286.
87 Lerner, *The Heresy of the Free Spirit*, p. 8.
88 I owe these remarks on chastity to a number of conversations with Lisabeth During.
89 "The Compilation Concerning the New Spirit," in *The Essential Writings of Christian Mysticism*, ed. McGinn, p. 491.
90 FS 115.
91 C 162.
92 Michel Foucault, *Sécurité, territoire, population: Cours au Collège de France (1977–1978)*, ed. Michel Senellart (Gallimard/Seuil: Paris, 2004), p. 200. I'd like to thank Roberto Nigro for bringing this passage to my attention.
93 C 148.
94 C 149.
95 C 114.
96 C 176.
97 Jacques Lacan, *On Feminine Sexuality: The Limits of Love and Knowledge*, trans. B. Fink (Norton, New York, 1998), pp. 76–7.
98 Ibid., p. 76.
99 Ibid., p. 77.
100 Ibid.
101 GB 99.
102 FS 94.
103 FS 249.
104 FS 254.
105 FS 241.
106 FS 246.
107 FS 195.
108 Raoul Vaneigem, *A Declaration of the Rights of Human Beings: On the Sovereignty of Life as Surpassing the Rights of Man* (Pluto Press, London, 2003).
109 In this connection, see the following: Michael Löwy, "Revolution Against 'Progress': Walter Benjamin's Romantic Anarchism," *New Left Review*, No. 152 (1985), pp. 42–59; and Michael Löwy, *Redemption and Utopia: Jewish Libertarian Thought in Central Europe: A Study in Elective Affinity* (Athlone Press, London, 1992).
110 Gustav Landauer, "Anarchic Thoughts on Anarchism," trans. J. Cohn and G. Kuhn, in *Perspectives on Anarchist Theory*, Vol. 6, No. 11

(1) (Fall 2007). Originally published as "Anarchistische Gedanken über Anarchismus," *Die Zukunft* (October 26, 1901), pp. 134–40.

111 Landauer, "Anarchic Thoughts on Anarchism," p. 85.

112 Ibid., p. 88.

113 Ibid.

114 Ibid.,

115 Ibid., p. 89.

116 Ibid.

117 Ibid.

118 Ibid., p. 91.

119 In this connection, see George Bataille's *The Unfinished System of Nonknowledge,* trans. M. Kendall and S. Kendall (University of Minnesota Press, Minneapolis and London, 2001). Especially useful is Stuart Kendall's "Editor's Introduction," pp. xi–xliv.

120 *Notre Musique* (2004), J-L. Godard (dir.) (France/Switzerland: Avventura Films, Péripheria Suisse, France 3 Cinéma et al.).

121 See the documentation collected in *Theanyspacewhatever* (Guggenheim Museum, New York, 2008).

122 H-U. Obrist, "In Conversation with Raoul Vaneigem," *e-flux journal*, available at e-flux.com. See Nicolas Bourriaud, *Relational Aesthetics* (Les Presses du Réel, Paris, 2002).

123 Liam Gillick, "Maybe It Would Be Better if We Worked in Groups of Three?," *e-flux journal*, available at e-flux.com.

124 For more information on the "Tarnac 9" see http://tarnac9. wordpress.com. See also the commentary by Alberto Toscano, "The War Against Pre-Terrorism: The Tarnac 9 and The Coming Insurrection," *Radical Philosophy*, No. 154 (March/ April 2009).

125 *L'insurrection qui vient* (La Fabrique, Paris, 2007); translated anonymously as *The Coming Insurrection* (Semiotexte[e], Los Angeles, 2009).

126 Ibid., p. 101.

127 "Julien Coupat Released," available at http://tarnac9.wordpress. com.

128 "Statement From the Tarnac 10," available at http://tarnac9. wordpress.com.

129 *L'insurrection qui vient*, p. 83.

130 The obvious connection here is between *The Coming Insurrection*

and Agamben's *The Coming Community*, trans. Michael Hardt (University of Minnesota Press, Minneapolis, 1993).

131   See *Call*, available at http://bloom0101.org, p. 57. *Call* was an earlier text by the Invisible Committee circulated anonymously in 2004.

132   In *Politics Is Not a Banana* (Institute for Experimental Freedom, 2009), p. 156 and p. 162.

133   See "A Point of Clarification," a statement from January 2009 that appears at the beginning of the American edition of *The Coming Insurrection*, pp. 5–19, see esp. p. 16.

134   Ibid., p. 12.

135   PB 51–2.

136   PB 52.

4. YOU ARE NOT YOUR OWN: ON THE NATURE OF FAITH

1   Adolph von Harnack, *History of Dogma*, Vol. 1, trans. N. Buchanan (Williams & Norgate, London and Edinburgh), p. 136.

2   Ibid.

3   Giorgio Agamben, *The Time that Remains: A Commentary on the Letter to the Romans*, trans. P. Daily (Stanford University Press, Stanford, 2005), p. 112 (hereafter abbreviated as PA).

4   Jacob Taubes, *The Political Theology of Paul*, trans. D. Hollander (Stanford University Press, Stanford, 2004), p. 83 (hereafter abbreviated as PT).

5   Heidegger, "Letter to Father Engelbert Krebs," in *Supplements*, p. 69.

6   *The Writings of St. Paul*, ed. W. Meeks (Norton, New York and London, 1972), p. 435 (hereafter abbreviated as PW).

7   Daniel Boyarin, *A Radical Jew: Paul and the Politics of Identity* (University of California Press, Berkeley, 1994), p. 2.

8   PT 24.

9   PT 11.

10   PT 1.

11   Alain Badiou, *Saint Paul: The Foundation of Universalism*, trans. R. Brassier (Stanford University Press, Stanford, 2003), p. 4–15 (hereafter abbreviated as PB).

12   For a rather different, but wonderfully detailed account of Paul's politics, that attempts to show the extent of Paul's debt to the traditions of Hellenistic popular and political philosophy, see Bruno Blumenfeld, *The Political Paul* (Sheffield Academic Press, London, 2001).

13   PW 241.

14   All references to Paul, unless indicated, are to the Revised Standard Edition, given in *The Writings of St. Paul*, ed. Meeks (PW). I have also, on occasion, checked translations from the Greek using *The Parallel New Testament Greek and English* (Oxford University Press, Oxford, 1933 [1882]).

15   PW 409.

16   See Martin Buber, *Two Types of Faith*, trans. N.P. Goldhawk (Syracuse University Press, Syracuse NY, 1994).

17   PB 4.

18   PT 54.

19   On this point, see Terry Eagleton's "The Scum of the Earth," in *Reason, Faith and Revolution*, p. 23.

20   PA 51–2.

21   PA 62–72.

22   PA 7.

23   Eagleton, *Reason, Faith and Revolution*, p. 31.

24   See *Infinitely Demanding*, Chapter 2.

25   PA 138–45.

26   Jacques Derrida, *Specters of Marx*, trans. P. Kamuf (Routledge, London and New York, 1994).

27   See, for example, the final paragraph of Agamben, *State of Exception*, p. 88, which begins, "To show law in its nonrelation to life and life in its nonrelation to law." We will come back to this phrase below.

28   PA 135.

29   PA 114.

30   PA 136.

31   See PA 133–4, where Agamben is referring to unpublished lectures by Foucault given in Leuven in 1981 called "Mal faire, dire vrai." This is closely related to the also unpublished fourth volume of the History of Sexuality, *The Confessions of the Flesh*, which deals with the practice of confession and monastic discipline.

32   This is worked out more thoroughly in my *Infinitely Demanding*, Chapters 1 and 2.

33   PA 128.

34   As Agamben relatedly writes in *The Coming Community*: "The lover wants the loved one *with all its predicates*, its being such as it is. The lover desires the *as* only insofar as it is *such*—this is the lover's particular fetishism" (p. 2).

35   PA 144.

36   Martin Heidegger, *Letters to his Wife 1915–70*, ed. G. Heidegger and trans. R.D.V. Glasgow (Polity Press, Cambridge, 2008), p. 50 (hereafter abbreviated as HL).

37   HL 50.

38   HL 54.

39   HL 55.

40   Martin Heidegger, *Being and Time*, trans. J. Macquarrie and E. Robinson (Blackwell, Oxford, 1962), p. 46 (hereafter abbreviated as SuZ). All references given to the German pagination, given in the margins of the English translation.

41   HL 57.

42   HL 58.

43   HL 59.

44   I discuss this topic in more detail in "Originary Inauthenticity," in Simon Critchley, *On Heidegger's* Being and Time (Routledge, London and New York, 2008).

45   Heidegger, *Supplements*, p. 69.

46   Ibid., p. 70.

47   Martin Heidegger, *The Phenomenology of Religious Life*, trans. M. Fritsch and J.A. Gosetti-Ferencei (Indiana University Press, Bloomington and London, 2004), p. 47 (hereafter abbreviated as PH).

48   PW 239.

49   PH 236.

50   See the reference to Harnack on PH 50.

51   PH 67.

52   PH 73.

53   Harnack, *History of Dogma*, Vol. 1, frontispiece.

54   PH 49.

55   PH 83.

56   PH 56.

57   PH 95.
58   PH 79.
59   PH 79.
60   PH 70.
61   PH 88–9.
62   PH 88.
63   PH 89.
64   See Adolf Deissmann, *Paul: A Study in Social and Religious History*, trans. W.E. Wilson (second revised ed., New York, 1926); and Albert Schweizer, *The Mysticism of Paul the Apostle*, trans. W. Montgomery (New York, 1931).
65   See Martin Dibelius, "Mystic and Prophet," in PW 395–409.
66   PH 57.
67   PH 73.
68   PH 73.
69   PH 73.
70   PH 73.
71   PH 80.
72   PH 80.
73   PH 82.
74   PH 102.
75   In Walter Benjamin, *Reflections*, ed. P. Demetz (Schocken, New York, 1978), pp. 312–13.
76   PT 72.
77   Cf. PB 46–7.
78   PB 56.
79   PA 1.
80   PA 18.
81   PA 24–5.
82   PA 33.
83   PII 83.
84   PH 84.
85   PH 84–5.
86   PH 86.
87   PH 86.
88   PH 87.
89   PH 87.
90   PA 34.

91   SuZ 179.
92   Agamben, *The Coming Community*, p. 14.
93   SuZ 180.
94   SuZ 371.
95   PA 34.
96   PT 87.
97   PT 54.
98   SuZ 269.
99   SuZ 271.
100 On the applicability of the terms *conversio* and *aversio* to Heidegger's distinction between authenticity and inauthenticity, see Reiner Schürmann, *On Heidegger's Being and Time*, ed. S. Levine (Routledge, London and New York, 2008), pp. 61–2.
101 SuZ 273.
102 SuZ 271.
103 SuZ 275.
104 SuZ 281, emphasis mine.
105 SuZ 276–7.
106 Jacques Lacan, *The Ethics of Psychoanalysis*, trans. D. Porter (Norton, New York, 1992), pp. 270–87.
107 SuZ 277.
108 SuZ 280.
109 Friedrich Nietzsche, *On the Genealogy of Morals*, trans. W. Kaufmann (Vintage, New York, 1967), pp. 62–3.
110 SuZ 289.
111 SuZ 284.
112 SuZ 323.
113 SuZ 285.
114 SuZ 286–7.
115 Martin Heidegger, *Introduction to Metaphysics*, trans. R. Manheim (Yale University Press, New Haven, 1959), p. 158.
116 SuZ 287.
117 SuZ 289.
118 Martin Heidegger, "Letter on Humanism," in *Basic Writings*, ed. D.F. Krell (Harper & Row, New York, 1977), p. 193.
119 See Jacques Derrida, *Of Spirit: Heidegger and the Question*, trans. G. Bennington and R. Bowlby (University of Chicago Press, Chicago, 1991).

120   Samuel Beckett, *Molloy* (Grove Press, New York, 2006), p. 79.
121   PW 239.
122   PW 240.
123   On this point see Boyarin, *A Radical Jew*, pp. 40–56.
124   PT 60.
125   Adolf von Harnack, *Marcion: The Gospel of the Alien God*, trans. J.E. Steely and L.D. Bierma (Labyrinth, Durham NC, 1990), pp. 1–14 (hereafter abbreviated as MG). The other important source for a discussion of Marcion is Hans Jonas, *The Gnostic Religion* (Beacon, Boston, 1958); see esp. pp. 130–46. Although I cannot take up Jonas's argument in this context, what is fascinating is the implicit link he makes between Gnosticism in general, and Marcionism in particular, and Heidegger's existential analytic. See *The Gnostic Religion*, pp. 320–40. I intend to pursue this question on a separate occasion.
126   MG 80.
127   Harnack, *History of Dogma*, Vol. 1, p 223.
128   Ibid., p. 267.
129   MG 23.
130   For a selection of the writings of the Apostolic Fathers, see *Early Christian Writings*, ed. A. Louth, trans. M. Staniforth (Penguin, London, 1987).
131   MG 12.
132   MG 66.
133   MG 111.
134   MG 96.
135   PT 58.
136   PT 61.
137   MG 134.
138   PA 95–6.
139   PA 108–11.
140   See Agamben, *State of Exception*, p. 87.
141   Ibid., p. 88.
142   PB 35.
143   PB 35.
144   PB 48, 49.
145   PB 49, emphasis mine.
146   PH 97.

147   See, for example, SuZ 130, where Heidegger writes, "*Authentic Being-one's-Self* does not rest upon an exceptional condition of the subject, a condition that has been detached from the 'they'; *it is rather an existentiell modification of the 'they'—of the 'they' as an essential existentiale.*"

148   MG 139.

149   On love as the fulfilling of the law, see Kierkegaard's *Works of Love*: "But there is no quarrel between the law and love, no more than there is between the sum and that of which it is the sum." Søren Kierkegaard, *Works of Love*, trans. H. and E. Hong (Harper Perennial, New York, 2009), p. 111 (hereafter abbreviated as WL).

150   I owe these thoughts to conversations with Lisabeth During.

5. NONVIOLENT VIOLENCE

1   Judith Butler, "Critique, Coercion, and Sacred Life in Benjamin's 'Critique of Violence',", in *Political Theologies*, eds. H. De Vries and L. E. Sullivan (Fordham University Press, New York, 2006), p. 202 et passim. I'd like to thank Judith Butler for sending me some of her unpublished writing on the question of violence and nonviolence. As will become clear, I am trying to think about the question of violence and nonviolence in the same neighborhood as Butler.

2   Slavoj Žižek, *In Defense of Lost Causes* (Verso, London and New York, 2008), p. 472 (hereafter abbreviated as ZI). The context for the quotation from the *London Review of Books* is Žižek's response to a letter from David Graeber. Žižek writes: "It is truly weird that David Graeber thinks my 'real message' is that 'intellectuals have always been, and always must be, whores to power.' On the contrary, isn't it the advocates of resistance from the interstices of power, such as Simon Critchley, who claim that direct engagement with power turns intellectuals into whores? In my view, the withdrawal to such a safe moralising position is the highest form of corruption" (Letters, *London Review of Books*, January 24, 2008).

3   Just for the record, the dispute began with Žižek's critical response to my 2007 book *Infinitely Demanding: Ethics of Commitment, Politics of Resistance*. Žižek's piece ("Resistance is Surrender," *London Review of Books*, November 15, 2007) occasioned some interesting responses,

notably from T.J. Clark, Chris Harman, and André Bénichou (see Letters, *London Review of Books*, December 13, 2007). Žižek's critique was then republished in *Harper's Magazine* in February 2008, to which I replied in a later issue (May 2008). Žižek published a greatly extended version of his critique of my position in *In Defense of Lost Causes* (ZI 337–50). I responded in an article called "Violent Thoughts about Slavoj Žižek," *Naked Punch*, Free Supplement, Issue 11 (Autumn 2008), pp. 3–6. Žižek then responded at length in the Afterword to the paperback edition of *In Defense of Lost Causes* (ZI 463–88). Another noteworthy intervention in the debate is Robert Young's "The Violent State," *Naked Punch*, Free Supplement, Issue 12 (Spring 2009), pp. 1–11.

4 Slavoj Žižek, *Violence* (Profile Books, London, 2008), p. 2 (hereafter abbreviated as V).

5 Slavoj Žižek, *The Sublime Object of Ideology* (Verso, London and New York, 1989).

6 See the stunning first chapter of *The Sublime Object of Ideology*, "How Did Marx Invent the Symptom?," pp. 11–53.

7 V 171.

8 V 183.

9 Slavoj Žižek, *The Parallax View* (MIT Press, Cambridge MA, 2006), pp. 375–85.

10 V 180–3.

11 Žižek, *The Parallax View*, p. 385.

12 Walter Benjamin, "Critique of Violence," *Selected Writings*, Vol. 1, ed. M. Bullock and M.W. Jennings (Harvard University Press, Cambridge MA, 1996), p. 242 (hereafter CV).

13 CV 242.

14 CV 243.

15 CV 243.

16 CV 245.

17 Georges Sorel, *Reflections on Violence*, ed. J. Jennings (Cambridge University Press, Cambridge, 1999).

18 CV 246.

19 CV 247.

20 CV 247.

21 CV 248.

22 CV 249.

23 CV 249–50.
24 Butler, "Critique, Coercion, and Sacred Life," p. 217.
25 CV 250.
26 Butler, "Critique, Coercion, and Sacred Life," p. 211.
27 CV 250.
28 CV 250, emphasis mine.
29 CV 250.
30 Butler, "Critique, Coercion, and Sacred Life," pp. 218–19.
31 I owe some of these insights to conversations with Robert Gibbs.
32 CV 252.
33 CV 252.
34 ZI 485.
35 Wallace Stevens, "The Poems of our Climate," in *The Palm at the End of the Mind*, ed. H. Stevens (Vintage, New York, 1990), p. 158.
36 See in particular Jacques Derrida, *On Cosmopolitanism and Forgiveness*, trans. M. Dooley and M. Hughes (Routledge, London and New York, 2001).
37 Emmanuel Levinas, *Totality and Infinity*, trans. A. Lingis (Duquesne University Press, Pittsburgh, 1969), p. 21 (hereafter abbreviated as TI).
38 TI 22.
39 TI 24.
40 TI 25.
41 TI 27, emphasis mine.
42 Walter Benjamin, "Theses on the Philosophy of History," in *Illuminations*, trans. H. Zohn (Fontana, London, 1973), pp. 263–4.
43 Emmanuel Levinas, *Otherwise than Being or Beyond Essence*, trans. A. Lingis (Nijhoff, The Hague, 1974), p. 194.
44 See my "Anarchic Law," *Law and Humanities*, Vol. 1, No. 2 (Winter 2007), pp. 248–55. In this regard, see also Desmond Manderson, *Proximity, Levinas and the Soul of Law* (McGill—Queen's University Press, Montreal, 2006).
45 I refer to the unpublished typescript of a lecture given in London in 2007.
46 TI 199.
47 TI 199.
48 TI 198.
49 Emmanuel Levinas, *Basic Philosophical Writings*, eds. A. Peperzak,

S. Critchley, and R. Bernasconi (Indiana University Press, Bloomington, 1996), p. 167.

50 TI 199.
51 Levinas, *Otherwise than Being or Beyond Essence*, p. 185.
52 TI 199.
53 Levinas, *Otherwise than Being or Beyond Essence*, p. 185.
54 Ibid., p. 177.
55 See Žižek, "Resistance Is Surrender." This is expanded with some elisions in *In Defense of Lost Causes* (ZI 346–50).
56 Žižek, "Resistance Is Surrender."
57 SR 16.
58 SR 55.
59 SR 56.
60 SR 55–6.
61 SR 33.
62 GM 202.
63 GM 288.
64 SR 48.
65 SR 55, emphasis mine.
66 SR 18.
67 SR 80.
68 *Bakunin on Anarchy*, pp. 314–15.
69 GM 191.
70 On Marx's critique of Bismarck, see "The Civil War in France," in *Marx's Later Political Writings*, ed. T. Carver (Cambridge University Press, Cambridge, 1996), pp. 186, 193, 205.
71 GM 196.
72 GM 391–2.
73 GM 392.
74 GM 476.
75 This and following quotations in the paragraph are from GM 477.
76 See Carl Schmitt, *Theory of the Partisan*, trans. G.L. Ulmen (Telos Press, New York, 2007), pp. 54–61.
77 GM 511.
78 SR 106.
79 GM 353.
80 GM 361.
81 See my *Infinitely Demanding*, pp. 111–14.

82 ZI 346.
83 On this point see David Graeber's response to Žižek in the Letters pages of *London Review of Books*, January 3, 2008. See also *Infinitely Demanding*, pp. 105–11.
84 See Letters, *London Review of Books*, December 13, 2007.
85 SR 80.
86 Žižek, "Resistance is Surrender," emphasis mine.
87 Jacques Lacan, *The Other Side of Psychoanalysis*, trans. R. Grigg (Norton, New York, 2007), p. 207.
88 ZI 475.
89 ZI 475.
90 ZI 476.
91 ZI 472.
92 ZI 348.
93 See Dietrich Bonhoeffer, *Ethics*, ed. C. J. Green (Fortress Press, Minneapolis, 2005), p. 273. See also Clifford Green's helpful introduction to this volume, pp. 1–44.
94 Ibid., p. 275.
95 Young, "The Violent State," p. 5.
96 Ibid., p. 4–5.
97 Ibid., p. 4.
98 See Frantz Fanon, "Colonial War and Mental Disorders," in *The Wretched of the Earth*, trans. R. Philcox (Grove, New York, 2004), pp. 181–233.
99 Ibid., pp. 15, 17, 19 et passim.
100 Ibid., pp. 44, 51, 52.
101 Ibid., p. 2.
102 Ibid., p. xlviii.
103 Ibid., p. lv.
104 Hannah Arendt, *On Violence* (Harcourt, Orlando, 1970), p. 83; see also p. 12 and p. 20.
105 Fanon, *The Wretched of the Earth*, p. 23.
106 Ibid., p. lviii.
107 David Gracber, "The New Anarchists," *New Left Review*, No. 13 (2002), p. 66.
108 To be brutally honest, I think that my defense of nonviolence in relation to neo-anarchism in *Infinitely Demanding* suffered from this dogmatism. Having listened to objections and reflected on

them, the present chapter represents an effort to rethink my position on the question of violence and nonviolence.

109   CV 247.

110   I'd like to thank Jacob Blumenfeld for clarifying my thoughts on this and other issues.

111   Tiqqun, *Introduction to Civil War*, trans. A. Galloway and J. Smith (Semiotext[e], Los Angeles, 2010), p. 209.

112   Žižek, *The Parallax View*, p. 385.

113   ZI 479.

114   ZI 474.

115   ZI 475. In this regard, see Žižek's continuation of this line of thought and his rather surprising citation of Gandhi's mantra "Be the change you want to see in the world" (which, a friend tells me, was used by Oxfam on a fridge magnet) in the final pages of *First as Tragedy, Then as Farce* (Verso, London and New York, 2009), p. 154. Indeed, perhaps even more surprising is the context in which Gandhi is cited, which is in connection to the Hopi saying "We are the ones that we have been waiting for." Žižek wants to give a Hegelian spin to this remark, as indicating a shift from substance to subject. If this is true, however, then Barack Obama is a formidable Hegelian dialectician, as he famously cited this Hopi saying on numerous occasions in speeches during 2008. That said, and without wanting to be too unfair, *First as Tragedy, Then as Farce* makes many perspicuous critical points and is the closest that Žižek has given us to a manifesto.

116   ZI 483.

117   V 172–3.

118   ZI 477–82.

119   ZI 478.

120   ZI 486.

121   ZI 485.

122   ZI 485.

123   CV 250.

124   ZI 484.

125   ZI 485.

126   CV 250.

127   ZI 349–50.

128   I owe this insight to conversations with Jacob Blumenfeld.

6. CONCLUSION

1   WL 345.
2   WL 345.
3   See, in particular, the extraordinary discussion of love in Book Two of Rosenzweig's *The Star of Redemption*, trans. W. Hallo (Notre Dame Press, Notre Dame IN, 1985), pp. 156–253.
4   WL 345.
5   WL 112–13.
6   WL 351.
7   WL 346.
8   WL 347.
9   WL 347.
10 WL 348, emphasis mine.
11 WL 348.
12 Rosenzweig, *The Star of Redemption*, p. 176.
13 Ibid., p. 177.
14 WL 171 (Rom. 13:8).
15 WL 172.
16 WL 352.
17 WL 352.
18 WL 352.
19 WL 352–3.
20 WL 353.

Index